INSIGHT

SYLVIA BROWNE

with Lindsay Harrison

INSIGHT

Case Files from the
Psychic World

DUTTON

DUTTON
Published by Penguin Group (USA) Inc.
375 Hudson Street, New York, New York 10014, U.S.A.
Penguin Group (Canada), 90 Eglinton Avenue East, Suite 700, Toronto, Ontario M4P 2Y3, Canada
(a division of Pearson Penguin Canada Inc.); Penguin Books Ltd, 80 Strand, London WC2R 0RL, England;
Penguin Ireland, 25 St Stephen's Green, Dublin 2, Ireland (a division of Penguin Books Ltd); Penguin Group
(Australia), 250 Camberwell Road, Camberwell, Victoria 3124, Australia (a division of Pearson Australia Group
Pty Ltd); Penguin Books India Pvt Ltd, 11 Community Centre, Panchsheel Park, New Delhi - 110 017, India;
Penguin Group (NZ), cnr Airborne and Rosedale Roads, Albany, Auckland 1310, New Zealand (a division of
Pearson New Zealand Ltd); Penguin Books (South Africa) (Pty) Ltd, 24 Sturdee Avenue, Rosebank,
Johannesburg 2196, South Africa

Penguin Books Ltd, Registered Offices: 80 Strand, London WC2R 0RL, England

Published by Dutton, a member of Penguin Group (USA) Inc.

First printing, July 2006
1   3   5   7   9   10   8   6   4   2

REGISTERED TRADEMARK—MARCA REGISTRADA

LIBRARY OF CONGRESS CATALOGING-IN-PUBLICATION DATA
has been applied for.

ISBN 0-525-94955-0

Printed in the United States of America
Set in Fairfield LH Light
Designed by Leonard Telesca

To the generous clients who bravely and openly
shared their stories
and made this book possible

CONTENTS

ACKNOWLEDGMENTS

In addition to our usual intrepid team of Brian Tart and Bonnie Solow, we want to give a special, heartfelt thanks to Linda Rossi and Michael McClellan, who tirelessly (or not) tackled, read and sorted decades' worth of letters and affidavits in anticipation of this book—and, come to think of it, so diligently kept them on hand in the first place.

We appreciate you and love you.

Sylvia and Lindsay

INTRODUCTION

This book is my Golden Anniversary celebration. As most of you know by now, I've been psychic since the day I was born, a family legacy that can be traced back at least three hundred years. But not until I was almost twenty, half a century ago (you do the math), did I allow myself to ease, informally at first, into a life of private readings—one-on-one sessions, in person or on the phone, with those who have an infinite variety of questions and are willing to hear the answers that come not *from* me, but *through* me, from the Source of all answers, wisdom and life itself.

Fifty years of readings. In a threadbare storefront office in San Jose, California, so tiny that I actually hung drapes on a blank wall to create the illusion of a window. In an equally tiny space in my cramped house, with my sons' diapers drying on a clothesline just outside the door. In countless hospital rooms and nursing homes and pediatric care facilities. In five-star hotel suites, mansions, mud huts and deerskin tents. On riverbanks, desert sand dunes, glistening beaches and freezing cold mountaintops. At the foot of the Sphinx, the Great Pyramids, the Eiffel Tower and a grove of baobab trees. On six of seven continents (Antarctica and I seem to be maintaining a mutually respectful distance) I've done thousands upon thousands of readings in this past half century, for clients of every age, race, creed and circumstance. And at this fifty-year benchmark, I'm looking back with profound gratitude and coming to some indisputable conclusions about the part of my life that continues to be devoted to my clients:

I've received far more than I could ever give, and learned far more than I could ever teach.

When we cut through the superficial differences between us, the meaningless variations in geography, skin color, cultural traditions and the specific words by which we worship God, we citizens of this earth who haven't turned away from Him, we're all the same at our core. We yearn to love and be loved. We yearn to hear that we're on the right path, or how to find our way back to it if we feel we've wandered off. We yearn to be stronger, wiser, healthier, more courageous and less afraid. We yearn to understand what confuses and debilitates us. We yearn to experience our connection to our Creator, and our own eternal spirits, rather than just hope against hope that they exist. We yearn to know beyond all doubt that there's more than this, that *we're* more than this, and that, for ourselves and for everyone we've ever loved, there really is no end. We yearn for peace of mind, and access to the ultimate peace our spirits possess through our divine birthright.

In varying forms, those are the issues with which my clients have entrusted me through all these years. And again, the answers I offer have nothing to do with me, other than my willingness to stay out of the way, accurately repeat the information I'm given (whether it makes the slightest bit of sense to me or not) and rest assured that I'm only given whatever information my clients are meant to know, which is not my call to make.

As essential to my readings as God Himself are the affidavits I ask for from every client I "read." I don't just want validation, I *need* validation. I need to know if what I've passed along is accurate and helpful. If it's not both of those things, it's time for me to close my doors.

I'm not talking about 100 percent accuracy. God is the sole possessor of that phenomenon. My accuracy level has been clinically tested, and frequently, at somewhere between 85 to 90 percent. That's my yardstick, and the standard to which I expect my clients to hold me each and every day.

Contained in this book is just a fraction of those affidavits, from clients who've come to me for help with everything from health and relationship problems to missing and murdered loved ones to grief issues to spiritual confusion to the perpetual and ever-popular "When will I meet Mr./Ms. Right?" These written validations and thousands more are on file in my office, thanks to my tireless, meticulous staff, and the comparative handful I've included in these pages were culled only from those who specifically indicated their permission for me to quote them. Still, because I consider my clients' privacy to be sacrosanct, I won't use their real names as I tell their stories. If they care to "go public" about it—again, that's their call to make, not mine.

Just to clarify, by the way—some of the validations you'll read are addressed to me directly. Others are accounts of readings that were sent to my staff, and they refer to me in the third person. It might have been less confusing for me to transform them all into "Dear Sylvia" letter form, but I had my heart set on re-creating these validations in the form in which they arrived in my office.

In case you're wondering what accounts of other people's readings could possibly have to do with you, there are a couple of very simple answers to that question. For one thing, some of the greatest insights we can achieve in this life come from the best and the worst of shared experiences. For another, far more important thing, these stories offer a steady stream of reassurance that whatever you've been through, or are going through, or are bracing yourself to go through, someone else has been there too, and you're not alone.

To every client over this past half century, with or without an affidavit, whether you're contained in this book or not, I thank you from the bottom of my heart for all you've taught and given me, and for the courage it took to ask me the questions that mattered most to you, knowing I would never lie to you or give you false hope even when that's what you might have thought you wanted.

God bless you and love you. I do.

INSIGHT

Chapter 1

THE WORLD'S PSYCHIC HISTORY

As long as humankind has occupied this planet, we've felt a little vulnerable, a little afraid and more than a little Homesick for the Other Side, where we're accustomed to living in God's perfection. We've looked, listened and prayed for something or someone to tell us with some authority that life on earth isn't as random and illogical and pointless as it often seems.

Prehistoric man hoped to increase his odds of success at hunting food for his family.

Kings, pharaohs and warriors sought divine guidance on upcoming battles.

Presidents and prime ministers throughout history, eager to maximize their power; doctors, scientists, psychiatrists and law enforcement officers in search of solutions to mysteries that have eluded them; loved ones of the missing, the murdered with no suspect, the critically ill with no diagnosis; the singles in search of Mr. or Ms. Right; children with night terrors, or genius far beyond their years; adults with debilitating fears, or simply the quiet, urgent need to know that they matter, if only to God . . .

In doubt, in desperation, in grief and in spiritual hunger, humankind of every circumstance, in every culture, religion and civilization since time began has turned to those who seem to have some sort of special insight, an "inside track" from some Greater Power, to answer their most practical and most intangible questions.

By whatever name they've called them, they've turned to psychics.

It's not easy to narrow down exactly what a "psychic" is. In general, a psychic is anyone who's able to receive and accurately interpret messages that originate from sources that are normally imperceptible to the five senses of sight, hearing, touch, taste and smell—in other words, sources that are "extrasensory." That would correctly mean that every person on earth is psychic, since every one of us has "gut feelings," "impulses," "instincts," "intuitions" and other signals we act on that have nothing to do with the five senses. I like to use the analogy that the difference between "being psychic" and "being a psychic" is like the difference between "playing the piano," which anyone can do, even if they use their foot or elbow, and having the gifts that elevate some to becoming concert pianists.

READINGS THROUGH THE AGES

There's no written history of the first time an African tribe turned to an anointed witch doctor to dispel a curse or summon the gods to guarantee a safe return home after a long hunt. We can't know when the East Indians elevated a select few to be their shamans, or healers, or when the first accurate fortune-teller, seer or soothsayer attracted their first believers in the villages of Eastern Europe and northern Africa.

We do know that around 2000 B.C., the Chinese turned to the I Ching, or "Book of Changes," and to the masters who could interpret the messages from beyond, thought to be found in the patterns formed when I Ching sticks or bones were cast on the ground.

We know that several centuries before Christ the ancient Greeks flocked to the sacred temple of Apollo near the town of Delphi to receive spiritual wisdom and prophecies from the Oracles who presided there. The most revered of the Oracles at Delphi was Sibyl, who was consulted about everything from battle strategies to which laws should be enacted. King Croesus of Lydia probably received the most infamously misinterpreted message from the Oracle in 550 B.C., when he asked about his plan to attack Persia. He was told that if he proceeded, "Croesus will destroy a great empire." Since that was exactly what he had in mind, he led the invasion of Persia, where he and his army were soundly defeated, leading to the Persian conquering of Lydia. Croesus bitterly demanded to know how the Oracle could have told him a lie of such magnitude, to which the Oracle replied that there was no lie, that her prophecy had been fulfilled. Croesus had indeed destroyed a great empire. It just happened to be his.

Entire libraries have been written about the prophets—David, Isaiah, Joseph, Moses, Samuel, Hosea, Ezekiel, Micah, Buddha and Muhammad, to name a pitifully tiny handful—without whom the world's great religions wouldn't exist.

The Old Testament of the Bible, which was written between about 1450 B.C. and 430 B.C., is filled with the writings of prophets, including some stunningly prophetic images of the birth, life and crucifixion of Jesus Christ, events that were still hundreds of years in the future.

The fifth chapter and second verse of the Old Testament book of Micah, for example, reads, "But thou, Bethlehem Ephratah, though thou be little among the thousands of Judah, yet out of thee shall he come forth unto me that is to be ruler in Israel; whose goings forth have been from of old, from everlasting." Almost eight hundred years later, Jesus was born in the little Israeli town of Bethlehem.

Isaiah, the great prophet whose book appears in the Old Testament, was born in Jerusalem seven hundred years before Jesus's birth and wrote extensively about the coming Messiah. For example, Isaiah 7:14 reads, "Therefore the Lord himself will give you a sign; Behold a virgin shall conceive, and bear a son, and shall call his name Immanuel [which means 'God with us']."

Matthew 1:18–21 in the New Testament describes the birth of Christ: "When his mother Mary had been betrothed to Joseph, before they came together she was found to be with child of the Holy Spirit; and her husband Joseph, being just a man and unwilling to put her to shame, resolved to divorce her quietly. But as he considered this, behold, an angel of the Lord appeared to him in a dream, saying, 'Joseph, son of David, do not fear to take Mary as your wife, for that which is conceived in her is of the Spirit; she will bear a son, and you shall call his name Jesus, for he will save people from their sins.'"

Isaiah also predicted, accurately, that Jesus would be crucified with criminals and buried in the tomb of a rich man, while the prophet Zechariah, in the ninth chapter and ninth verse of his Old Testament book, said that the Messiah would ride into Jerusalem on a donkey, just as Jesus did.

The prophet David, who was Israel's greatest king, is credited with writing the Old Testament book of Psalms. Psalm 22 contains some heartbreakingly prophetic images of the crucifixion of Christ a thousand years before it occurred. It reads, in part:

> *All who see me mock at me,*
> > *they make mouths at me, they wag*
> > > *their heads;*
> *"He committed his cause to the Lord;*
> > *let him deliver him,*
> > *let him rescue him, for he delights in him!"* . . .
> *Yea, dogs are round about me;*
> > *a company of evildoers encircle me;*
> > *they have pierced my hands and feet—*
> *I can count all my bones—*

they stare and gloat over me;
   they divide my garments among them,
      and for my raiment they cast lots.

Matthew 27:28–40 in the New Testament is an eyewitness account of Christ's crucifixion and reads, in part:

They stripped him and put a scarlet robe upon him, and plaiting a crown of thorns they put it on his head, and put a reed in his right hand. And kneeling before him they mocked him, saying, "Hail, King of the Jews!" And they spat upon him, and took the reed and struck him on the head. And when they had mocked him, they stripped him of the robe, and put his own clothes on him, and led him away to crucify him. And when they had crucified him, they divided his garments among them by casting lots . . . And those who passed by derided him, wagging their heads and saying, "You who would destroy the temple and build it in three days, save yourself! If you are the Son of God, come down from the cross."

Throughout his thirty-three years on this earth, Jesus himself expressed his awareness of and reverence for the great prophets who preceded him, but never did he state it more eloquently than in his beautiful Sermon on the Mount: "Think not that I have come to abolish the law and the prophets; I have come not to abolish them but to fulfill them" (Matthew 5:17).

The Jewish Torah, which is God's teachings in written form, corresponds, of course, to the Old Testament, with the prophets considered to be God's messengers and teachers on earth. In Judaism the greatest of all prophets was Moses, who delivered the Israelites from their slavery to the pharaoh to the Promised Land of Canaan. It was Moses whom God summoned to the sacred peak of Mount Sinai to present him with the stone tablets on which the Ten Commandments were written. According to the Jewish faith, Moses saw the combined prophecies of all other prophets still to come. And it's worth mentioning that Moses's birth was predicted to the pharaoh by his own team of personal astrologers, who had significant influence over the pharaoh's decisions and, by definition, over the politics of Egypt itself.

Muhammad, born in Mecca in A.D. 570, was the founder of the Islamic faith and is considered by the followers of that faith, called Muslims, to be the last of the great prophets and messengers sent by God to guide and teach mankind about the one Creator, the all-knowing, all-merciful, supreme and sovereign God, whom they call Allah. Muhammad was forty years old when, during one of his meditative retreats near Mecca, he was visited by the Angel Gabriel and received the first of what would ultimately be twenty-three years of revelations from God, the core of the great religion of Islam.

And then there was a brilliantly gifted child named Siddhartha Gautama, born in northern India twenty-five hundred years ago to Queen Maha Maya and her husband King Suddhodana. After twenty-nine years of luxury in the palace as a cherished prince, Siddhartha abandoned his royal legacy, his wealth and his family and set out alone to find a cure to the tragic cycle of birth, deprivation, illness, dying and death that he'd seen outside the palace walls and found to be unbearably devastating. Six years later, after a journey that included both debilitating deprivation and loneliness, he sat down in a forest beneath a spreading fig tree and vowed, "Though my skin, my nerves and my lifeblood go dry, I will not abandon this seat until I have realized Supreme Enlightenment." He meditated there all night long, through a raging storm, as his prayers of clarity and understanding were answered one by one, and as dawn broke, Prince Siddhartha had been transformed into the great Buddha Shakyamuni, the Enlightened One, founder of the beautiful, active, self-propelled religion of Buddhism. Among the Buddhist scripts is a prophecy of a future Buddha, who currently resides in the *Tutshita,* or heaven. His name, the prophecy says, will be Maitreya, which means "The Best of Men," and his description reads, in part:

He will have a heavenly voice which reaches far; his skin will have
a golden hue; a great splendor will radiate from his body; his chest
will be broad, limbs well developed, and his eyes will be like lotus
petals. His body is eighty cubits high and twenty cubits broad. He
will have a retinue of eighty-four thousand persons . . . And those
who have listened to his Dharma [ways of protecting ourselves
from ignorance] *will be assembled in a park full of beautiful flow-*
ers, and his assembly will extend over a hundred leagues. Under
Maitreya's guidance, hundreds of thousands of living beings shall
enter upon a religious life.

Not all prophets inspired great religions, of course, but their contributions to both the earthly and paranormal worlds are still profound
and still being intensely studied today, long after the seers themselves
headed Home.

There's Nostradamus of France, born in 1503, who wrote a series
of 942 prophetic four-line verses, or quatrains, that have been translated and interpreted and marveled over and scoffed at for more than
five hundred years. One of his most often quoted prophecies concerned one of three Antichrists he warned of, a master manipulator he
referred to as a "great enemy of the human race":

Out of the deepest part of the west of Europe,
From poor people a young child shall be born,
Who with his tongue shall seduce many people,
His fame shall increase in the Eastern Kingdom.

He shall come to tyrannize the land.
He shall raise up a hatred that had long been dormant.
The child of Germany observes no law.
Cries, and tears, fire, blood, and battle.

It's hard to ignore the "coincidence" (as if there were such a thing)
of Adolf Hitler's birth to a poor Austrian family in 1889, and the

subsequent havoc he wreaked more than three hundred years after Nostradamus's uncannily accurate description of his obscene impact on the world.

There's Madame Helena Blavatsky, born in Russia in 1831, an exotic, eccentric spiritualist and psychic whose occasionally outrageous presentation sadly compromised her undeniable prophetic gifts from time to time. On the downside, for example, is an infamous (and frankly almost hilarious) "actual photograph" of Madame Blavatsky seated in front of three "Ascended Masters" she routinely channeled at séances, who conveniently materialized, one of them in an ermine cloak, to pose with her. On the upside, there were her recorded predictions that atoms could be divided, that atoms are in perpetual motion and that matter and energy can be converted, all of which were proven to be true after her death in 1891. In fact, Ascended Masters and other questionable behavior to the contrary, her book *The Secret Doctrine,* filled with insights and prophecies on a staggering variety of subjects, was one of a handful of volumes Albert Einstein was known to keep within easy reach on his desk.

There's the British author and prophet H. G. Wells (1866–1946), who's most popularly known for such science-fiction novels as *The War of the Worlds* and *The Island of Dr. Moreau.* Among his verifiable predictions were the atomic bomb, the London Blitz, the use of airplanes in the military, computers, uranium bombs, television sets and VCRs.

There's Sir Arthur Conan Doyle, author of the legendary Sherlock Holmes novels and short stories, who devoted the last half of his life almost exclusively to his fervent belief in spiritualism. He began channeling his Spirit Guide Phineas and, shortly before his death in 1930, shared a series of prophecies he'd received, including "earthquakes of great severity and enormous tidal waves" that would destroy a large portion of the human race and "roughly three years of upheavals and disturbance" in the Eastern Mediterranean basin, "where not less than five countries will entirely disappear." His prophecies ended with a conclusion I think all of us know to be true in the core of our souls: "Mankind can be saved by returning to its spiritual values."

There's the wonderful "Sleeping Prophet," Edgar Cayce, born and raised in Kentucky in the late 1800s, who, with no medical training, cured countless illnesses "by remote" for clients hundreds or thousands of miles away, through information that came to him during self-induced trances. He ultimately expanded his work to include an amazing variety of metaphysical exploration, from brilliant reincarnation studies to such prophecies as (in 1939) the deaths of Franklin Roosevelt in 1945 and John Kennedy in 1963, and (in 1935) an approaching cataclysm in Europe involving Germany, Austria and ultimately Japan.

There are too many other historically prominent prophets and psychics to even list for this discussion, let alone explore—Aldous Huxley, Eileen Garrett, Mother Shipton, Maria Esperanza—and those names barely scratch the surface of those who've left their indelible marks on the world and paved the way for the rest of us.

Then, of course, we can't overlook the astrologers, who, it's thought, since ancient Babylonia have looked to the cosmos for signs of the choices and the hurdles that lie ahead of us, and our best possible responses to them.

There are palmists, who interpret the past, present and future through the natural markings of the hands.

There are the numerologists, who use a combination of numbers and the alphabet, and the subject's birth date and full given name, for signs of what's gone before, what lies ahead and what's in the way.

There are the tarot card readers, who use a deck of symbolic, specifically defined cards to spell out a subject's potential, stumbling blocks and most advantageous courses of action in virtually every area of life.

There are the channels, who receive spirit communication by entering an altered state of consciousness and allowing spirits to literally speak through them.

There are mediums, who receive spirit communication and pass it along by simply repeating it in their own voices.

There are shamans, who, in their classic definition, heal through the nature around them and all the wisdom that living nature contains.

There are clairvoyants, who see and interpret information from other dimensions.

There are clairaudients, who hear and interpret information from other dimensions.

There are clairsentients, who *feel* and interpret information from other dimensions.

There are (or *were,* since they've all but disappeared) phrenologists, who interpreted significant meanings in the natural shape and surface of the head.

There are tasseographers, which is the formal name for those who interpret information found in the varying shapes of tea leaves.

There are alchemists, who use an arcane set of herbal and other natural formulas, including an utterly elusive substance called the Philosopher's Stone, to heal and to reveal divine information.

There are those who look for spiritual messages of hope and doom in everything from rising smoke (capnomancists) to burning twigs (botanomancists) to the movements of fish (ichthymomancists) to randomly opened books (rhapsodomancists) to the behavior of snakes (ophiomancists).

And again, I'm just scratching that particular surface.

It's no surprise that the world of psychic and paranormal phenomena has been studied, tested, researched, celebrated, revered, scoffed at as one giant global con job and reviled as "the devil's work." Madame Blavatsky and Colonel Henry Olcott, an American journalist and researcher who served on a commission investigating the Lincoln assassination, founded the Theosophical Society in 1875 to study, among other things, spiritualism and the occult. The Society for Psychical Research was founded in England in 1882 by no less than a Cambridge professor named Henry Sidgwick, who was soon joined by none other than Sir Arthur Conan Doyle. Well-known medium Arthur Ford created the Spiritual Frontiers Fellowship in 1955. The Stanford Research

Institute and Duke University have exhaustively investigated every corner of the psychic arena. The CIA and the Defense Intelligence Agency chimed in with Project Star Gate in 1975, gathering a team of "remote viewers," or those who can perceive and describe details about a specific location that they're separated from by time, distance or a physical barrier. The government hoped that remote viewing skills could pinpoint everything from covert enemy arsenals to missing hostages. (Project Star Gate was officially disbanded in 1995, and its twenty years of research, its intended targets and its roster of participants remain classified.) I created my own Nirvana Foundation for Psychic Research. The list of organizations devoted to researching and testing psychic phenomena in the last century and a half goes on and on and on.

The skeptics, who are legion, take the position that even after all that intense scrutiny, no one has been able to scientifically prove that psychic phenomena exist.

The rest of us take the position that firsthand eyewitness experience is all the proof we need.

And to be fair, there's no arguing the fact that for every legitimate, gifted, honest psychic who's ever existed, there have been thousands upon thousands of frauds.

Some are skilled at simple magic tricks and sleight-of-hand, particularly illusions that involve wrapping your cash in a handkerchief and, after you've closed your eyes in prayer for a few critical moments, seeing the handkerchief opened again to reveal nothing but a pile of charred, worthless ashes. Why? Because your money was ill-gotten and therefore cursed—or, more accurately, because it was switched with an identical handkerchief full of ashes and is now residing in the psychic/medium/spiritualist's pocket.

Others go to the trouble of rigging a room with "ghostly" visions, sound effects and levitating tables. Even the prophetically gifted Madame Blavatsky sadly resorted to some very cheesy, completely phony apparitions with the help of hidden partitions and well-designed lighting.

Then there are the blatant extortionists whose effectiveness at removing a curse (which never exists in the first place unless you believe it does) or securing the love, health or success you're after is directly dependent on how much money you're willing to hand over.

There are those who do very well, particularly among the superstitious, selling specialty items that have been "blessed" or endowed with specific powers thanks to (imaginary) rituals and prayers—usually candles, herbs or small vials of "holy" (aka "tap") water. The effectiveness of these items is invariably related to their cost. A $40 candle intended to make you irresistible to a potential love interest, for example, will allegedly pale in comparison to the results you'll get from the $80 candle. But for maximum effectiveness, an especially magical $120 candle can often be retrieved from a back room "only for you" if you happen to be paying with cash as opposed to a check or credit card, on which payment can be stopped when you get home and realize you've just paid $120 for a $2.50 candle. If the hilariously expensive candles, herbs or holy water don't seem to be accomplishing as much as you'd hoped (and they won't), and you make a return trip to complain, you'll invariably be told that the real fault is yours. It's your negativity that's blocking the results, or that pesky curse you're afflicted with, or your unwillingness to believe, or, worst of all, your stinginess, for which God is clearly punishing you. There's only one solution—you've simply got to prove your sincerity and devotion by being more generous. And what luck, your savings account, or your jewelry, or your car just might do the trick. Which leads to the most obvious question that too few trusting, earnest people remember to ask themselves in time: what possible use does God have for cash, jewelry or a car?

Most common, particularly on "psychic hotlines," are the cold readers, who artfully display uncanny accuracy without the callers ever realizing that it was they who provided all the significant information.

All despicable, all immoral, all cashing in on people's faith, vulnerability and basic human need for reassurance.

As most law enforcement authorities will confirm, there are two primary reasons why so many of these lowlife thieves get away with their crimes and avoid prosecution: they're very skilled at leaving town and disappearing as soon as they sense the threat of exposure; and, sadly, most of their victims are too embarrassed by their gullibility, stupidity and willingness to turn to a "psychic" in the first place to step up and file a formal complaint or participate in an investigation.

If you're one of those victims, please, *please* ask yourself which is more embarrassing in the long run—trusting a con artist when you were vulnerable and then helping expose them, or trusting a con artist when you were vulnerable and then, by your silence, letting them move right along to other victims, partially funded by your hard-earned money?

A third reason these frauds are often more successful than they have any right to be is possibly the one that upsets me the most: their victims are frightened of retribution from the con artist. Let me put that fear to rest right now. For one thing, if these supposed psychics/mediums/spiritualists had any real power to significantly change your life for better or worse, they wouldn't be frauds to begin with and you wouldn't be feeling so ripped off. For another thing, if there really were such things as curses, "evil eyes," "bad mojo" and all the other threatened dark clouds that keep these people in business, I would have dropped dead years ago of some mysterious affliction for all the con artists I've helped to expose.

Professional debunkers would probably be surprised at how many frauds I've personally busted and reported to various district attorneys around the country, as have many of my predecessors and current colleagues. Those of us who experience the paranormal every day of our lives and treasure its God-given potential are probably more offended than anyone else by those who reduce it to just another quick, easy scam. Whether the Skeptics Society and other debunkers take it as good news or bad news, they and I have much more in common than they might think.

Take the client who showed up in my office one day for a reading, very upset about some dire predictions she'd received from another psychic.

She listed some of them for me, and I was horrified, not only by how wrong they were but also by how vague and unhelpful they were. ("Be very careful of a woman with dark hair," for example, is an example of an inane but all too common "prediction." What specific woman with dark hair? Who is she? Why be careful of her? What's she going to do, when is she going to do it, and for what purpose? With no more information than that, you're in danger of being uneasy around every dark-haired woman you come across. What are you supposed to do, run screaming from every plane you step onto where you're greeted by a stewardess with dark hair, or choose exclusively blond female friends, coworkers, service people and caregivers from now on? Anyone who leaves you with more fear than comfort in the course of a reading is getting their information from somewhere other than the loving, compassionate God and spirit world where the only truth can be found, I guarantee it.)

Once this poor client had finished her litany of the hazy "predictions" that had caused her who knows how many sleepless nights, I couldn't resist asking, "Who on earth told you all this?"

I think my hair literally stood on end when the client replied, "The woman in Texas who does readings for you."

My shriek of "What?!" could probably be heard for miles around.

It seems that a "psychic" in Austin, and others I've unearthed since, was claiming to be some kind of endorsed representative of mine, seeing clients on my behalf since, after all, I can't be in all places at all times. I can't stress enough: *No one reads for me. I have no team of endorsed psychic representatives around the country, or around the world, filling in for me to take up the slack in my waiting list.* That has never happened, and it never will, for the same reason I've turned down multimillion-dollar offers to create my own psychic phone hotline. I can't guarantee or control the quality, validity or integrity of any readings but my own, nor would I ever, not even for millions of dollars. If you ever doubt how seriously I take my psychic gifts and my insistence on using them only for the humanitarian purposes God intended when He gave them to me, call the woman in Austin who was "reading for me" and ask how much of her was left by the time I finished with her on the phone. Between my efforts and those of the Austin district attorney, let's just say she was successfully persuaded to make a career change.

And then there was the "spiritual adviser" in San Jose who was luring clients by offering $10 readings and then invariably discovering that they were the unwitting victims of potentially fatal curses that—what luck—the spiritual adviser could dispel for $4000, *cash only*. The San Jose district attorney and I made short work of her too, just as we did with a Vallejo "reader" who had a comparatively bargain rate scam going: her charge for dispelling curses was only $2500. A steal. And I really mean that.

My dear friend Montel Williams and I shut down an outrageously corrupt "psychic" in Manhattan whose name was Madame Zorro, or Madame Zara, something like that. Come to think of it, the "reader" in Vallejo was a Madame "Z" too—Zina, or Zita. Presumably "Madame" followed by a name that starts with one of the less common letters of the alphabet is meant to sound exotic, mysterious and otherworldly. More often than not, it's simply a harder alias to trace than if there was a last name involved.

Most outrageous, though, might have been a scam artist who advertised her psychic hotline in a whole array of national tabloids. Her name? Silvia Brown. "Internationally Renowned Psychic and Television Star" Silvia Brown, if I'm remembering correctly. Eerily close to the name Sylvia Browne, don't you think? The battery of lawyers I unleashed on her thought so too, and believe me, I took particular pleasure in putting a stop to her.

It's worth repeating: there never has been and never will be a psychic hotline that I'm involved with in any way. Period. If you hear of one that claims I have anything to do with it, *please* call my office and your local district attorney, in whichever order you prefer.

I'm sure the very nature of the psychic/spiritual/paranormal "business" (that always seems like such an odd way to refer to my life's purpose and passion, but it's appropriate for this discussion) prevents people from thinking about this when they're booking a reading. But before you make an appointment, don't be shy about checking out the psychic in question. Word of mouth is worth paying attention to, obviously, and no psychic has any longevity at all without a great track record. Why stop there, though? Why not find out if they have a business license, and/or if they're members of the Better Business Bureau and, if so, whether or not there have been complaints about them? Your first reaction to those questions might be "Who cares, as long as I get a legitimate reading?" But what's wrong with making sure ahead of time that the legitimate reading you're after is coming from a legitimate businessperson? Let's face it, being "legitimate for the most part" is like being "a little bit pregnant"—there is no such thing. You either are or you aren't. And because I know how hard my legitimate colleagues and I have to fight for every ounce of credibility we've got, I can't encourage you enough to take every possible precaution, before you even walk in the door, to protect yourself from the frauds who make a mockery of this profession I cherish.

In the meantime, I'll continue posting fraud alerts on both of my websites—*www.sylvia.org* and *www.novus.org,* and I'll keep right on working with law enforcement to try to close down every scam, fraud, thief and con artist you bring to my attention. The damage they do financially is bad enough. But the emotional, psychological and spiritual damage they're capable of doing is incalculable.

So speak up, without embarrassment or fear, if not for yourself, then for the next victim who may not have as much courage as you do. Let's face it, we're all in this together, learning and growing as best we can in this rough school of life on earth, our purpose boiling down to three simple basics you've probably heard me say a million times:

Do good,

Love God,

Then shut up and go Home.

Chapter 2

MY OWN PSYCHIC HISTORY

Compared with the earth's psychic history that's existed "since humankind first set foot on this planet," my family's three-hundred-year psychic lineage makes us seem like a bunch of newcomers. Be that as it may, as many of you know, I was born in Kansas City, Missouri, on October 19, 1936, and I've been genetically psychic since that day.

I'm asked all the time what it's like to be psychic, and the best I can do to describe it is to answer the question with a question: "What's it like to be *you*?" I've never experienced not being psychic, so I have nothing to compare it with, just as you've never experienced being anyone but you. I did learn very early in my childhood that I was seeing and hearing things that those around me weren't. If my wise and brilliantly psychic grandma Ada hadn't been there to explain what I was experiencing, and to help me think of it as a gift rather than a burden, I'm sure I would have grown up frightened, self-conscious and desperate to hide my apparent insanity from the rest of the world.

Instead, with Grandma Ada's comforting guidance, I learned to pay attention to the sights, sounds and silent knowledge that seemed to be seeking out me of all people, this child who yearned to be "normal." I learned to pray that I not be given information I could neither handle nor do anything about—no visions of melting faces on those who were about to die, please; no random violent "movies" of plane crashes with no telltale flight numbers, or twisted mangled cars full of bleeding accident victims without enough details to warn someone ahead of time; no involuntary collage of crime scenes unless they were accompanied by the names or faces of the criminals involved. I learned to accept, and ultimately embrace, my Spirit Guide, who burst into my life from the Other Side one night when I was eight years old and, once I recovered from my initial terror of her, even accepted my insistence on changing her name from Iena to Francine. I learned that the nuns at the Catholic school I attended were insistent on the reality of spirits who survive death, and of Angels, but had no patience whatsoever with my announcement that I routinely saw and communicated with those same spirits and Angels. (I thought the nuns would be delighted that I was able to confirm the existence of this spirit world they kept carrying on about. Instead, it inspired them to consider me a discipline problem who needed to keep her fairy tales to herself.)

Nuns and confusion aside, I decided that if I had to be stuck with "knowing things," as the euphemism went, I might as well stop keeping those things to myself, whether anyone wanted to hear them or not.

Sometimes it caused problems—like when I informed my mother that my father had a girlfriend, including what she looked like and how long he'd been seeing her, even though there had never been the slightest hint that a girlfriend existed.

Sometimes it was literally a Godsend—like the day my father and I were sitting in a movie theater and, in the middle of the movie, I felt a sudden, ice-cold panic and screamed at him that we had to go home *right that second.* My baby sister, Sharon, couldn't breathe, I told him. She was turning blue, and she would die if we didn't get there to help her. We were met in the driveway by Mother, who managed to tell us through her frantic sobs that something was desperately wrong with

Sharon. She was burning up with fever and gasping for air. Mother had tried to call an ambulance, but the phone was inexplicably dead. Daddy sped Sharon to the hospital with only minutes to spare, the doctors told him later, but she did successfully recover from what turned out to be double pneumonia.

Dispensing both important and trivial unsolicited information to everyone around me became second nature to me throughout my childhood. But to this day I remember the first time someone actually sought me out for an answer to something that had been troubling her. Technically speaking, it was my first official "psychic reading."

I was eight years old. My Spirit Guide, Francine, and I were beginning to communicate with some regularity, still a bit hesitantly and skeptically on my part, but there was no denying the fact that she was interesting and seemed to know what she was talking about.

One day a classmate named Mary Marguerite approached me after school, pulling me aside so that we'd be out of earshot of the other children. Mary Marguerite and I had been friends since we were five years old. She'd become completely accustomed to my psychic gifts, which translated through the lovely, simple acceptance of a child's eyes as my just knowing things that other people didn't. Looking back, I don't think she or any of my other childhood friends thought any more of my "knowing things" than we thought of the fact that our friend Louise could touch the tip of her nose with her tongue and our friend Cindy could voluntarily burp.

"Sylvia," Mary Marguerite whispered, "I'm really worried about my mom. She doesn't seem very happy, and I don't know why. Is there something wrong with her?"

I had no conscious awareness of asking Francine, or Anyone Else, for that matter. And in retrospect, I wish I'd had a more insightful answer to give her. But an answer did come to me instantly, and I shared it with her. "I don't know, but she needs to be careful, because she's going to fall down and break her arm." I admit it, I was amazed at how clearly I saw and knew that, on command, in response to a question, rather than simply at random as usual. And it turned out I wasn't finished. "Your father's going to lose his job too."

Within two months Mary Marguerite's mother had broken her arm and her father had lost his job. My first official "reading," and even at eight years old it didn't count as far as I was concerned until and unless I turned out to be right.

REJECTING AND EMBRACING THE GIFT

I "read" my way through high school, for girlfriends anxious to hear if their boyfriends were faithful and/or would marry them someday, for a few sheepish members of the faculty who couldn't resist privately checking out their supposedly psychic student, for virtually everyone but myself—and if my teenage years proved nothing else, they proved that I don't have a psychic bone in my body when it comes to my own life. As high school ended and college began, I was mourning the loss of my cherished grandma Ada and the end of a relationship with a man I was sure would be the greatest and the last love of my life. (Not even close, needless to say.) And as much as I appreciated the challenging stimulation of my courses at St. Theresa's College, tackling double majors in education and literature, with a minor in theology, I felt lost, empty, afraid and alone.

I can't trace exactly when depression compelled me to start actively "tuning out" my psychic gifts in general and Francine in particular. But I do know that denying the essence of who I was made me physically ill, persistently flat on my back with everything from the flu to bronchitis to full-blown pneumonia. I also know that the self-doubt I was struggling with took root and flourished as I began adding abnormal psychology courses to my already overloaded curriculum and discovered that at least four of the seven primary levels of mental illness seemed to describe me perfectly.

Believe me, I'm well aware that most of you who've taken psychology courses were as unnerved as I was by the creepy suspicion that those infernal lists of psychotic symptoms hit a little too close to home. I had some added bonuses, though, that many of you had the luxury of ignoring. All my life I'd seen visions no one else saw. All my life I'd heard voices no one else heard. The conclusion seemed unavoidable and paralyzing: I was obviously schizophrenic.

That realization would have been devastating enough all by itself, but as far as I was concerned it also meant the end of my dream of becoming a teacher. It was the only career I'd ever imagined for myself, and I truly believed I'd be good at it. There wasn't a chance, though, that I was going to jeopardize innocent children by exposing them every day to a teacher who also happened to be a raving lunatic. I'm sure Grandma Ada would have "grounded" me and pulled me back on track, but she was gone, and I plugged my ears to Francine by redefining her as the ultimate proof of my terrible mental illness. I finally confided in my doctor and in a priest I'd known for many years, both of whom were compassionate, understanding and insistent on sending me to a psychiatrist. I went, convinced that he would confirm my self-diagnosis. My doctor and my priest admitted later that they fully expected what actually happened: after an endless barrage of interviews and tests, the psychiatrist sat me down, pulled his chair close to mine and calmly concluded, "You're perfectly normal, but something paranormal is going on as well."

It was better than "In my professional opinion, you're nuts." But I still wasn't completely persuaded that I could safely unleash myself on hapless classrooms full of children. After all, I had proof of my dementia, that constant, chirping presence named Francine who'd been part of my life, part of *me,* since I was eight years old, that haunting voice that no one else could hear. The more I read, the more I studied, the more I agonized over her, the clearer it became that not only was Francine not a being from the spirit world, not only was she not my Guide, she wasn't even real. That's why I was the only person who'd experienced her. She was imaginary, just some alternate personality my own pathetic mind had created as an escape, a diversion from my abusive mother, a textbook coping mechanism I'd been foolish enough to indulge. If I could get rid of her once and for all, it would mean I'd managed to integrate myself into one cohesive being again, and could maybe even look forward to being sane someday.

It sounded so logical to me, and I was so convinced that saying good-bye to the imaginary Francine was a giant leap toward mental health, that I actually gave her a ceremonial farewell speech. I explained everything I'd been going through and everything I'd been thinking, building to the grand finale of unmasking her Spirit Guide facade and telling her that finally, thank God, I knew my imagination had conjured her up, which meant that it could just as easily eliminate her.

She listened with her characteristic patience, neither defending herself nor resenting me. She didn't say a word until I was finished. Then she made a suggestion, which I was free to accept or reject, completely my choice: if the issue was that no one had ever experienced her but me, and she was unable to make that happen, then I could go right ahead and dismiss her as imaginary and she'd never bother me again. But if she really was my Spirit Guide, an actual living entity from the Other Side as she claimed to be, and others besides me could experience her as a being completely separate from me, it should prove once and for all that my sanity was perfectly intact.

"What are you suggesting?" I asked her, almost afraid to hear the answer.

"Gather your family," she said. "I will show myself to you, and to them. Then you will know."

In all these years, I'd never seen Francine. She'd described herself to me: five feet nine inches tall, slender, with olive skin, very large dark eyes, and black hair that she wore in a thick braid that fell to her waist. Oddly, the subject of her manifesting herself had never even come up. Now she was offering, as the ultimate proof of my own mental health or lack of it, which made it an offer I couldn't refuse.

"When?" I asked.

"Tonight," she replied. My hands were shaking as I dialed my parents' number.

It was raining. Of course. Daddy, Mother and my sister, Sharon, were with me in the darkened room full of candles Francine had asked for. (Spirits can see candlelight more clearly than electric lights, by the way, in case you've ever wondered.) They were almost giddy with the anticipation of meeting and actually seeing this woman I'd been carrying on about for all these years. In sharp contrast, I was anxious, almost terrified, torn between an odd fear of Francine materializing and a dread of her not materializing, of the four of us sitting there hour after hour, waiting and watching for nothing at all, which would prove beyond all doubt how nuts I really was.

There was an empty rocking chair beside me. Daddy, Mother and Sharon were sitting across from me. We were all silent. The only sound was the heavy rain outside my small apartment windows. It was Daddy's eyes I noticed first, as they moved to the rocking chair and began widening in amazement. Within moments Mother's and Sharon's eyes were fixed there too, mirroring Daddy's look of something approaching awe.

I couldn't bring myself to look directly at the rocking chair where their stares were held. Instead I just watched peripherally as, very slowly and gracefully, without a sound, a pale blue dress began to take shape, its soft opaque folds draping from the seat of the chair to the dark wood floor.

Then the long, slender fingers of a hand with impossibly smooth burnished gold/olive skin appeared against the pastel blue, resting in the lap of the dress. An arm, thin and muscular, revealed itself gradually above the hand, as if a transparent veil was being lifted.

At that point my father suddenly blurted out, "Don't anyone speak until she's gone, so we won't take a chance on influencing each other about what we saw." No one answered him. He seemed to be the only one of us in the room who was able to find a voice.

As I continued to watch out of the corner of my eye, a long, thick braid of black hair fell without warning from the front of the shoulder to lie against the arm.

And that was all I could take. While my enthralled family continued to gape, I turned away and never glanced back. That's all I saw of Francine, all I wanted to see and I've never seen her again in the half century since.

Dr. John Renick, the psychiatrist whom I'd come to trust and value, was quick to point out the obvious the next day: Francine was clearly real. There were witnesses to verify it. So much for my alternate personality/imagination theory, my last feared "symptom" of insanity.

"Why did you turn away?" he asked, with total compassion and no criticism or disapproval.

I rarely let other people see me cry, but there was no stopping my tears that day. "Because I have to live in this world," I told him. "I hear and see so much that normal people don't have to put up with. I don't want to be some airy-fairy weirdo. I want to be a teacher. I'm goofy enough. I can't afford to be any goofier, and I was afraid that if I let myself sit there and look at Francine as if she was just another person in the room, it might push me right over the edge."

He smiled, and I'll be grateful all my life for his reply that resonated with sincerity and affirmation. "Sylvia," he said, "what a perfectly sane thing to say."

I took that in and finally smiled back through my tears, and I never questioned my sanity again.

I started my teaching career shortly thereafter, at the age of nineteen. And slowly but surely I welcomed Francine back into my life. To this day, when I make jokes about my mental health, she temporarily stops speaking to me.

I loved being a teacher. I loved being a psychic teacher even more. I knew what any or all of my students were up to at any given moment, and it was an exercise in futility to try lying to me about why they hadn't done their homework or why they were late for school, since I was always able to tell them the real reason before they'd even finished the story they were making up as they went along.

Of far more importance, I knew without asking what was going on with each of them emotionally, and at home—who was being nurtured, who was being neglected, whose parents had substance abuse or anger problems, whose parents were too lazy or self-involved or just plain absent to provide something as simple as breakfast or a hug—so that I could find ways to make up the difference and see to it they never left my classroom without knowing that someone believed in them. I told my students every day of every week of every school year that I loved them, and because they were children, psychic little truth barometers that they are, they knew I meant it.

One morning early in my first year of teaching I was doing an involuntary psychic scan of each child as they all filed into the classroom, when I suddenly felt almost overwhelmed by the infinite array of physical, emotional and spiritual burdens these little bodies were being asked to bear, usually while trying to act as if nothing at all was wrong. There were the pathologically shy ones, the physically challenged ones who were the targets of every bully in school, the overly aggressive ones who were trying to hide deep insecurities, the ones to whom learning did not come easily no matter how hard they tried, the ones to whom school was a refuge because home was a nightmare, the ones who'd been told since the day they were born that they'd never amount to anything, the ones whose egos were so overfed that they were in danger of losing their compassion—every variation of the human condition, wrapped up in packages too small to contain them, let alone know how to cope with them.

I wanted to help them and calm them and reach their spirits in some meaningful way that would stay with them long after they left my classroom, and I also needed to ease the empathetic pain I was feeling for them or I'd never make it through a productive day of teaching without dissolving into an emotional puddle.

And so, on pure impulse, I stood up in front of them once they'd taken their seats and said, "Before we get started this morning I want you all to do something for me. Put your feet flat on the floor, rest your hands in your laps, let your bodies relax and close your eyes."

There was a bit of hesitation and confusion, but they followed instructions. "Now, take a few slow, deep breaths, in and out, in and out, and every time you breathe out I want you to think of something that's bothering you or making you sad and picture it flying away from you and disappearing into the sky."

They did. It became very quiet in the room, and I could feel the chaos in the air slowly dissipating.

And thus began what became a regular exercise in my classroom, what I guess could be called "subversive meditation." Not once did I actually use that word, to the class, or maybe even to myself. This was decades ago, in the heart of the Midwest, after all. If word had spread that Miss Shoemaker (my maiden name) was teaching children to meditate in her classroom, I'm sure I would have been fired, and I might have found myself on the receiving end of a public stoning. During those few minutes while my students quietly closed their eyes and relaxed, I talked them through such visualization techniques as picturing themselves becoming what they most wanted to be when they grew up, or spending the happiest, most perfect day they could imagine. I gave them simple affirmations for their health, their self-confidence, the God-given talents that each of them had and their value in this world that no one could ever take away from them.

Five minutes every day or two at most, and slowly but surely, it made a difference. Some of the changes were obvious—better grades, better behavior, better attitudes in general. Some of them were subtle—smiles from children who looked as if they hadn't smiled and meant it for far too long, shoulders slumped with discouragement straightening with some newfound pride, little gestures of kindness from students who'd previously been too self-involved to notice or care, new friendships formed I would have bet against, an enthusiasm for learning and participating that continued to grow as the year progressed. I don't want to create the false impression that I meditated my classrooms into little Shangri-las where there was never an imperfect moment and that every child magically sprouted a halo and wings thanks to me by the time summer vacation arrived. But I do want you to know that I never met a child who wasn't helped by a few minutes of quiet, focused creative visualization and affirmation on a regular basis.

My teaching career was a joy, as was my renewed acceptance of my God-given paranormal gifts and of Francine's constant presence.

And then there was my personal life, which was in an agonizing state of disrepair as I tried to recover from an inevitable breakup with my first real true love. Look up the term "rebound relationship" in any dictionary and you'll see a wedding photo of me and a young blue-eyed policeman named Gary Dufresne, too soon after that breakup. To be appropriately grateful, though, I walked away from that turbulent short-lived marriage with two sons I adore and a fresh start in northern California, where my passion for psychic readings evolved from a pastime into a full-time, lifelong joy.

MAKING THE COMMITMENT

I've only experienced one addiction, and I have no intention of trying to overcome it: I'm a learning junkie. I love school, I love studying, I love research, I even love the fact that the more I learn, the more I find I don't know. So it's no surprise that almost before I'd unpacked my bags in San Jose after a rushed move from Kansas City, I'd enrolled at San Francisco University, aiming toward my master's degree in literature.

SFU irreversibly changed the course of my life, in more ways than I could ever have anticipated. Or, to be more precise, a man named Bob Williams at SFU changed the course of my life. On a small scale, he was my creative writing instructor. On an infinitely larger scale, he was brilliantly well read and thought provoking about the worlds of the metaphysical and paranormal that I'd still never given myself full, unapologetic permission to explore. We'd talk and talk, late into the night, for more hours than I can possibly count, about those worlds, challenging and stimulating each other, sharing ideas and making me feel energized rather than inappropriate about my gifts and their potential. One day he pulled me into a small, eccentric bookstore and began loading a shopping basket with books by psychic healer Edgar Cayce, theosophist Madame Helena Blavatsky, prophets like Nostradamus and Arthur Conan Doyle, and even the philosophers Jean-Paul Sartre and Bertrand Russell. Laughing at what was quickly becoming a basket so full that books were overflowing onto the floor, I asked what he was doing.

"Giving you your next assignment," he said. "As your instructor, I officially order you to read every one of these books."

"I already have," I told him proudly.

It didn't faze him one bit. "Then read them again. Only this time, put them to use. The authors of these books are no different from you. They had gifts as controversial as yours. But they used them to blast through conventional boundaries and break new ground, without waiting for permission. They devoted their lives to learning everything they could about the unique insights God gave them, and then they used what they knew to heal, enlighten, comfort or just bring a glimpse of hope to this hard, scary world. You can do what they did, and your work can be as important as theirs was if you'll commit to it and stay committed."

"You really believe that?" I wasn't fishing for a compliment, I was insisting on the truth from him.

"I believe in you," he said, and those four simple words from that vibrant, loving, generous man ignited a fire in my spirit that has never gone out.

As if to put his money where his mouth was, Bob surprised me in our creative writing class a few days later. We'd finished our discussion of *Ulysses* with a half hour left to go before the bell rang, and suddenly, so nonchalantly that I knew he'd planned it, he announced that Sylvia

Dufresne would be happy to give a demonstration of psychic readings if anyone would care to volunteer.

There were fifty students in the room. Fifty hands went up. I gaped at Bob like a deer in the headlights, and he grinned confidently back, as I made my way to the front of the class. I honestly don't remember a thing about the readings I did that day, due to some combination of nervousness and shock. But I do remember excitement and applause when the bell rang a half hour later, and being treated with conspicuously increased respect from that day on. Unbeknownst to me at the time, and thanks entirely to my dear friend Bob Williams, Sylvia Shoemaker Dufresne had just established the beginnings of "a following."

I'll always think of it as one of the great tragic ironies of my life that Bob, my biggest fan and most trusting believer, didn't listen the one time I begged him to pay attention. For a long time he'd been planning a one-year trip to Australia that he was wildly excited about. And I, without having any specifics to offer, psychically knew beyond any doubt that if Bob went to Australia, I would never see him alive again. If he went to Australia, he would come home in a coffin. I was sure of it, and I didn't just ask him not to go, I pleaded with him not to go.

"What do you think is going to happen to me?" he asked, much too lightheartedly.

"You'll die, Bob."

"Of what?"

"I don't know. That's all I'm getting. That you'll die in Australia. And I can't bear the thought of that."

It was a conversation we had a thousand times, and it always ended with him hugging me and promising me he wasn't going to let anything happen. He often added, "If nothing else, I'm too much of a coward to die in Australia, because I know if I do, you'll kill me!" He always laughed at that. I never did.

So off went Bob, and a large part of my heart, to Australia, happy, healthy, already looking forward to coming home again so we could pick up where we left off. One day about three months into his trip he was taking a shower and happened to notice a small lump under his arm. When it didn't go away after a few weeks, he went to a doctor to have it checked out. The diagnosis: lymphatic cancer. Less than six months later he was dead, and he came home from Australia in a casket. There hasn't been a day since when I haven't missed Bob Williams and thanked him for throwing such a loving, unmistakable spotlight on the path I was meant to take.

Several weeks after Bob's death, a few friends and I went to hear a well-known psychic who was giving a lecture to a standing-room-only crowd in San Francisco. I arrived eager, ready to be inspired by someone who'd arrived at a place I aspired to go. Within ten minutes, I was getting annoyed. At the half-hour mark, I was angry. After an hour, I was so furious that it took every ounce of self-control not to storm out in protest.

I managed not to detonate until later, when my friends and I were safely seated in a booth at a nearby diner. "Any idiot can stand there and claim they predicted this and they saw that before anyone else did, and such-and-such celebrities don't take a breath without checking with them, and if it weren't for them that movie star wouldn't even have a career. First of all, where's the proof of all those claims they made? Where's their validation? Second of all, whose business is it of anybody's who their clients are? Could they have been any less discreet? What are they, publicity junkies? And third of all, how dare they take one bit of credit for their information? Have they spent two seconds wondering where the information really comes from? Have they studied and researched the psychic world at all, and learned that it's not about us, it's about God? Period. It starts and ends with Him, and that's where all the credit and thanks should go. But did you hear the word 'God' even once tonight? I didn't!"

I finally took a breath, and during it I heard Bob Williams's voice, clear as a bell, as if he were sitting next to me: "What are you going to do about it?"

The next morning, after a sleepless night, I founded and committed my life to the Nirvana Foundation for Psychic Research, in Bob's memory. Its purposes were to teach psychic development, to confirm the survival of the spirit after death according to God's promise of eternity, to exhaustively research every facet of the paranormal world, to insist on validation every step of the way, and to find every way I could to serve God as my way of thanking Him for this gift He'd given me. And what more personal, intimate way to go about it than to use that gift to bring comfort, hope and insights from the Other Side to every one of His children who looked to me for help?

That's how my "career" of psychic readings began, although the word "career" can't begin to encompass the honor, and the soaring awareness of God's grace, that continue to fill my heart every time a client tells me their reading made a difference.

Of course, from the beginning I've been the target of a whole lot of professional close-minded skeptics, atheists and a whole lot of dogmatic fundamentalists who've called me everything from a fraud to a scam artist to the devil's handmaiden. My position was, is and always will be that I respect everyone's right to their own beliefs, and if psychic phenomena don't happen to be among them, that only means we've had vastly different life experiences. When I experience and see proof of something over and over and over again, day after day, week after week and year after year, I happen to think I'd be the biggest fool on earth to disbelieve.

One of my most outspoken critics/accusers in the past several years has been James Randi, professionally known as the Amazing Randi, a stage magician, atheist and debunker who's expressed his opinion on national television that I'm a quack and a complete phony who uses cheap mental tricks to capitalize on people's fears and vulnerabilites to make myself rich and famous. To the best of my knowledge, Randi has never read a book of mine, or talked to a single client. But he offered me a challenge: if I could pass a series of psychic tests of his design to his satisfaction, he would give me a million dollars. I've rejected the challenge, not feeling the need at this stage in my life and career to jump through hoops to prove myself to him or to anyone, and I've suggested he take the million dollars he's raised and donate it to a legitimate, worthwhile charity who will see to it that it goes to those who could put it to such good use.

Randi has also never deliberately subjected himself to a reading from me. But one night on CNN's *Larry King Live* he got a spontaneous one that was as big a surprise to me as it was to him. Here's a partial transcript of that "reading," which aired on September 3, 2001:

BROWNE: But I'll tell you something about you, Randi. You've got to look into your left ventricle in your heart. Now, you can say I'm just full of, you know, whatever, but you've got to check your left ventricle.

RANDI: They've been telling about my kidneys and about my prostate, about my feet, about my heart, my lungs, I'm in very bad shape.

BROWNE: No, no, no, I'm very serious. You've got something wrong in your left ventricle.

RANDI: Yes, well, we'll check it out, and I'll let you know.

KING: Now, Randi, supposing you went to a cardiologist tomorrow and he said—this is just hypothetical—and he says to you, "Whew, your left ventricle . . ."

BROWNE: It's all screwed up.

KING: What would you say?

RANDI: I would get back to you immediately, Larry.

KING: You would?

RANDI: And I would tell you that it is true.

KING: And would that give you a plus toward maybe Sylvia has something?

RANDI: Well, as a matter of fact, I will call my cardiac surgeon tomorrow, and I will get back to you on e-mail, Larry, or by phone call if you will, and I will give you a complete report on the condition of my heart.

KING: He'll have to see you, though.

BROWNE: You can't just call him up.

Randi subsequently denied having any heart problems, although whether or not he actually provided Larry King with a complete report on the condition of his heart I have no idea.

What I do know is that on February 2, 2006, James Randi underwent emergency coronary artery bypass surgery. According to accounts of his admission to the hospital, this heart surgery "appeared to be unexpected."

Randi, I took no pleasure in that news, and you're in my prayers for a speedy, complete recovery.

As I said, I've grown accustomed to attacks on my psychic gifts. I've reached a point where I simply roll my eyes and shrug and go right back to work. It's like trying to convince avowed, close-minded atheists that God exists—they have some kind of stake in their absolute disbelief, so my absolute certainty that we experience God every second of every minute of every day, with every breath we take, is guaranteed to fall on deaf ears. I've lost interest, frankly, in the whole debate over the validity of paranormal phenomena. I know it's the truth. The dim, repetitious chorus of "no sir!" from professional debunkers has become too tedious to dignify with any other response but "I'm sorry, but you'll have to bore someone else with this noise. I'm busy."

What I don't tolerate, however, is a word of skepticism about the depth of my spirituality, and my absolute certainty of God's sacred promise of immortality. I've studied world religion since my late teens, including all twenty-six versions of the Bible, and I stand proudly among those who believe as I do:

- From Christianity: "The gift of God is eternal life, through Jesus Christ our Lord."

- From Judaism: "The dust returneth to the earth as it was, and the Spirit returneth unto God who gave it."
- From Islam: "Those who have believed and done the things which are right, these shall be the inmates of Paradise."
- From Jainism: "I know there will be a life hereafter."
- From Confucianism: "All the living must die and, dying, return to the ground, but the Spirit issues forth and is displayed in light."
- From Hinduism: "He becomes immortal who seeks the general good of man."
- From Sikhism: "Why weep when a man dieth, since he is only going home?"
- From Buddhism: "Earnestness is the path of immortality."
- From Shinto: "Regard Heaven as your father, Earth as your mother, all things as brothers and sisters, and you will enjoy the divine country which excels all others."
- From Taoism: "Life is going forth. Death is a returning home."
- From Zoroastrianism: "The soul of the righteous shall be joyful in immortality."
- From the Baha'i: "Make mention of Me on earth that in My Heaven I may remember thee."

If all those great, beautiful faiths and I are wrong and we're not going to the Other Side when these lifetimes are over, then I'll be perfectly happy to go wherever they're going.

But we're not wrong. You know that in your heart as surely as I know it in mine. You don't have to take my word for it. Take God's. He promised it in every language on earth.

READINGS AND FRANCINE

I want to clear up a common misconception even among those who know my work very well: my Spirit Guide, Francine, is *not* an active participant in my day-to-day readings. This is not a perpetual puppet show that she and I have going, in which I just sit down with a client and let her chirp away in my ear while I dutifully parrot whatever it is she has to say. My sources of information during readings are as widely varied as the readings themselves, all God-centered spirits from the Other Side as Francine is, but very often with far more experience on earth.

We each choose our Spirit Guide on the Other Side before we come here for another incarnation, trusting that guide to be our constant companion, our most intimate confidant and our subtle, objective mentor throughout this lifetime. One of the basic requirements for a Spirit Guide is that they have to have experienced at least one incarnation themselves, so that they can empathize with the countless temptations, fears, problems and inane, sometimes cataclysmic mistakes that are an inevitable part of being an earthly human. And one incarnation is all Francine chose to subject herself to. She was Aztec/Incan and lived in Colombia from 1500 to 1520. Before and after that, she's resided exclusively on the Other Side.

As I describe in detail in my book *Life on the Other Side*, we live in a state of perpetual bliss at Home, busy and perfect in an atmosphere alive with the Divine. There is no such thing as time, no past, present and future. Everything is "now," and eternity isn't just a concept, it's a fully understood fact, and the context in which everything is perceived.

And in the context of eternity, from a vantage point in which everything and its purpose are brilliantly clear, such genuinely traumatic earthly events as "I lost my job" or "my boyfriend dumped me" or even "my child is very ill" are, to put it bluntly, trivia. Our entire lifetimes on earth amount to the blink of an eye against a backdrop of the eternal, and the residents of the Other Side know that no matter what happens to us here, we'll be Home "in a minute" anyway. Spirit Guides who have experienced several incarnations are likely to empathize, at least to some extent, with the fact that our day-to-day problems sometimes feel insurmountable to us.

Again, though, Francine only experienced being human once, for about twenty years, half a millennium ago. She would never trivialize my worries and fears, nor would she trivialize anyone else's. But for the most part, when I turn to her about any of my "earthly" concerns, the response I'm likely to get is "Everything is going to be fine."

And she's right, of course. In the big picture, we all have an eternity to look forward to in the perfect, sacred bliss of the Other Side. So yes, everything *is* going to be fine, sooner or later. But if your child is sick, or your spouse has left you, or your refrigerator is empty and you have no money for groceries, you need words of wisdom that are a little more practical and immediate.

Where Francine can be very helpful during readings is in telling me whether or not a client's loved one is dying, whether or not they've died, exactly when they died and exactly what they died of. It's just as common for the deceased loved one to give me that information themselves, but Francine is a brilliantly reliable source.

A famous story about Francine, which I've written about before but which bears repeating, happened many, many years ago. A friend named Dr. Bill Yabroff was a psychology professor at the University of Santa Clara, and he was what I call with deep appreciation an "open-minded skeptic" about many areas of my life and work, including Francine. He'd attended several of her lectures about theology and the Other Side, and one day he asked if I'd be willing to trance her and let him test her authenticity. He didn't tell me in advance what "test" he had in mind, but I trusted him, and I knew him to be fair and objective, so I frankly welcomed the idea.

The "test" turned out to be Bill sitting down with Francine and a stack of twenty files, of twenty deceased former patients, randomly selected from his and his colleagues' archives. One by one Bill read the patients' names, and only their names, out loud, and asked Francine to tell him the cause of death of each patient. If Francine was legitimately addressing him from the Other Side as she claimed, she should have access to that information from the deceased patients themselves, Bill theorized. If she was a fraud, she'd make a fool of herself trying to guess her way through the list.

Francine correctly and very specifically identified the cause of death of nineteen of the twenty patients in Bill's stack of files.

Bill was stunned. The odds against her guessing with that much accuracy were incalculable. And he'd even taken the added precaution of not looking at the causes of death himself until after Francine had given her response, so he could rule out the possibility that she was reading his mind.

The twentieth cause of death, Francine's one "miss," was a drug overdose in which Francine said there were three substances involved. The autopsy report only designated two. Bill was so swept away by Francine's accuracy, and so curious, that he called the patient's family. It turned out they had requested a second autopsy, which revealed the presence of three substances, not just two.

So if Francine is more accurate than some coroners, and can pass a test like that, you bet I'll trust her on those occasions when clients need answers from the Other Side and their own loved ones aren't quite ready or willing to speak up yet.

While Bill never published the details and results of that test, he did take it upon himself to write a letter "to whom it may concern" before that particular encounter with Francine even happened. I've kept it for all these decades (my apologies that the date on the letter is no longer legible) and proudly reprint it here as one more thank-you to William Yabroff, Ph.D.

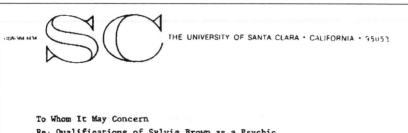

THE UNIVERSITY OF SANTA CLARA · CALIFORNIA · 95053

To Whom It May Concern
Re: Qualifications of Sylvia Brown as a Psychic
From: William Yabroff, Ph.D. Director, Counseling Psychology.

It is with pleasure that I recommend Sylvia Brown both as a person and a psychic. I have known Sylvia professionally for five years and find her to be an unusually authentic psychic as well as a highly ethical person, qualities which seem rare these days in the psychic field.

Sylvia seems to have the ability to accurately read the physical and emotional states of persons who come to her. She is specific in her readings rather than general, and encourages people to check-out the specificity of these readings. I have referred a number of clients to her and have been gratified by the client's reports of how helpful her sessions became in the course of therapy.

I have also had the opportunity to evidence her ability to find people and objects on a number of occassions. These include the finding of a valuable piece of jewelry, the location of metal objects underground, the accurate prediction of earth tremors and quakes, and descriptions of former structures which had been removed from the premise long before her services were called upon.

No psychic is %100 percent accurate and Sylvia is the first to call attention to this. Her own work reflects a surprising accuracy level and has inspired confidence with a number of professionals in Santa Clara Valley.

I recommend her for your most serious consideration, with enthusiasm and without reservation.

William Yabroff, Ph.D.
Associate Professor
Counseling Psychology

A PERSONAL NOTE

The next chapter will describe the specific elements of readings from my point of view. In the most ridiculously general terms, though, it all boils down to the following steps:

- Formulate a question, silently or out loud.
- With all the faith and trust in the world, say from the depth of my spirit some version of "Hit it, God."
- Shove my own mind out of the way to make room for whatever answers come from a far more reliable Source than I.
- Have the courage to accept and repeat those answers with no editing or judging or equivocating.

Other psychics might disagree, but for me, the most difficult of those steps is without a doubt the last one. It's become easier over all these years. But there are still moments when I receive information that seems so preposterous I almost brace myself for the client to get up and storm out of my office with a parting "If you're just going to sit here and spout nonsense at me, then good-bye forever, you phony."

An example of that very moment happened years and years ago, when a well-dressed, beautifully pulled together woman with the confident air of a successful corporate executive came to me to ask what I saw for the upcoming career change she was planning.

I silently went through the above-mentioned steps in less than a second. An answer came through loud and clear. The problem was, it sounded ridiculous. Every ounce of logic in me told me it couldn't possibly be right and I could kiss my credibility good-bye if I allowed myself to repeat it out loud. But the commitment I'd made to God not to edit, judge or equivocate was far stronger than my pride, so I threw caution to the wind, took a deep breath and repeated verbatim what I'd heard so clearly:

"You have a worm farm."

And as much of a cliché as it is, I believe it was true in this particular case—you literally could have knocked me over with a feather when she nonchalantly replied, "Yes, I do."

I told that story in my first book for Dutton, *The Other Side and Back.* A few weeks ago I was doing a book signing of my eighth Dutton book, *Phenomenon,* when a woman arrived at the table, extended her copy of the book and smiled, "Hi, Sylvia. I'm the 'worm farm' woman."

I'll be the first to admit, I can't be counted on to remember clients' names or faces. But greet me with a warm smile and your version of "I'm the 'worm farm' woman," and chances are that, just as she did, you'll make my day.

Chapter 3

HOW I READ

The readings I do fall into three basic categories as far as sheer mechanics are concerned:

- "Walk-ins," or face-to-face, in-person readings, definitely *not* to be confused with Ruth Montgomery's soul/spirit switching concept of walk-ins that I happen to find physically, physiologically and spiritually impossible
- Phone readings, which allow me to have the worldwide clientele I've enjoyed for all these decades
- Letter readings, for clients who have a few specific questions and understandably want answers more quickly than the waiting lists for the first two options allow

I personally respond to each letter reading, by the way, but my responses are passed along in phone calls from my ministers and staff. Not as "hands on" as I'd like, but it can save weeks or months of delay in getting questions answered, and again, the answers are exclusively mine.

Not a day goes by when someone doesn't ask about the difference in my accuracy between walk-ins, phone readings and letter readings. It's a fair question, with a very simple answer:

There's not one bit of difference for me, or for my accuracy, between the kinds of readings I do. I've been tested by more psychologists, scientists, doctors, psychiatrists, hypnotherapists and researchers than I can count, with the result that my accuracy rate averages between 87 and 90 percent. (If any psychic you go to claims 100 percent accuracy, don't bother with the rest of your reading. You've already been lied to.) My percentage stands whether we're in the same room or halfway around the world from each other, and whether or not we ever hear the sound of each other's voice.

For that to make the perfect sense it really does, all you have to do is understand the elements of a reading from my point of view.

If only *I* completely understood them.

READINGS THROUGH MY EYES

I don't honestly know how I do what I do. I just do it. And because I was born with this gift, I don't know what it's like not to do it, or exactly how to break it down into individual components to explain it. It's a bit like my asking you, "How do you breathe?" There's no question that you do it, that you've done it all your life and that you give little or no thought to doing it. You know that you inhale and exhale. But if I pushed you for more details than that, the physiological processes your muscles and organs and cells go through to accomplish taking a breath, I think the vast majority of you would be stumped. (I certainly would be, and I know quite a bit about how the body works.)

What I will happily do, though, is discuss elements of how I do what I do, any one or more of which are likely to come into play during a reading. As for what percentage of one element or another I use in a "typical" reading (not that there really is such a thing), your guess is as good as mine.

And so, in no order of importance whatsoever, here are some of the tools I use with every client, whether or not we ever spend a moment together in the same room or hear the sound of each other's voice.

INFUSED KNOWLEDGE

Infused knowledge is information that's directly transferred from one mind to another, with the receiver being given information they had no knowledge of before, and having no conscious awareness of where it came from.

Infused knowledge is one of the most common ways that the Other Side communicates with us here on earth. When I'm giving a reading and suddenly "know" that your blood sugar is low when you haven't mentioned your health; or your child needs to see an endocrinologist even though you haven't mentioned your child; or there's going to be a breakthrough in Norway in six months in the treatment of an illness your best friend is suffering from when you haven't said a word about your best friend, chances are it's a classic example of infused knowledge. It's brand-new information to me, it's nothing you told me, and in cases like those there are often no spirit voices chirping the information into my ear. I didn't know. Then I knew. And I have no idea how. That's infused knowledge.

When I do readings or make predictions, as I routinely do on television and as I did in my book *Prophecy*, I can't even guess how often I've had to turn to a dictionary after I've passed along some of the infused knowledge I've been given, particularly in the areas of medicine and technology. It's an understatement to say that I don't have college degrees in either of those subjects, and it's not unusual for me to hear myself repeating terminology I can't begin to spell, let alone define.

Infused knowledge is hardly exclusive to me, or to psychics. It's far more common than it gets credit for, probably because it's so silent and subtle. The spirit world on the Other Side, for example, is constantly working on cures, scientific breakthroughs, inventions and countless other contributions to our well-being here on earth. It's through infused knowledge that spirits pass that information along to the appropriate researchers, scientists, physicists, doctors and the other brilliant minds among us who can transform the information into tangible reality.

And then there are those nights when you go to sleep with a problem on your mind and wake up knowing the solution, or where to find it. It's not because you remembered something while you slept, or because your mind was finally relaxed enough to think clearly. It's because something just "came to you" that, if you really stop to notice, is brand-new information, and you have no idea where it came from.

It came from Home, and it's another example of infused knowledge, one of my most valuable and completely involuntary reading tools.

CLAIRVOYANCE

Clairvoyance is the ability to see beings, objects or information that originate from some other dimension. It's sometimes called "second sight," and it's a God-given gift that allows some people eyes to perceive a wider range of input and frequencies than "normal."

I'm clairvoyant. It's what allows me to literally see and accurately describe what spirits from Home are around you, where a missing child or object can be found, the final moments in a murder victim's life whether it was ten minutes or ten years ago, or the person you're going to marry three years from now. Clairvoyant visions originate in other dimensions, and earth is the only dimension where we have this limiting concept called time. Everywhere else there's only "now," so in dimensions beyond ours, past, present and future aren't necessarily factored into a vision. It takes skill and practice to translate a timeless vision into earthly parameters, so that, for example, I can "see" a client in a car accident and know whether it's already happened or it's something they need to take precautions against in the future.

The gift of clairvoyance isn't limited to us psychics, as millions of you already know. You're seeing things you either don't want to see or don't understand, and/or your children are seeing them and becoming confused or frightened by them. (Although more often than not, your children will take them in stride, for reasons we'll discuss in the "Children" chapter.) To those of you who know exactly what I'm talking about, let me pass along an important lesson my grandma Ada taught me when I was five years old and started having my first very scary clairvoyant experiences. (For example, I suddenly saw my great-grandmothers' faces melting one night at a family dinner, which was pretty disgusting, not knowing it was my child's-eyes psychic awareness that they were both going to die within the next couple of weeks.) I was terrified by the idea of spending my life being a sitting duck for any random, violent, grotesque images that happened along, whether I was strong enough to handle them or not. I still remember telling Grandma Ada that I didn't want to see any of these things, I didn't want to be psychic, I just wanted it all to go away and be a normal five-year-old.

She explained that my psychic gifts, my gift of clairvoyance and any information that came as a result of those gifts had the same Source—they were from God. Which meant they were to be honored, respected and used for His work or not at all. And since He gave them to me for a reason, He was the first place I should turn for any help and guidance I might need. "Ask and it shall be given."

So, with a little coaching from Grandma Ada, I gave Him my word that I would devote these gifts to His best purpose, if He would please only send me clairvoyant images I could do something about. If I have to see a plane go down, show me enough information to let me warn the right people. If I have to see a house in flames, give me a town, an address, something to help me make sure no one's inside when it burns, or tell me how they can prevent the fire in the first place. Don't show me a diseased heart without telling me whose it is and what they need to do about it, or a shipwreck without a location where rescuers can find it.

I prayed and prayed and prayed for useful clairvoyance or none at all, and it worked. As I said, if you, a loved one or especially a child you know has been given the gift of clairvoyance, learn as I did from my grandma Ada: thank God for the gift, honor it, devote it to Him and pray to only be given visions you can work with to further His divine purpose.

During a reading, then, when I tell you there are four Angels around you, or ask you about the short stocky man with the bald head and handlebar moustache who's standing right behind you, or tell you not to get in a red car for the next six months, or comment on your house burning down two years ago, it's all a result of the gift of clairvoyance.

CLAIRAUDIENCE

Clairaudience is a French word that means "clear hearing." Whoever coined it obviously never experienced the high-frequency, chirping, hyperspeed sound of spirit that takes every ounce of concentration to understand. "Clear" isn't one of the adjectives that leaps to mind.

In addition to being clairvoyant, I'm also clairaudient, which means I have the ability to hear communication from other dimensions. If you've seen me on television giving names and details about audience members' deceased loved ones that I'd have no way of knowing, you've seen my clairaudience in action. Some information comes through infused knowledge, or telepathically, as you'll read about in the next few pages. But much of it comes directly from the spirits on the Other Side who are invariably standing in line to talk when they know someone is able to listen and pass along messages.

And it's amazing how often the person I'm passing the message to draws a complete blank on what they're hearing, in readings, during lectures or on television, only to realize later that it couldn't have been more obvious. And while they're drawing a blank, the friends they came with gape at them as if they've completely lost their minds. One of the most memorable examples happened during a live two-hour pay-per-view special on national television. I was answering a question for a gentleman in the audience when a very distinct spirit appeared right behind him.

"Who's the short, slender, dark-haired woman with the heart-shaped face and high cheekbones who's with you?" I asked him.

Once he figured out that I was referring to a spirit and not to one of the friends he was with, he replied as if he couldn't have been less surprised, "That's my mother."

"She wants me to say hello to Keith," I said, since this woman was chirping, "Hello, Keith!" in my ear at the top of her lungs. "Who's Keith?"

He shrugged a silent "not a clue" and started to pursue his original question. In the meantime, his friends were staring at him slack-jawed, and his mother was giving me a headache with her relentless, "Hello, Keith!"

I had to cut him off. "I'm sorry, but I've got to say hello to Keith. Who is Keith?"

He had no idea who Keith was. His friends were beside themselves. And since his mother wasn't about to let it go, neither was I. We went back and forth like that at least two or three more times before a sudden look of recognition lit up his face and he announced, "Oh. *I'm* Keith."

That's clairvoyance.

And let me add one important note to those of you who also happen to be clairvoyant, whether you completely understand the gift or not. This is an unequivocal fact: no voice from God, or from the God-centered joy of the Other Side will *ever* say something angry, or mean, or threatening, or that encourages you to do anything harmful or destructive to yourself or anyone else. I say this as someone who has infinite respect for my many friends and colleagues in the mental health community: if you hear voices and they're demeaning, profane, violent or negative in any way, *please* get to a reputable, licensed therapist right away and let them help you, or call my office and we'll be happy to refer you to an experienced professional.

TELEPATHY

Telepathy is the direct transfer of information or feelings from one being to another without the use of any of the five physical senses. A "sender" silently passes signals to a "receiver," sometimes over great distances, and it can happen deliberately or without either the sender or the receiver being aware of it.

Telepathic information is usually meant to have an impact on the receiver and/or to be acted upon, so the conscious mind is usually let in on it sooner or later. The information is received in many different forms: words or phrases that pop into the mind for no apparent reason, sudden flashes of images, unusually clear dreams, or maybe inexplicable thoughts about a person we haven't seen or thought about in a long time.

We've all heard and read stories about twins, or other very close family members and kindred souls on earth, "knowing" what each other is thinking, or when one or the other is in pain or in trouble. Those are classic examples of earthly telepathic communication. And the spirit world is particularly adept at telepathy. Ask anyone who's had encounters with a deceased loved one, and they'll frequently describe entire conversations in which neither of them spoke a single word. Communication with Angels is exclusively telepathic, since Angels never speak.

If you have the joy of being close to an animal, by the way, you don't need me to tell you how much those divine spirits telepathically "send" if you'll simply take the time to tune in and "receive."

You may be wondering what if any difference there is between telepathy and infused knowledge. And there is a difference, subtle as it is: with a telepathic message there's a specific "sender," but infused knowledge invariably comes from a nonspecific, unidentified source.

There are "experts" in the field of telepathy who believe that some of us are natural telepathic "senders" and others of us are "receivers." I don't happen to believe that, or maybe I just don't believe it matters. What does matter is that telepathic communication is yet another gift our spirit minds retain from our lives at Home for those times on earth when it comes in handy.

PSYCHOMETRY

The spiritual and emotional energy we humans emanate is extremely powerful. You know that as well as I do. The most obvious example that springs to mind is when you walk into a room in which there's just been a nasty argument. I don't care how calmly everyone might be sitting there trying to act as if everything's just fine, you can still feel the residual anger. "You could cut the tension in the air with a knife" is an observation we've all heard, and we've all experienced it too.

A subtle but very real side effect of that spiritual and emotional energy is that the inanimate objects around us, if they're there for any length of time, absorb and continue to contain the energy with which they've come in contact.

Psychometry is the ability to sense and interpret the energy in an inanimate object and use it to connect with its original owner or location. Psychics who specialize in psychometry when working with law enforcement, for example, can hold an article of a missing child's clothing and, by reading the child's energy contained in that clothing, receive images, smells or sounds from the child's surroundings, sense whether the child is frightened or cold or hungry or being well cared for, and/or perceive any injuries the child might have. Or, during a more conventional reading, a psychic might find it helpful to hold an object belonging to the client, or the living or deceased loved one the client wants to discuss.

I rarely use psychometry during readings. For the most part, I use it the way you do—I pick up an object while shopping, let's say, and react to whatever feeling it gives me. I might see a purse, or an antique necklace, that's exactly what I've been looking for, but when I pick it up and hold it there's "something about it" that makes me put it back and keep looking. That's psychometry. Or I'll be house-hunting or apartment-hunting and walk into a place that's ideal in every way, with the one exception that "for some reason" I can't wait to get out of there. That's psychometry.

When I do use it with clients, it tends to involve their questions about a specific item they're curious about. If you've watched me on *The Montel Williams Show* with any regularity, you've probably seen this in action. An audience member brings an object they've bought, found or inherited. Most typically, it has some financial or sentimental value to them, but either they have an uneasy feeling about it or, "Ever since I brought it home it seems as if there's a lot of tension in the house."

Sometimes I'll ask to hold it, and over the years I've found myself handling objects that filled me with dread, "felt" peaceful and calming, or seemed completely neutral. Other times I don't even need to hold the object, I can "feel" at twenty paces that I want no part of it. (One particularly memorable item was an antique doll. Montel and I still talk about it. Lindsay and I still talk about it. I never got far enough to know how it "felt." I couldn't get past the fact that it was, without a doubt, the ugliest, creepiest doll I've ever seen in my life. That thing would have been in my fireplace in the blink of an eye if someone had brought it into my house, sentimental value or no.) Or, I can "feel" at twenty paces that there's no problem with the object and something else is going on.

I admit, it does fascinate me when a client walks into my office with some item and says, "This has been in my family for generations, but I've always felt as if there might be something evil about it. Should I get rid of it?" You don't need a psychic to answer that question. But it's important to clarify that it's the absorbed energy in those items that creates our psychometric response to them. The items themselves aren't "haunted" or "possessed" or "evil." Spirits and ghosts can manipulate inanimate objects, and they can contribute to the energy held inside them, but they can't occupy them. "Inanimate" means "not alive," and "not alive" means they're uninhabitable for anything living, from earth or from the spirit world.

Whether you're consciously aware of your psychometric skills or don't believe a word of it, I still hope you'll pay attention to what you "pick up" from the objects you surround yourself with. Understanding what you're feeling (accumulated energy) and what you're not feeling (hauntings or possessions) in the material world around you can help you discard some of the negativity in your life, and who among us can't use all the help with that we can get?

THE SOURCES

All those tools are meaningless, of course, without places to apply them. Try being a successful builder with a truckload of state-of-the-art tools and no building materials. That's a rough idea of what it would be like for me to have all these ways of accessing information without the available information itself. And thanks to God and the infinite perfection of this universe He created, there's no limit to that information.

Again in no particular order, simply depending on the specific needs of each individual client, here are the general sources of knowledge I draw from during any given reading.

THE OTHER SIDE

There would be no such thing as legitimate psychic readings if there were no such place as the Other Side. It is our Home, the place we left for our brief visits here and the place we'll return to when these lifetimes end. It is God's embrace, in real physical form, our Source and our Destination, and with the rarest exceptions the general source of what I transmit to each and every client.

The Other Side, believe it or not, is right here among us, another dimension superimposed on ours, a mere three feet above our version of "ground level." Its vibrational frequency is simply much higher than ours, which is why we don't perceive it. Its topography is a perfect mirror image of ours, with one exception—because there's no erosion or pollution on the Other Side, its landscape is an image of earth's from thousands of years ago, when bodies of water were pure blue and mountains and coastlines were perfectly intact. On the Other Side, Atlantis and Lemuria, the earth's "lost continents," thrive. So do the world's great architectural and artistic masterpieces, even the ones that have long since been destroyed here.

There is no negativity on the Other Side, no aggression, no ego or jealousy or pride, and no judgment. God didn't create those emotions. We did. And yet, incredibly, it's those exact human-made emotions that inspire our seemingly inane choice to leave the Other Side from time to time and slog through another round of what we whimsically call "life." We take occasional brief trips away from the glory of the Other Side for the growth and education of our souls, because it's our journey and our joy to make the most of our spirits in honor of their Creator.

And when these brief trips are over, we return to our *real* Home and resume our blissful, blessed *real* lives with even deeper understanding and more knowledge than we had before.

HALL OF RECORDS

We've all heard of the legendary tunnel that takes us Home when each lifetime on earth is complete. That tunnel is perfectly real. And it doesn't descend from somewhere in the depth of the cosmos to take us "up" to the Other Side. It rises from our own bodies, out of our own etheric substance, at maybe a thirty-degree angle, since, remember, our destination is only three feet above where we are right now.

No matter where on this earth our lifetimes end, no matter what our culture or religion or circumstance, all tunnels lead to the same place, the same impossibly beautiful entrance to the Other Side, where a cluster of gorgeous white marble buildings tower above the meadow that greets us when we arrive. First among the cluster of buildings is a triumvirate of Halls called the Hall of Wisdom, the Hall of Justice and the Hall of Records.

The Hall of Records, like its two companions, is Greco-Roman in structure, with spectacular columns and a soaring dome. It also happens to be the busiest, most constantly bustling hub of this white marble triumvirate, for the most fascinating reasons.

To get an image of the inside of the Hall of Records, picture an infinite number of aisles, lined on either side with an infinite number of shelves filled with an infinite number of scrolls, books, documents, maps, artwork, blueprints, etc., every shelf in perfectly kept order. Now take each of those infinite numbers of aisles, shelves and contents, multiply it by any other infinite number that springs to mind and you have some idea of the scope of the Hall of Records' breathtaking expanse. Its purpose requires every square inch of that expanse, although the laws of physics on the Other Side, limitless as they are, prevent it from ever being filled to capacity.

The Hall of Records houses every historical and literary work ever written, drawn, drafted, sketched or painted on earth and at Home. That includes precious documents and artwork whose "originals" have been destroyed here, from those that perished in the burning of the legendary libraries of Alexandria two thousand years ago to the brilliant tomes swallowed by the sea when the continents of Atlantis and Lemuria were lost.

It also houses every detailed chart of every incarnation of every one of us who's ever lived on this planet. And each of those charts is impeccably preserved on scrolls, scripted in flawless Aramaic, which is the universal language on the Other Side, and kept in perfect order for us or for anyone else at Home to review, study, research and learn from.

Access to all those charts is one of the reasons the Hall of Records is such a popular center of activity. We can astrally travel to the Hall of Records during sleep, meditation or hypnosis while we're still on earth, and we often do, but we're never given access to our own charts. (It would fall loosely under the category of cheating on a major exam—it's just not done.) Once we're on the Other Side again, though, we can study all our own charts for as long as we like, for context and perspective on the journey of our soul. We can study the charts of loved ones we've left behind on earth, for insights into our interactions with them, good and bad, and to see what lies ahead for them and why. We can study the charts of historical figures we've admired or despised or never understood, or of people still on earth whose impact seems significant, personally or globally, and track the future of that impact. We can even "merge" with a chart, a process in which our spirit becomes a literal eyewitness to any event or life it chooses without ever leaving the gleaming infinite aisles in the vast Hall of Records.

As functional and endlessly fascinating as the Hall of Records is to the residents of the Other Side, it's also among the most sacred places, because it's within the Hall of Records that the Akashic Records are preserved, the complete written body of God's knowledge, laws and memories.

THE AKASHIC RECORDS

There seems to be general agreement among the majority of the world's faiths, cultures and philosophies that the Akashic Records exist. What's not quite as unanimously agreed upon is where they exist and how to describe exactly what they are.

The Hindus believe in a universal substance called "akasha," from which the natural elements of fire, water, air and earth were created. Eternally imprinted on that substance is every thought, word and action in the history of the universe, collectively called the Akashic Records. The brilliant prophet and clairvoyant Edgar Cayce perceived the Akashic Records to be the collective memories and histories of every thought, sound, physical and emotional vibration, major event and incidental moment in eternity, an atmospheric presence that affects us all and which we all affect with every breath we take. Carl Jung, the noted psychologist, described the Akashic Records as a tangible universal force of nature that he called the Collective Unconscious, an eternal and infinite embodiment of the principle that for every action there's an equal and opposite reaction.

My definition of the Akashic Records doesn't contradict any of those philosophies, it just simplifies them and enhances their power. The Akashic Records are the entire sacrosanct body of God's knowledge, laws and memories. They're absolutely imprinted on the ether of every planet, solar system and galaxy God created. But they also exist in written form, perfectly printed in the universal language of Aramaic, in the Hall of Records on the Other Side.

We have the honor of perpetual access to the Akashic Records when we're at Home on the Other Side. Our spirits, safely housed in our subconscious minds, have perpetual access to them as well during our fleeting incarnations here on earth. During sleep, hypnosis, meditation or physiological unconsciousness, when our noisy, chaotic conscious minds are temporarily out of the way, our spirits know exactly where the Akashic Records are and how to get there. We turn to them more often than we consciously realize for answers, for clarity, for comfort and for the nourishment only God can provide.

Remember, there's no such thing as "time" anywhere but on earth. Everywhere else in this eternal universe, including on the Other Side, there is only "now." So God's written body of knowledge includes everything that ever has been and everything that ever will be.

Could I ask for a better Source than that for readings and predictions?

THE CHART

As I mentioned, the Hall of Records also houses every chart ever written of every incarnation ever lived by every person on this earth. Reading your chart, or your loved one's chart, from this life or your past lives, is another of the clearest, most efficient ways for me to tell you about everything from your career path to the name and particulars of Mr. or Ms. Right to present and future health issues to any past life issues that might be affecting the life you're living now. To fully understand that fact, you have to fully understand what your chart is to begin with.

We make these brief trips to earth to learn and grow through first-hand experience, for the progress of our souls on their eternal journey. It's a different education than we could ever hope for on the Other Side, where everything is infused with God's perfection. As my Spirit Guide, Francine, rhetorically asks me when I complain to her about an especially rough time in my life, "What have you learned when times were good?"

So we choose to come here, as often as we feel the need, and we choose what we hope to learn and work on this time around. And just as we would never head off to college without deciding which college can offer the exact education we're looking for, what courses we'll need along the way, where we should live and with whom, and countless other details to give ourselves the best odds of what we want to accomplish, we wouldn't consider anything as haphazard and potentially pointless as coming to earth unprepared. Nor would God "hang us out to dry" like that.

And so before we come here, we write our chart. It's an understatement to call it "detailed." From the broad strokes to the most trivial incidents, we leave nothing to chance in pursuit of our eternal growth.

I don't know anyone, including myself, who can imagine having deliberately chosen some of the unpleasantness, ugliness and tragedy in their life. But let me just remind you, and myself, again: we write our charts in preparation for coming to a very rough boarding school, so the charts themselves are bound to be filled with difficult challenges and lessons learned the hard way. If what we were in search of was a happy, carefree, perfect life, we'd stay Home.

And then there's the bliss that is our constant state of mind on the Other Side, including when we're writing our chart. We're fearless at Home, we're confident, we're our most loving selves and we're eternally, timelessly surrounded by nothing but the tangible presence of God's unconditional love. Writing our chart in that state of mind is like going to the grocery store with a full wallet on an empty stomach—it's a recipe for sheer greed in our eagerness for spiritual progress.

We begin with the broad strokes, the powerful inner drives that spur us along our various chosen paths toward the finish line we're determined to reach.

Life Themes

One of those broad strokes is our Life Theme, which is the answer to the question "What is your purpose this time around?" There are forty-four Life Themes, from Activator to Winner, and I've listed them and their descriptions in my books *The Other Side and Back* and *Life on the Other Side.*

We write two Life Themes into our chart—the Primary Life Theme and the Secondary Life Theme. The Primary Theme essentially defines the overall goal we intend to accomplish, and the Secondary Theme is usually the conflicting emotional drive we set up for ourselves to overcome in achieving that goal. For example, my Primary Theme, what I chose as the driving force in this lifetime, is Humanitarian. But my Secondary Life Theme is Loner, a yearning for solitude that would make my Humanitarian theme impossible if I allowed myself to indulge in it. A pessimist would say that the Secondary Theme is the main obstacle in our path toward our Primary Theme. An optimist would say, more accurately, I'm sure, that the challenge of our Secondary Theme is what gives us the added determination to see to it that our Primary Theme is successful in the end.

Option Lines

In addition to determining our Life Themes, we also choose one specific area of life we just can't seem to get right, no matter how hard we try or how successful we might be in everything else we do. That one specific area is your Option Line, i.e., the hardest course we sign up for in this rough school called life on earth.

There are seven Option Lines. I have a feeling you'll recognize yours instantly, simply by answering the question "Even if the rest of my life is going beautifully, I can always count on my (fill in appropriate Option Line) to mess me up":

- health
- spirituality
- love relationships
- social life
- finance
- career
- family

Exit Points

As attached as we can get to our lives on earth, it's important to re-member that our real lives, the lives that bring us the most joy and in which we're most genuinely "alive," are our lives on the Other Side. And we wouldn't dream of leaving Home to make these brief visits to "boot camp" without guaranteeing ahead of time that we're heading off on a round trip that will get us safely Home again when this particular visit has served its purpose.

The ways and means we prearrange for getting back to the Other Side when we're ready are called Exit Points, which are yet another as-pect of our charts. We design five Exit Points into our lifetimes on earth, and we don't necessarily wait until the fifth one to head Home. We might decide when our first Exit Point comes along, or our second, or fourth, that we've accomplished all we need to on this trip. And we don't necessarily space them out evenly when we create them. We might write in two Exit Points for the same year, for example, and then not schedule another one to come along for twenty or thirty years.

The most obvious Exit Points include critical illnesses and surgeries, potentially fatal accidents and any other events that could have resulted in our death but didn't—not because of "luck," but because we simply chose not to take that particular Exit Point. Other Exit Points, though, are so subtle that we might not even recognize them when they happen: de-ciding "for no reason" to drive a different route than usual to work; "triv-ial" delays that keep us from leaving the house on time; a last-minute change in travel plans; canceling a commitment because we suddenly "just don't feel like it." Countless incidents that seem utterly meaningless could easily be a subconscious memory of an Exit Point that we wrote into our chart but decided not to take advantage of after all.

Another way that memories of our Exit Points sometimes surface is in the form of recurring dreams. Pay close attention to any recurring dreams about an unfamiliar but very specific person, place or situation that makes you feel uneasy. If that dream ends up manifesting itself in "real life," it might mean the dream was prophetic. But just as often, it's the memory of an Exit Point you wrote that your spirit mind is shining a spotlight on, to signal you that you're about to have a choice to make.

One of the most important reasons to embrace the truth of Exit Points is to liberate ourselves from feeling so responsible when a loved one dies despite our most exhaustive efforts and our most impassioned prayers. We all have our Exit Points. Each and every one of us. And in the end it's no one's choice but our own which one we opt to take. Please stop suffering over the loss of a loved one for whom you think you could have or should have done more, or could have or should have prayed more. Most of all, never let it enter your mind that God ignored your prayers. That never happens. Just remember and respect that for reasons of their own your loved one simply said yes to an Exit Point, designed long before they came here, and it will make perfect sense to you when you see them again back Home.

The Akashic Records and the vast details of clients' charts, with all their "subcategories," are obviously infinite Sources of every reading and prediction I give.

But sometimes, understandably, clients want a close encounter with a specific loved one. And that's where the actual residents of the Other Side come in.

SPIRITS

As I mentioned earlier, when our bodies die, most of us experience the brilliantly lit tunnel, not descending from some faraway place in the sky but actually rising from our own bodies. We travel with gorgeous, weightless freedom through this almost sideways tunnel, never for one instant feeling as if we've died but instead feeling more thrillingly alive than we could ever imagine here on earth. All our worries, frustrations, anger, resentment and other negativity melt away, replaced by the peace and all-loving, unconditional understanding we remember and are about to reunite with at Home. God's sacred white light waits to embrace us at the end of the tunnel, along with loved ones from every lifetime we've ever lived. Even our pets from every lifetime are there to greet us, so eager with the joy of seeing us that the human spirits have to wait their turn to get to us. And once we've arrived on the Other Side, we resume the busy, active, exquisite lives we temporarily left behind to further our spiritual education in the tough school earth provides.

If you've had encounters with spirits from the Other Side, or talked to or read accounts from those who have, you've noticed that very often the descriptions include the impression that the spirits were "floating" a few feet above the ground. While that's often exactly what it looks like through our eyes, what's really happening is that the spirits are simply moving on their ground level at Home, which as you read earlier is only three feet higher than ours.

By the time spirits come back from the Other Side to say hello and let us know they're still very much alive, they've already transcended to and been living in a place of emotional and spiritual bliss, not to mention perfect physical health. Any unhappiness they experienced during their latest lifetime on earth, any negativity they carried around, any illnesses or infirmities or injuries they suffered have all been resolved. What that means is that we never need to spend a moment wondering if our deceased loved ones at Home are well and happy. In the blessed perfection of Home, they can't possibly be anything less.

Spirits are invariably eager for us to recognize exactly who they are, which means they'll either appear in a form that's familiar to us, they'll create a scent we'd associate with them, they'll offer a light touch to our hair or the back of our neck or our shoulder that was their habit during their lifetime, or they'll manipulate an object that will offer hints to their identity. They'll repeatedly move a framed photograph of themselves so that it's facing a different direction or lying flat on a table or dresser, play with the flame of a candle we've lit in their honor, superimpose their face on a painting or snapshot, rock their favorite rocking chair, play a music box they gave us—the possibilities are as limitless as the imaginations of our loved ones themselves, and all we have to do is be receptive and pay attention.

Because spirits have to cross back into our dimension in order to visit us, they often attach their energy to such powerful conductors as electricity and water in order to help with their "reentry." Eager to make their presence known, they'll create bizarre behavior in TVs, appliances, telephones and other objects and electrical devices, and they're especially active between the hours of 1:00 A.M. and 5:00 A.M., when the night air is at its dampest and the dew is at its heaviest. Please don't misunderstand if and when you experience your telephone chronically ringing with either no one or static on the other end when you answer, or your television set suddenly doing a full rotation of all its channels while its remote control sits idle on the coffee table. Your belongings are not "possessed," any more than they're "possessed" when you use them yourself. Instead, it's very possibly a spirit, simply manipulating something tangible that you'll be sure to notice, to say, "I'm right here, watching over you." (I'm too much of a realist not to add that the spirit world is hardly responsible for every malfunction around the house. Sometimes all you need is a good repairman.)

Finally, just as spirits from the Other Side are incapable of negative thoughts and actions, they're also incapable of visiting us for anything but the most positive of reasons. Even though it can be startling to see or hear them when you're not accustomed to it, spirit visitations are never intended to frighten or intimidate or threaten or chase us away. All they want is to love us, comfort us, reassure us that they've never really left us and never will.

There are two questions I'm most often asked by clients about their deceased loved ones. One is some variation on "Are they still mad at me/disappointed in me/upset that I wasn't there to say good-bye?" The other is "Do they have a message for me?"

The answer to the first question is and always will be the same for every client and every deceased loved one, and I just can't stress this enough: *There is nothing but joy and pure, sacred bliss on the Other Side. If your loved one is there, they've long since forgotten what negative emotions even feel like.*

The answer to the second question, nine times out of ten, is that your loved one has the most wonderful message of all for you: by the grace of God who created us, they've survived death just as He promised, and we really are eternal after all.

GHOSTS

While I've investigated hundreds of hauntings and met hundreds of ghosts over all these years, I've never had a ghost appear around a client during a reading. I've advised a tiny percentage of clients that their loved ones haven't crossed over yet, which I invariably learn from Francine—she can tell me whether or not someone's arrived on the Other Side, and if we know they're no longer on earth, as she puts it, "Everyone's got to be somewhere."

Even though it comes up rarely during readings, I do want to explain what ghosts are and how they differ from spirits, just for clarification.

There's one tragic quality shared by every ghost in the world: not one of them has the slightest idea that they're dead. Unlike most spirits who, when their bodies die, eagerly proceed through the tunnel that will take them Home, ghosts turn away from the tunnel, refusing to acknowledge its existence for reasons of their own and, as a result, remain earthbound, desperately confused and lonely, often angry, sometimes aggressive and petulant, trapped in a futile effort to make sense of an existence that by definition makes no sense at all.

Of course, ghosts do leave their bodies like all of us do when our bodies stop functioning, and by leaving their bodies they also leave this earthly dimension. But by rejecting the tunnel and God's loving, healing white light on the Other Side, they don't transcend to the higher-frequency dimension of Home either, which means that their spirits are left quite literally "neither here nor there." That fact alone makes them very different from spirits from the Other Side in a number of ways:

- Living in neither earth's dimension nor the dimension of the Other Side, ghosts are typically more visible and distinct than spirits. I've used this analogy several times, but it seems effective enough that I'll unapologetically use it again: the easiest way to picture the three dimensions we're talking about—earth's dimension, ghosts' dimension and the dimension of Home—is to visualize an electric fan. At its slowest speed, the fan's blades are well defined and easy to see. That represents the dimension on earth, the one we all function in and are accustomed to. At the fan's medium speed, the individual blades begin to blur into each other and are harder for our eyes to distinguish. That represents the dimension in which ghosts are trapped. Turn the fan to its highest speed and its blades seem to disappear completely, creating the illusion that the blades aren't there at all, as false an illusion as the idea that the Other Side and its resident spirits don't exist just because we can't readily see them. The fact that some people are able to see and hear ghosts and spirits while others aren't doesn't prove that some people are crazy while others aren't. It just proves that some people's physical senses are more finely tuned than others'.
- Because they haven't yet experienced the love and healing of the Other Side, ghosts will bear visible signs of any injuries or illnesses or deformities that were present when their bodies died. You will *never* see a spirit from Home who's wounded or sick or in any kind of physical or emotional pain.
- When spirits are among us, their ultimate motivation is their love for us, and their efforts to get us to notice them are meant to express that love. Ghosts are much more complicated. Their reasons

for turning away from the tunnel and refusing to accept the fact of their death are widely varied. Some cling to their earthly lives out of a confused sense of loyalty to a loved one or a property or even a job. Some stay behind for revenge. Some stay behind to search or wait for a lost love. Some stay behind out of fear that God is too displeased with them to let them come Home (which is impossible, by the way—His arms are always open to us). Whatever their confused purpose for rejecting the truth that they're dead, they're among us out of a distorted sense of reality. The world through a ghost's eyes is locked in a time warp of their own disturbed creation. From their point of view, *we* are the intruders in *their* world, not the other way around. So we shouldn't be too surprised that in their encounters with us, they're sometimes angry, desperate, resentful, cranky or annoying. Occasionally, when they realize that someone is seeing, hearing or acknowledging them in any way, they can be appreciative and even playful, especially with children. But overall, like most unhappy, chronically disoriented beings, they can be unpredictable, not to mention depressing.

- Having not transcended, ghosts exist in our dimension, not in the dimension of Home three feet above our ground level on earth. That's why, while spirits appear to be "floating" as they move along the ground level of the Other Side, ghosts accurately appear to be functioning on exactly the same level we are.

- As we discussed earlier, spirits, because they're so eager for us to know it's them, will appear in a form that will help us recognize them. Ghosts couldn't care less whether we recognize them or not, since they're among us out of confusion having nothing at all to do with comforting us. They might show up as images of their own earthly bodies, they might appear faded and unformed, or they might even present themselves as balls of heavy mist. They have neither the divine skill nor the self-control of spirits from Home, so the physical appearance of ghosts is simply one more way in which they can be frustratingly unpredictable.

Unpredictable, surly, terribly confused, sometimes even perfectly pleasant and sympathetic—I've met ghosts of every disposition, in every possible circumstance. The one thing I have never met and don't believe I ever will, because I don't believe for one minute that it happens, is a ghost who will do actual bodily harm to anyone. I heard a quote once that will always make me smile: "I don't believe in ghosts, but I've been afraid of them all my life." There's no doubt about it, they can be scary if you're not expecting them, and they can be even scarier if they're being obnoxious and trying to drive you away. But if your fear of them is centered around the idea that they'll hurt you, put that one back in the "myth" file and promise yourself that if and when you do meet a ghost, you'll focus as best you can on kindly and compassionately talking them Home where they belong.

PROTECTING MYSELF

Averaging fifteen to twenty readings a day, many of which are highly sensitive and emotional, would be completely debilitating if I hadn't learned early on how to prevent it. A small part of it involves maintaining my objectivity—not my distance, just my objectivity—which I do as much for my clients' benefit as for my own. As any of my family members and close friends will tell you, the minute I lose my objectivity with someone, I also lose my psychic ability where they're concerned. I get as caught up in worrying, second-guessing and letting my heart overrule my head as the least psychic person on earth. So objectivity is essential to a clear reading and also to keeping me from being drained by the end of the day.

My most powerful arsenal in the battle to keep my positive spiritual, emotional and physical energy thriving is something I call Tools of Protection. They're not tools that work exclusively on me. They'll make a difference in your life too, for shielding yourself against the negativity, illness and darkness we all confront in the course of simply leading our lives. They also serve the exquisite purpose of visualizing, in a variety of ways, God's pure, impenetrable love wrapping around you, reminding you that you are adored, divine and eternally invincible.

Tools of Protection are designed to surround us like a divine force field wherever we go. Use any or all of them that appeal to you—in fact, the more the better. And "using them" means nothing more than firmly fixing the images in your conscious mind and your spirit mind. Take an hour meditating these images around you, or take two minutes visualizing them before you go to sleep and during your morning shower. It doesn't matter. Any amount of time, day or night, is fine, as long as you get into the habit of using your Tools of Protection and reach a point when you'd feel naked without them.

If you don't believe they'll work, try it for a week or two to prove me wrong. They certainly won't do you any harm. They also won't make your life free of negativity for the rest of your time on earth. But when it comes to the interference around you that undermines your confidence, blurs your focus and tries to pull you off track, a combination of God and your Tools of Protection will make a difference, you have my word.

- *The White Light of the Holy Spirit.* If there's any Tool of Protection I advocate more than any other, as many times a day and night as you think of it, it's simply visualizing God's purest, most brilliant, most cleansing and loving white light radiating from the top of your head to the soles of your feet, a glowing sacred aura several inches thick. Let it stimulate the flow of your blood. Let its healing warmth find and cure every pain and infirmity you suffer from. Let it purify the air around you so that every breath you take is deep and nourishing. Let all the negativity and fear and stress and worry and self-doubt and sadness you're carrying leave your body and be resolved in God's light that you'll wear like a hallowed birthmark from this day forward, a genetic legacy from your Creator. Imagine that everyone around you can see it as your declaration that you are proud to be your

Father and Mother's child, and that you know with every step you take that you are loved.

I never fall asleep or get out of bed in the morning without surrounding myself and my loved ones with the White Light of the Holy Spirit. And no client leaves my office or hangs up the phone from a reading with me without my surrounding them as well, whether they're aware of it or not. A silent gift from me, and by far the most valuable I can give.

- **The Circle of Mirrors.** Picture yourself inside a perfect circle of mirrors, taller than you, facing away from you. White entities are drawn toward mirrors, while dark, negative entities are repelled by them. This is also a favorite of mine, because for reasons they never quite understand, when you've surrounded yourself by the Circle of Mirrors, rude, aggressive, chronically obnoxious people suddenly go out of their way to avoid you.
- **Gold and Silver Nets.** The image is a fisherman's net, of fine-spun gold and silver gossamer, strong but light as air, its fibers braided and glistening with the white light of the Holy Spirit. Drape it over yourself, to cover and protect yourself from head to toe in divine white light. As you move through your day, drape a matching gold and silver net over any dark entities you encounter, to contain and neutralize their negativity.
- **Worry Beads.** Borrowed and blended from the Catholics, the Greeks and the Tibetans, with thanks. Either buy or make yourself a four-to-five-inch-diameter circle of beads. It's essential that the beads be made of a natural material, preferably wood—nothing artificial. Every night before you sleep, go one bead at a time around the little circle, assigning one thing you're worried about to each separate bead. When each bead has its own designated worry, place the circle of beads in a small container of sand on your nightstand, to let the sand absorb the worries from the beads and neutralize them.

Those are a few of the Tools of Protection that keep me from becoming depleted after a day of even the most emotionally charged readings. Please by all means borrow them, use them and create your own. They'll be the same source of strength for you that they've been for me for all these many years.

THE FOLLOWING PAGES

You'll find more specifics of how I read as the upcoming chapters unfold. Topics like regressive hypnosis and cell memory are important enough to deserve their own spotlights, in the places in this book where their relevance is most apparent.

What follows are stories of actual readings, all excerpted from affidavits, letters and audiotapes from those readings, and all shared with the clients' permission. Still, it's my nature to be protective of them, so I'll be using their initials and/or pseudonyms and leave it to them to decide whether or not they want to point to one of these stories and say, "That's mine!"

And make no mistake about it—these are not my stories. They're yours. Every one of you of every age and culture and circumstance and belief system I've ever read, and every one of you still to come, will find some part of yourself in these pages and know that whatever you've been through, or whatever you're going through now, someone else has been there too, and understands.

As for me, I am, as I always have been and will be until I go Home, simply a grateful messenger who thanks you and loves you all.

Chapter 4

OUR LOVED ONES ON EARTH: RELATIONSHIPS, FAMILIES, CHILDREN AND PETS

We were all created by the Embodiment of Love itself, so it's no surprise that to some extent, love is one of the major forces that form the essence of our lives, both on earth and at Home. On the Other Side, we love perfectly, gracefully, unconditionally, as easily and naturally as we breathe. Here on earth, we're frankly not always that good at it. And God bless us, with our lovers and spouses, with that collection of people called "family," with the children who define our future and with the Angels on earth called animals, when it comes to love, we never stop trying to get it right.

Whether we're looking for love, falling in love, trying to hold on to love, trying to give or receive love without being either too suffocating or too distant, falling out of love, grieving over a love that slipped away or wishing we were immune from ever loving again, there's one fact we all know in our souls: in our last hours on earth, it's how we honored love while we were here that will shape both our final thoughts and the legacy we'll leave behind.

RELATIONSHIPS

You've seen it with your own eyes, I'm sure. I'm at a lecture, I'm in front of a television audience, or I'm on television or radio taking phone calls, and it's guaranteed that someone is going to ask when Mr. or Ms. Right is going to come along, and/or if they're with them already. Have you noticed that everyone around them smiles?

I've decided that some of the smiles are from people who simply saw the question coming.

Some of the smiles are from people who appreciate the hope and romance of it.

And some of the smiles are from people who've been there, done that, and are thinking, "Better them than me."

If you think the same question comes up in private readings with the same reliable frequency, you're exactly right. One on one, though, we can go into more detail, and more of the inevitable variations and complications seem to emerge in the course of the conversation. Because, as we all know if we're past the age of about twelve, finding Mr. or Ms. Right carries no guarantee of leading to "and they lived happily ever after."

That's one of the reasons I pitch such a fit when someone asks when they're going to find their "soul mate." You know if you've seen me or read my books what my answer will always be. But if you're new to my philosophy on this subject, here it is: Your soulmate is on the Other Side having a great time right this minute, waiting for you to come Home. Don't drive yourself crazy looking for them here on earth, because 999.9 times out of a thousand, you're setting yourself up for a lot of frustration and disappointment. You'll have much greater success keeping your eye out for your kindred spirits instead.

Understanding the difference between a soul mate and a kindred spirit will clarify things considerably, and they really are entirely different entities.

When God created each of us, He endowed our spirits with both male and female aspects. At the same instant we were created, our identical twin spirit was created too, with male and female aspects that are essentially mirror images of our own. That identical twin spirit is our only true soul mate. They're not our "other half," any more than anyone is our "other half" or "completes" us as so many hyper-romanticized articles and "experts" enjoy claiming. Encouraging a search for our "other half" to "complete" us implies that we're a planet full of half-people walking around incomplete until we meet that one person who fills in our missing pieces. Isn't that silly? I'm already a whole, complete person, all by myself, thanks. You are too, and don't let anyone convince you otherwise. And I feel safe in assuming that the list of qualities you're searching for in your ideal life partner doesn't include "dependent on others to make them whole and complete." I'm not sure which would be worse—being that desperately needy, or being attracted to someone that desperately needy.

While we're living on the Other Side, we share a close bond with our soul mates, like most identical twins. But we each have our own friends, our own interests, our own talents, our own careers and passions, our own distinct personalities—in other words, our own identities. And, as with all spirits on the Other Side, we make our own decisions about when and how often, if ever, we want to incarnate on earth for the advancement of our soul's eternal journey. The odds against our deciding to come here at the exact same time as our soul mate are overwhelming, not to mention that the experience would be redundant—we see each other at Home all the time, always have, always will. Why feel any need at all to synchronize our watches and charts to make sure we see each other all the time on our brief trips away from Home as well? I get claustrophobic just imagining that.

Kindred spirits, on the other hand, are simply souls we've known in one or more of our past lives, here or on the Other Side or both. They're those occasional people we meet for the first time and feel an inexplicable familiarity with, so that instead of saying, "Nice meeting you," we're almost tempted to say, "Oh, look, it's you!" Reconnecting with a kindred spirit from another life can be thrilling, comforting, stimulating and incredibly enriching, for the obvious reason that the two of you share a past together whether either of you consciously knows it or not. You only have one soul mate, one identical twin soul. You have more kindred spirits than you can count, and that fact alone increases the odds of finding a life partner among them with whom you can build a truly fulfilling, mutually empowering commitment.

The myth of meeting your soul mate creates false hope, disproportionate significance and, all too often, a much more difficult recovery if a relationship doesn't work out. "Soul mate" seems to inspire temporary amnesia about the fact that whoever we fall in love with, they're going to turn out to be human beings. Discovering that your "soul mate" leaves wet towels on the bed, hogs the closet space, spends money faster than you can earn it, makes rude noises when they eat, occasionally cheats, lies or treats your family like dirt is a lot more discouraging and harder to walk away from than learning those same things about a human being/kindred spirit who seemed like a good idea at the time, but oh, well.

When I give a client a name or physical description of a kindred spirit, and the approximate time they'll meet them, I'm getting the information from the chart the client wrote. And that can be as misleading as the soul mate concept. "I charted this person into my life" shouldn't necessarily be unrealistically romanticized into the idea that therefore they're "destined" to be with you. We write people into our charts for any number of reasons, the bottom line of which is invariably because our spirit will somehow profit from knowing them. That might translate to joy, and a fulfilling, reciprocal relationship. It might translate to an enduring friendship, romantic or not. It might translate to learning more through that person about who we are, what our priorities are and what our boundaries are. It might translate to finally finding the strength to walk away when we realize we're involved in something unhealthy, rather than staying out of pride or complacency or a fear of being alone. In one particular case I can think of, it translated to a path to a whole other invaluable experience—one of my closest friends is someone I would never have met if she hadn't called for a reading to help her through a particularly hideous breakup. To this day, as much pain as she was in at the time, she still says, "If that's what it took to get here, he was worth it."

So when I tell a client about the Mr. or Ms. Right they charted, they'll never hear me guarantee a happily-ever-after for the relationship itself. But I will always be sure that they charted that person for some reason, and they, like you, have the power to recognize in the end what those reasons were.

And it doesn't take a psychic to guarantee this, to my clients and to you: the more content you are being single and independent, and the less you need a relationship, the better your chances of finding a healthy, fulfilling one. That's a fact, and a promise.

Somewhere in this sampling of the thousands of letters and affidavits from clients with relationship issues you'll find someone who reminds you of you, for better or worse. Smile, and give them and yourself all the credit in the world, remembering that, again, when it comes to love, we never stop trying to get it right.

> I asked Sylvia if she saw me marrying the boyfriend I was with at the time. I was disappointed when she urged me to "dump the couch potato." Then she asked me if I knew or had met yet a tall, husky, hazel-eyed guy with dark brown curly hair, because that's the man I would marry, sometime in the spring. (My reading was in November.)
>
> I would have sent my affidavit sooner, but I just got back from my honeymoon with the tall, husky, hazel-eyed guy with dark brown curly hair I met during the holidays, shortly after I "dumped the couch potato."
>
> Thank you, Sylvia, for making it so easy for me to recognize the man I was really meant to be with.
>
> from Lily

I didn't even come to Sylvia to talk about relationships. I was there to tell her I was moving from California to Arizona to start a new life thanks to a business opportunity, and I wanted to make sure the business opportunity was a sound one.

To my surprise, Sylvia was adamant that my life was in California, and that if I did move to Arizona it would be a very short trip. She then described, in great detail, the man I was going to meet, and marry within six months of meeting him. She said he lived in the same area of California I did, that we would meet at a party thrown by mutual friends and develop a serious relationship very quickly, that a major health problem of mine wouldn't cause him the slightest hesitation about getting involved with me, and that the Reno area played a very important part in his life.

I met him at a party thrown by mutual friends. We became serious very quickly. He wasn't fazed in the least by my health problem. He and I lived within twenty miles of each other, but he was developing several real estate holdings in the Reno/Lake Tahoe area. And we were married six days prior to the six-month anniversary of the night we met.

from Janeen

Dear Sylvia,

I wonder how many letters you get ten years later from people you've met. But here's one of them now. You were the guest speaker at a group I belonged to all those years ago. My mother was sitting next to me and kept nudging me, whispering, "Ask her! Ask her!" and I kept telling her to be quiet. Finally you walked right up to me and said, "Go ahead, ask me."

My mother wanted to know more than I did if I would ever get married again. You said I would. You went on to describe in exact detail a man I had just had a first date with earlier that week, and you said we would have three children. I already had two children from a previous marriage, so I assumed you meant that someday I would have one more.

Well, here I am ten years later, married to that gorgeous man you described to me, and we have three children together, in addition to the two I already had. And praise God, he's a wonderful man, and we're so happy.

from Phyllis

My reading with Sylvia was amazing, positive and very successful, with one exception. She told me the current man in my life was basically just "taking up space" and that our relationship wasn't as significant as I was trying to convince myself it was.

Six months later, I told the man in my life he needed to move out, and it's thrilling how much my life has opened up and expanded since he left. I was upset with Sylvia right after the reading and thought she was very abrupt when she talked about this man. I recently listened to the tape again and was shocked to discover that I was actually the one who was abrupt, not Sylvia. She was telling me something I didn't want to hear at the time, that turned out to be exactly what I *needed* to hear, and I'm very grateful.

from Nicole

Dear Sylvia,

I wrote to you a few months ago asking about the man I'm meant to be with, so that I'll recognize him next time after falling for "Mr. Wrong" over and over again. You told me his name is Dan, he's a good man and he's a financial adviser.

I recently got an e-mail from a former classmate I've known

since first grade and haven't heard from in years. His name is Dan, he just graduated from law school and he's an investment banker.

Is this the man you were talking about?

from Victoria

(Note from Sylvia to readers: Considering what you know about charts, shall I answer this one by myself, or shall we all say it in unison? *Yes, that's him!*)

Dear Sylvia,

"My problem with the guy I recently met is that you described him too perfectly! It was pretty much love at first sight on my end, and the three weeks we've been seeing each other have been thrilling for me, although nothing has really "happened" yet.

At dinner the other night I was staring at him, marveling over how exactly he fit your description, right down to just one dimple and bump on his nose. He asked why I was staring, and I just said I had a tape for him to listen to.

I played him the part of my reading where you talked about him. I thought he'd be flattered. Instead, he got very uncomfortable, said he didn't think it sounded like him and left. I haven't heard from him since, and he won't return my phone calls. I know if he'll just give me a chance to apologize for what I now understand was premature and presumptuous on my part, we can get back on track again. Since he's avoiding my calls, I'm thinking about stopping by his job after work one day to talk and straighten things out. Would that be a good idea?

from Jackie

(Another note from Sylvia to readers: This one we can do in unison. *No.* And don't worry, I've already talked to her, and she's better now.)

I had a phone reading with Sylvia. I'm a former psychotherapist, so I was admittedly cautious. But I'd been through a lot of changes in my life, including some surgeries that meant abandoning my chosen career, and among other things I was wondering if I had a chance at a happy relationship in my future, considering my new physical limitations.

Sylvia immediately described a 5'4" brown-haired green-eyed woman with a heart-shaped face, high cheekbones and big round eyes. She said her name started with "D," either Diane or Donna, she's a genuinely good person, beautiful both inside and out, and she'd be completely dedicated to me and not care a bit about my physical problems. She said I'd meet her in August, and there was no way I could possibly miss her.

Several months after my reading I signed up for a real estate class at the local city college. The first night of the class—on August 28—I was among the first to arrive and took a seat near the front of the room. Moments later a beautiful woman with brown hair, big green eyes and high cheekbones walked in, scanned the many empty desks and then walked over and said she thought she'd sit by me. We introduced ourselves. Her name was Donna.

We were nothing more than friends for the first few months, because she was married, and had been for fourteen years. But it was an unhappy marriage, and she filed for divorce not long after I played her the tape of my reading with Sylvia and Donna said she believed she was the woman Sylvia told me about.

Donna and I have been together ever since. It's a calming, relaxing, affirming relationship that almost seems too good to be true, and I look forward to spending the rest of my life with this woman, just as Sylvia said I would.

from Kevin

Shortly after my reading started Sylvia asked, "Who's Tom?" I told her Tom was a man I had gone out with a few times but stopped seeing because I felt smothered by him after only a handful of dates. She said, "Good. I don't like Tom. He doesn't respect other people's boundaries, and he never will, no matter what you say." We moved on to other subjects, and I didn't give it any more thought.

Several months later some close friends asked if I'd be interested in going out with the attractive, successful, smart, divorced and very nice real estate attorney who had just handled a property dispute for them. I would never describe myself as a frequent dater, or an especially enthusiastic one, but these were (and are) dear friends and their description of "T. J." made him sound like someone I might enjoy, so I finally agreed.

I never put myself in a stranger's hands, so I did as I always do and insisted on meeting T. J. at the restaurant rather than having him pick me up. He was definitely attractive and made a great first impression. We didn't even have our menus yet when I called him T. J. and he told me to call him Tom instead. I flashed back for the first time in ages to my reading with Sylvia. Of course I had assumed back then that she was referring to the Tom I had stopped seeing, and I still had no reason to believe she wasn't. But I'm sure I was a little more on guard with him that night than I would have been without Sylvia's words ringing in my ears. He wanted to go out again three nights later, and I was kind of relieved that I could honestly tell him I was leaving town on business the next morning for a week. I promised to call him when I got back, and I intended to.

Well, to make a long story short, he called more than fifty times during the week I was gone even though I tried to politely explain how busy I was, and the last straw was when he surprised me by being at my apartment door waiting for me when I got home from the airport. Then he was annoyed because I didn't seem happy to see him.

After trying to reason with him for three weeks about taking things slowly and feeling as if he was crowding me, and him pretending to understand but not changing his behavior a bit unless it suited him, I heard Sylvia's words again: "He'll never respect your boundaries no matter what you say." So, even though I've never done anything like this in my life, I told him if I ever saw or heard from him again I would take out a restraining order on him, and I couldn't imagine something like that would look good on an attorney's public record. He was furious, but it worked, and it's been quiet for almost four months now (except for all the apologies from the friends who set me up with him).

It was definitely Sylvia's warning that gave me the courage to threaten a restraining order on this Tom kook, and I would have gone through with it if it had been necessary. Please thank her for keeping my radar on high alert and giving me permission to choose protecting my boundaries over trying not to hurt someone's feelings.

from Sharon

Dear Sylvia,

When I saw you in November I spoke to you in the most glowing terms about my girlfriend Sherry, and I told you I was planning on giving her an engagement ring for Christmas. You urged me not to invest in the ring, because Sherry was unstable, was hiding a drug problem from me and had been "borrowing" money from my savings account with my ATM card. You also said she wouldn't still be with me at Christmas. I was sure you had to be talking about someone else. Sherry and I had been together for almost two years, and the picture you painted of her sounded nothing like the woman I was in love with. I told you you were wrong, and you simply said, "No, I'm not." I didn't say anything at the time, but I was still convinced you were wrong when I left the reading, even though other parts of it were accurate to the point of being scary.

A few days after my reading my curiosity started getting to me, and I went in person to my bank to get my savings account statement. (I pay close attention to my checking account statement, but not to my savings account, since it's something I rarely even touch.) I was sick to my stomach when I discovered that almost $1400 was missing. My girlfriend didn't admit to it, but from her response it was obvious she'd taken it. Then, two weeks later, I came home from work one night to an empty apartment. She cleaned the place out and took off, and I did find a glass pipe in the trash she left behind. I guess my questioning her about the missing money made her want to get as far away from me as possible before I started uncovering God knows what else.

I won't say I'm not heartbroken, but I'm also grateful as hell for you tipping me off that she wasn't who I thought she was and saving me from what would obviously have been a disaster of a marriage. Thank you, Sylvia. Thank you, thank you.

from Todd

Dear Sylvia,

A few months after my divorce I wrote to ask you when there would be another significant relationship in my life. You told me that by October I would meet a woman with short dark hair, 5'8" tall, slender, long-waisted, with long legs, an oval face, hazel eyes and a full mouth. She would also have a young child.

On my birthday, September 22, some friends took me to a small jazz club, and that exact woman was sitting at the next table with a group of her friends. I couldn't resist striking up a conversation with her, needless to say, although I wasn't about to tell her Sylvia Browne had described her to me—it sounded like a lame pickup line or something.

We had a couple of dinners together, and I met her three-year-old son. It was great, until she headed home to Toronto, and there I was in Augusta, Georgia, wondering if that was all there was. I wrote you again to ask if you still thought that was "her," and you said yes, be patient, you two won't be this far apart for much longer.

She and I kept in touch several times a week, although I think we were both reluctant to get involved in a long-distance relationship.

To our mutual surprise, four months later her father passed away, and she and her son relocated to take care of her elderly mom—right here in Augusta. They're who she was visiting when I first met her. We've been together ever since, she and her son are the joys of my life and I finally confessed to her that it was Sylvia Browne who told me who to look for and when. She asked me to be sure to say that this is a thank-you note from both of us.

from Philip

I had a private reading with Sylvia at a low point in my life. My 34-year-old wife had left me for a 19-year-old guy she met in a chat room (and got pregnant by two months after meeting him). She turned very vindictive and nasty during the divorce, and I was really scared when she decided to fight for custody of our two children, who were all I cared about at that point.

I asked Sylvia if I would end up winning custody of our children. She said I would, because my ex-wife's new boyfriend didn't want them and she would end up choosing him over them. That was exactly right. Out of nowhere she just stopped contesting my petition for full custody and didn't even ask for visitation.

What really saved me from making a terrible mistake for me and the children was when Sylvia warned me that my ex-wife would be getting in touch with me after her baby was born, saying she wanted to reconcile and put our family back together. Sylvia said not to fall for it, because it wouldn't have anything to do with loving me, it would be about wanting to "come in from the cold." When her baby was five months old, she started calling, telling me she'd never stopped loving me and wanted us to get back together. It didn't take long to find out that the 19-year-old had disappeared on her, after maxing out her credit cards and selling her car behind her back before he left, and she was just wanting the lifestyle back that she'd thrown away.

I'm helping her get back on her feet financially because of the baby and because she's my children's mother, but thanks to Sylvia warning me keep my eyes open, I'm not considering reconciling with her.

from Josh

FAMILIES

I think the most fascinating thing about those people collectively known as our family is the same thing that can make them the most challenging: we charted each and every one of them, but they came here with their own charts too. Which means this group of people who, on paper, are all supposed to adore one another and be genetically compatible and have things in common and enjoy one another's company have, in fact, agreed to be related, but beyond that, they each have their own journey to fulfill and their own lessons to learn. There are absolutely reasons we included one another in our charts, but just as with relationships, there's an endless variety to be found among those reasons. And they're not all for us to understand while we're here. They're for us to confront with honesty, courage and integrity, learn from and grow from—a microcosm of why we make these occasional trips to earth in the first place.

There's a very good chance that, like me, you charted a thumbnail sketch of the general population into your family, almost as if we provide ourselves with a captive group to practice on before we head out into the world. You probably wrote in at least one kindred spirit from a past life (my daddy and my grandma Ada), at least one dark entity (my mother) and at least one spirit you're meeting for the very first time (my sister). Tempting as it might be to assume, as I often do, that you must have been either drunk or insane when you wrote your chart, your family is likely to be your most glaring lesson that we—and they—all charted what will best serve the growth of our souls.

I haven't been a genius in my love relationships in this lifetime, and I've got the ex-husbands to prove it. But it's the area of family that most often reminds me of the old adage "Those who can, do; those who can't, teach." I have no trouble at all with clarity when it comes to the family problems my clients bring me. When it comes to my own family problems, I can be as clueless as the next person. Everything I know about charts and past-life connections and our designing our lifetimes for the purpose of taking necessary, important steps in the learning and growth of our spirits goes right out the window, always has, probably always will, when some kind of drama rears its head among these people I insisted on being genetically entwined with. In my spiritual and psychic lives, you'll never meet a more confident woman. In my lives as a daughter, sister, mother and grandmother, you'll never meet one who's felt more inadequate and more confused and more of a hand-wringing worrier from time to time. Yes, even I, with all my passionate, deep-rooted and utterly indestructible faith, forget too often to just "let go and let God" when it comes to my family.

A perfect example is the relationship between my sons Paul and Chris. I was looking something up a few weeks ago in Lindsay's and my first book for Dutton, *The Other Side and Back*, published in 1999, and I came across several paragraphs about the fact that the two of them didn't especially like each other, couldn't be in the same room for five minutes without an argument and wouldn't have cared if they never laid eyes on each other again. I agonized over that, lost sleep over it, tried every trick you can name to persuade them to be the great pals I'd always hoped they'd be and generally made a pest and a nag of myself in an effort to force them to have a close relationship that, let's face it, would have made *me* happy, regardless of what it did for them. I'm very close to both of them, so their estrangement made *me* uncomfortable.

Now, seven years later, my sons are friends. They like each other, they're there for each other and they're wonderful uncles to each other's children. And guess how much I had to do with it. *Absolutely nothing.* Life brought them together. Common circumstances brought them together. Following their respective charts brought them together. My staying out of the way and letting it be their and God's business brought them together.

I'm reminding myself as much as or more than I'm reminding you: when you're faced with family problems, as we all are sooner or later, make your best efforts, but don't ever forget where the real Power lies.

Come to think of it, if nothing else can be said for this family I charted, I've been outspoken enough about them that not once in fifty years has a client come to me with a family issue and been afraid that what they're about to tell me will sound too dysfunctional.

Dear Sylvia,

I just had to write you a quick note to tell you that, thank God, you were exactly right during my phone reading with you two months ago.

Just as you said it would, it became apparent during my grandchildren's custody hearing that my daughter-in-law, their mother, didn't want them, she just wanted as much child support as she could get her hands on. We were also able to establish her abuse of them without their being put through the ordeal of testifying against her.

My son got full custody of the children, and their mother is limited to supervised custody and has to pay *him* child support, which she's furious about and is going to appeal. You predicted every bit of it except her appealing the child support ruling, and my son couldn't care less about it. As he says, it's only money, while he finally has the joy of full-time custody and of knowing these beautiful children will be raised in a safe, healthy, happy home.

from Linnea

Dearest Sylvia,

My son James has always been a very private person. Even when he was a child he kept his emotions to himself and always tried to put on the appearance that everything was fine, no matter how upset or disappointed or depressed he might be. He's also been a wonderful son, as thoughtful and attentive toward me as he could be, and when he left home, went to college and got married there was still never a week that went by when he didn't call at least once or twice just to say hello and check up on me.

As you know, when I had my reading with you I was concerned about him because I felt he was distancing himself from me. I couldn't imagine what I'd done to make him pull away, and when I'd ask him if something was wrong between us he would assure me he loved me and nothing had changed at all, he was just busy. I could hear in his voice that he was holding back as usual, but I wasn't getting anywhere, so I asked if you knew what was going on.

You said he was avoiding me because if I spent too much time with him I would see how depressed and unhappy he was, and he didn't want me to worry. His wife was mentally and verbally abusing him, you told me, constantly nagging him, calling him a loser, embarrassing him in front of his friends and co-workers and taking advantage of the fact that she knew he wouldn't fight back. You said she married him for his stability after she'd left an abusive long-time boyfriend (exactly right!) and now it was like she was mocking him for the very same stability.

I couldn't imagine you were right. I'd never seen any hint of such a thing. But that weekend I went to see him when I knew she'd be gone for the day. I kept things casual at first, and he put on his best act of how fine and normal everything was, as usual. I could tell he wasn't himself, and that it was an act for my benefit, though. So finally, when we were sitting quietly on his porch, I came right out without giving him a chance to see it coming and asked, "Is J. abusing you?" He just looked at me with this shocked expression on his face and didn't say a word, and then all of a sudden he started to cry.

It turned out to be exactly what he and I both needed. Once he "let me in" I was able to help him find a good therapist, we've had a lot of great talks and even though he doesn't know yet what's going to happen with his marriage or what he hopes will happen, he knows that whatever it is, we'll get through it together.

Sylvia, without you, your honesty and your accuracy, I'm sure my son would still be depressed and unhappy and avoiding my calls, and I would still be trying to figure out what I did wrong. My daughter-in-law probably won't be writing you any thank-you notes, but on behalf of my son and me, our deepest gratitude doesn't begin to say it.

from Judith

I had a private reading with Sylvia eight years ago. She made several predictions for my family, and I admit it, I was angry when I left her office. I thought it was pure guesswork from a woman who must have been in a bad mood or something, and I didn't appreciate it.

Two weeks ago my husband and I were packing for a move to another city, and I came across the tape of my reading with Sylvia in the back of a drawer. I didn't even know I still had it. Just for something to listen to while I packed, I played it, and it gave me goose bumps. Every word of that "guesswork" that offended me so much had come to pass in the eight years since.

- Sylvia said my daughter and son-in-law would have a son. True.
- She said the baby would be born drug-addicted and have a lot of health struggles as a result in the first two years of his life, but eventually he'd be okay. True.
- She said when my grandson was four years old, he'd go to live with his paternal grandparents. True. (They won custody of him when Child Protective Services took him away from my daughter. By then my son-in-law was long gone.)
- She said my husband and I would end up fighting for and winning custody of him. True. That's why we're relocating. (His paternal grandparents developed serious health problems that made it impossible for them to care for him.)
- She said my daughter would keep disappearing and reappearing in my grandson's life, but until she was clean and sober she would continue to choose the wrong men over him because she's incapable of thinking clearly. Very true.

It still amazes me that not once as all these events unfolded did I say to myself, "That sounds familiar. Where have I heard that before?" Maybe if I'd listened more closely eight years ago instead of being so defensive and huffy I would have antici-pated some of it and done more "acting" than "reacting."

As it is, all I can do is say that eight years later, I'm now one of your biggest believers, and as of this morning I'm on your waiting list for another reading at your earliest convenience. I promise to leave my attitude at home this time.

from Madeline

Dear Sylvia,

I know I said thank you about fifty times as I was walking out of your office after my reading, but I have to say it again a month later now that I'm seeing, or more to the point, feeling, the changes for the better that are taking place in my life with your words ringing in my ears to inspire me.

I'm the guy with the brother—you made me laugh by calling him the "prodigal son impersonator." He's been a bully and a troublemaker pretty much all of his life, barely made it through high school with all the partying and drinking and smoking weed, goes from one job to another to another and keeps getting fired for things that are already somebody else's fault, has been to jail (never prison) a few times, and is now living back home with our parents, not working and treating them like slaves. I was an honor student, got my master's degree, have a beautiful wife and a baby on the way and just got my third promotion at the software company I've been with for five years, during which I bought my parents their house and both their cars. Bottom line: he's always been the apple of my parents' eyes, I've always been the one who felt like nothing I could do was ever enough. By the time I came to see you, I was so tired of it I was ready to throw up my hands and never see them again. You can only beat your head against a wall for so long before it starts to hurt.

Your explaining life charts to me, and the various past life connections that are at work among us (especially the one about my mother and brother being brother and sister in a past life—you have no idea how much sense that makes now that you mention it!), have been eye-opening and life-changing for me. Instead of looking at my family from the limited perspective of this life, and the over-simplified rules of "fair and unfair," I can look at a far bigger picture in which we're all in the process of learning and growing and getting what we need from each other, including me, based on what we're here to do. When I think of the dynamics between my parents and brother as essentially being none of my business, and of how I designed a perfect situation for myself to inspire the independence and success I'm enjoying, I find myself really appreciating these people and loving them without resentment, maybe for the first time. Not to mention the relief of letting myself off the hook for feeling like the more I do, the more I fall short in my parents' eyes, when the truth is, it doesn't have anything to do with that, or me, at all.

Your spiritual outlook and insights have given me a family I can now love for exactly who they are, not in spite of it, and that's a gift that will last me the rest of my life. Thank you, Sylvia Browne!

from Damon

CHILDREN

Children are the most psychic humans on this planet. Never doubt that. Never dismiss what they do and say as nothing but their little imaginations at work. Never discourage them from expressing themselves because their psychic wisdom confuses you or, as I've heard many parents complain, it "creeps you out." Children can teach you volumes about the spirit world, the Other Side, past lives and eternity itself if you'll pay attention and learn how to help them teach you.

There's an utterly logical reason for children's psychic sensitivity: they're newly arrived from Home, that sacred dimension from which we all came and to which we'll all return, and their memories of it are still fresh. They've been living busy lives as spirits among spirits in the higher vibrational frequency of the Other Side, and for years after their birth they're as "tuned" to that frequency as they are to this much lower, much slower one on earth. Interacting with residents of that place they've just come from is natural to them. So when a baby focuses on some spot in midair where you see nothing, and begins giggling and chattering in response to voices you don't hear, consider yourself blessed to be witnessing a reunion between the baby and a visitor from Home. And when an "imaginary playmate" enters the picture, ask questions. Almost ten times out of ten, there's nothing imaginary about that playmate at all, it's a spirit, the child's Spirit Guide or, if the playmate is unhappy, injured or challenged in some way, a ghost.

The more questions you ask, and the more you really listen to the answers with your conscious mind and spirit mind paying attention, the more your children can teach you about the spirit world, the Other Side and your own eternity. A simple "Who were you before this?" or "What did you used to do for a living?" even to a very young child, is likely to inspire a fascinating response, and it will be your loss if you jump to the conclusion that they're making it up.

And you don't have to take the word of a wacky psychic for it, either. Actor Blair Underwood has edited a lovely book about children's past-life memories, full of quotes and anecdotes from the uncoached children themselves. It's called *Before I Got Here: The Wondrous Things We Hear When We Listen to the Souls of Our Children*. It's charming and worth reading, particularly if you think I'm just making these things up. For the record, I don't know Blair Underwood, I had nothing to do with the book, and I don't get a dime of royalties from it. It just happens to add more confirmation to one of my favorite subjects, and I recommend you buy it, the minute you're done reading *Insight*, of course.

A distraught woman brought her four-year-old daughter, Casey, to me one day. It was one of those "wrong reason, right move" situations— because of the "crazy" things Casey had been saying almost since the first day she learned to talk, the woman had come to the conclusion that her daughter was "possessed" and wanted me to heal and bless her.

I don't believe in possession. I don't believe in any variation of it, any claim that another spirit, good or evil, has overtaken someone's body without their willing, conscious permission. It's a physical and spiritual impossibility. So I knew that whatever was going on with this child, we could rule out possession.

The mother started to give me a few examples of Casey's "craziness," but I cut her off, not wanting to have any predisposed ideas before I sat down with this seemingly happy, bright, outgoing little girl. With her mother's permission, Casey and I headed into my office alone. I was just closing the door when the mother hurried over to me and whispered, "Ask her about the bank near her grandma's house."

Casey had no trouble getting comfortable with me, settling into an overstuffed chair and chatting easily as if we were old friends. She was articulate and charming, with the most wonderful ready giggle, and I tried to imagine anyone having this child and being anything less than enchanted by her, let alone thinking she might need an exorcism. But again, I didn't want to leap to conclusions. So after a few minutes of idle conversation about how much we both loved our dogs and rice pudding and each other's dresses, I eased into what her mother had suggested would give me a hint at Casey's deep disturbance.

"Tell me about the bank near your grandma's house," I said.

She didn't bat an eye, and her tone implied that she was glad I'd asked, because she found this kind of interesting. "It used to be a grocery store," she said. "They had oranges outside, and apples, and sometimes peaches."

"Really? When was that?"

"When Mommy was a baby, and I used to take her there."

"Who were you to her? Do you remember? Were you *her* mommy?"

She giggled, as if I'd just said something hilariously silly. "No, I was her *uncle*. But I got shot in the war. Right here. See?" She lifted her Pooh T-shirt just enough to show me a faint brown oval birthmark just above her navel.

Several minutes later, after more of the same casual questions and answers, I put Casey in the safe hands of my staff to play and sat down in private with her mother.

"How did it go?" she asked, almost in tears. "Do you have any idea what's wrong with her?"

"I think so," I told her. "I think there's not a single thing wrong with her except a good memory of her past life that she'd love to tell you about if you'll just calm down and listen to her with an open mind. And I think you can validate that for yourself. Did there used to be a grocery store near her grandmother's house where the bank is now?"

"I have no idea," she said.

"Find out. And what about an uncle of yours who might have been killed in a war? Do you know anything about that?"

She thought for several seconds. "I think I may have heard something about an uncle I never knew, ages ago, but I'm not sure. Why?"

"Again, find out. Ask your family members. Someone can tell you one way or the other."

"Okay. But then what?"

"Then, if it turns out there really was a grocery store, and there really was an uncle who was shot and killed in a war, call me and I'll explain what a special gift you've been given who you keep calling crazy."

A couple of weeks later I got a call from Casey's mother. Sure enough, there used to be a little neighborhood grocery store and fruit stand where the bank now stood. And sure enough, Casey's mother's uncle Carl, her father's brother, had died in battle during World War II. According to the official military records, he'd been shot in the stomach and was killed instantly.

It wasn't easy, needless to say, to help this woman make the transition from "my daughter's possessed" to "my daughter's my reincarnated uncle." But I finally got her there, when she couldn't come up with any other possible explanation for this wealth of information her child had that was news to her. It was almost harder to convince her that not only was there nothing scary or all that unusual about Casey's past-life memories and their past-life relationship, but she and the rest of her family could learn a lot and even celebrate a reunion with a deceased relative if they'd simply ask questions and consider the probability that this little girl knew exactly what she was talking about.

As for Casey's birthmark, there was nothing especially uncommon about its connection to a past life. I began studying birthmarks decades ago, thanks in large part to a neurologist colleague of mine with whom I'd shared a lot of mutual referrals. He was convinced that there was more to birthmarks than just haphazard pigmentation or genetic whimsy, but he hadn't figured out what their significance might be and asked if I'd put my mind to it and call if I came up with anything.

I'd never paid much attention to birthmarks, nor had I been especially curious about them, but I agreed to help if I could. I promptly forgot about it until weeks later when I was doing a past-life regressive hypnosis session. The client was telling me about his death in his most recent previous life, how he'd bled to death from a knife wound in the back of his right leg, just below the knee. Something about his description of the wound and how specific he was jarred my memory of my neurologist friend's request. So when my client was "awake" again I asked if he happened to have any birthmarks. He did, he told me, and he rolled up his pant leg to show me a reddish-brown rectangular mark a couple of inches below his right knee.

It took several more of these birthmark "experiments" for me to be convinced enough to call the neurologist and tell him I thought I might have something. But once I started going out of my way to notice, there was no denying the fact that probably nine out of ten clients were born with some kind of marking on their skin that matched up perfectly with a serious or fatal wound from a past life that they'd remembered during regressive hypnosis. The correlation actually makes perfect sense when you think about the dynamics of cell memory, which we'll discuss in Chapter 9.

So if for some reason you find it awkward to ask your child a question like "Who were you before this?" or "Have you and I ever known each other before?" as a key to help them unlock their past life memories, don't hesitate to use their birthmark if they have one. Simply point to it and say, "What happened here?"

Then sit back and listen to more proof of the eternity of the spirit pouring with total acceptance from your own little resident expert on that particular subject.

I've been blessed to witness and share in countless experiences with clients and their children in my fifty years of readings. You'll find some of them here, in my clients' own words, and more of them in the "Healings" chapter, put more eloquently than I could ever hope to. Enjoy them. Better yet, marvel at them, and use them as even more motivation to appreciate the children around you as the incredibly psychic, wise, spiritual little beings they really are.

A very short story from my reading with Sylvia that I'll never forget. When my daughter was three or four years old, she used to ask me several times a week who the lady beside the dining room hutch was. Of course, I didn't see anyone beside the dining room hutch, and I assumed it was just a childhood game or something, so I always said I didn't know and paid no more attention to it.

I happened to mention it during my reading, and Sylvia immediately said, "That was her Spirit Guide. Her name is Elsa."

I hadn't had a chance to add yet that when she was asking about the lady beside the dining room hutch, my daughter would always follow it up by asking, "Who is Elsa?"

from Anita

To Sylvia & Staff:

Please accept this modest check as my way of saying thanks for what I feel was a free but life-changing "reading" from Sylvia without my ever meeting her or hearing her voice.

I've been a fan of Sylvia's for many years, and during my pregnancy with my first child (now eight months old) I read and was inspired by every word of *The Other Side & Back.* My husband and I are blessed with a beautiful, healthy, blonde-haired, green-eyed baby girl, for which we thank God every day.

The one problem, that came to really frighten us, was that from the very first time I tried to give Vanessa a bath, she began screaming the instant the water touched her skin. It wasn't angry "I don't like baths" screaming or sleepy, cranky "I'm not in the mood for this" screaming. (We've come to know the difference.) It was like she was in agony, being tortured. Naturally, I checked the water temperature, and it was fine. I settled for a sponge bath to try to calm her down, but that didn't seem to help. And the same exact behavior went on for the second bath, the third, the fifth and the tenth, in what was an otherwise good-natured, happy baby.

We were frantic. Friends and family members offered all sorts of advice, none of which worked, and tried to bathe her themselves, with no more luck than we had. We took her to her doctor more than once, and even though he saw it with his own eyes he couldn't find anything wrong and was as stumped as we were.

Like I said, I'd read *The Other Side & Back*, and finally, having run out of things to try (and without telling my husband, who would never have let me live it down), I took Sylvia's advice from that book and started talking to her while she slept. I had no way of asking her, obviously, but I thought maybe she'd drowned in a past life, or been tortured with water in a past life, or who knows what, since no one else had a better explanation for what was going on.

Taking Sylvia's word for it that even if my baby couldn't understand what I was saying, her age-old spirit could, I stood by her crib and watched her until she fell asleep at night, or for her nap. (I was relentless.) And then, as soon as I was sure she was sleeping soundly, I read to her straight from Sylvia's book:

My dear child, I feel blessed that you chose me as the care-taker and nurturer of your sacred spirit as it starts its new life on earth. I promise you the best effort of my soul to keep you safe, healthy, happy and connected to the God who created you and lives inside you with every breath you take. May you keep all the joy and wisdom your past lives have given you, and may all sorrow, fear, illness, and negativity from those past lives be released and resolved for all time into the white light of the Holy Spirit.

I have tears in my eyes as I write this, from awe and gratitude and relief and some disbelief, maybe, although I witnessed it— after only four days of repeating those words to her every time she slept, I found myself with a baby who doesn't make a sound when I put her into the water and who actually seemed to enjoy her baths from then on.

I've confided this "secret" to two of my friends and bought one of them a copy of *The Other Side & Back* for her baby shower gift. I haven't explained it to my husband, whose curiosity about how I accomplished this is almost out of control, but I think I'll just hand him the book and let him read it for himself. If he laughs, I'll just point to our daughter playing happily in her bath and tell him to laugh at that.

If I could write a "good" check for ten times this amount, or a hundred, I would, with great pleasure, and it would be worth it. I know you'll put this to the best possible use for someone who needs it, and again, it's my thanks for my peaceful baby and my "reading with no waiting list!"

from Teri

I've had the privilege of a long, genuinely spirit-altering relationship with the Make-A-Wish Foundation, through whom I've become friends with children who will always remain among my most inspiring teachers and heroes.

In honor of all the Make-A-Wish children, families, organizers and staff, I want to share a letter that will give you just a glimpse of the God-centered wisdom of a child's spirit. I'll use pseudonyms instead of their real names, out of respect for this wonderful family's privacy, but to the family: I love you, and I'll never forget you.

Dear Sylvia,

You've been speaking with my brother Gary for the past few days, and I just had to write you a note to express my thanks on his behalf and mine and my mother's.

I'm not sure if Gary has mentioned me to you yet, but my name is Louise and I'm 19 years old and I would do absolutely anything for my brother. When he got home from the hospital after a bunch of awful tests, and the doctors told him he's going to be paralyzed and only has a very limited amount of time left here I knew I had to do something. I couldn't stop crying and was so heartbroken that his four-year battle with cancer has come to this.

But all he keeps telling me is that he knows either way he will be fine and the Other Side is such a beautiful place where he will have no pain and really live happily. I don't know if I would ever be able to be that strong, but he always has been. He is so special.

So my mission from then on was to read your books with

Gary and my mom and try to become as strong as he is. As the pain got worse and his faith got stronger I knew I had to do something. I called the Marty Lyons Foundation to see if it was at all possible if Gary could speak with you, and after a few more calls they said YES!

I kept this a secret from Gary the whole time and only told him a few hours before you were to call. For the first time ever he was speechless and thrilled. You mean so much to him, I only wish you knew how much you have helped him (and my family) deal with such an awful disease.

After the first night you spoke with him he was able to move his legs, which he hasn't moved in a month or longer. We were all so shocked and thankful, I can't even find the right words to describe how we felt.

Your prayers mean so much to Gary, and to know that you, Sylvia Browne, are praying for him and care for him just makes him glow!

My mother, brother and I thank you, and Francine, for giving us so much hope and spirituality, and we love you for that.

Thank you again and again,

Louise

A month after this beautiful letter was written, my friend Gary went Home. There is no happier, busier, more joyful spirit on the Other Side.

To his sister and mother: from the bottom of my heart, I love you too.

\

ANIMALS

My grandmother used to say, "Never trust anyone who doesn't like animals." That rule has served me well all my life. In fact, finding out that someone doesn't like animals hits me in the same place, and in the same way, as finding out that someone enjoys child pornography. I can't get away far enough or fast enough.

This isn't an opinion, it's a fact: animals are among God's most perfect creations. Their spirits are more pure and more advanced than ours, so much so that they never have to reincarnate. They come to earth once, the closest thing we have to Angels living among us, and when they leave here they head straight back Home in the blink of an eye, where they're eternally cherished as the sacred beings they are.

Never doubt for an instant that every animal you've ever loved and lost is waiting for you on the Other Side, and that their powerful souls are still visiting you and watching over you here on earth. As you've heard me say before, and please don't think I'm kidding, if there are no animals on the Other Side, then I want to go wherever they are. In fact, an image I love, and cling to when one of my beloved dogs passes away, is that when we emerge from the tunnel into the perfect bliss of Home, the people who are gathered to greet us have to wait their turn. It seems that every pet we've ever owned from every lifetime we've ever lived is first in line, a sea of joyful leaping to welcome us with that same unconditional love they honored us with when we knew them here.

As for our departed pets' visits to us from Home, I used to almost scold clients for not staying tuned in enough to notice when they're being visited by one of their animals, because I know that very specific grief firsthand, and I'm so eager for my grieving clients to find the comfort those visits can bring.

The operative words are "used to." Then I, world-renowned psychic, in touch with the spirit world *all the time*, learned that I'm capable of missing visits myself, and I've never been impatient with a client about it again.

Many years ago a research team and I were investigating a haunting at an odd old Victorian mansion in New England. We did our usual exploration of the whole house for several hours when we first arrived. Then we divided up, each of us taking a separate room, with me and my trusty tape recorder settling into the master bedroom where the homeowner was sure the majority of the paranormal activity was centered. I unwrapped a blank tape from its plastic, slid it into the tape recorder, hit "record" and then sat inside the closed door of the room for hour after hour of total silence.

The team and I assembled the next morning to compare notes and play the tapes we'd recorded in our respective rooms. None of us had detected a thing in the way of spirit or ghost activity, and tape after tape of absolutely nothing supported our growing belief that the only thing going on in that house was a lot of draftiness and a need for some serious repair work.

To go through the motions of confirming our conclusion, I slipped my tape into the machine and hit "play." Again, all I'd heard that night in that room was hours of silence, and I'd been wide awake for every tedious minute of it.

So I couldn't have been more shocked as we sat there together listening to a tape in which we could clearly hear the distant, relentless, aggressive barking of what sounded like a very large dog.

It was impossible. The tape I used was brand-new and sealed, so there was no way we were listening to prerecorded barking. And I happen to have excellent hearing. I couldn't have missed such obvious noise while the tape recorder was picking it up.

My research team and I weren't about to shrug it off. We're not the group you want if you're hoping for an investigative conclusion of "Something's going on, but beats us what it is, so oh, well, and good luck with it." We went straight back to that house. One of us stayed to talk to the owner while the rest of us branched out to canvass the neighbors and even the local police who regularly patrolled that neighborhood. The results: the owner had never heard a dog in the five years he'd lived in the house, and neither the neighbors nor the patrolmen had heard a dog that night or any other night in longer than they could remember.

I finally turned to the only other person I could think of who might solve the mystery—I asked Francine where the impossible barking on that tape came from.

"That was your bull mastiff," she announced.

Instead of clearing things up, she'd only made them more complicated. I'd owned a lot of dogs, in a wide variety of breeds, but I'd never owned or even known a bull mastiff.

"Not in this life, no," she said. "He was your constant companion during your life in England, and he's with you in this life to protect you when he knows you're not feeling safe."

Do I remember a bull mastiff from a past life? No. Do I doubt Francine's explanation? Not for one second. If you've ever known and loved a dog, you have no more trouble than I do believing that their loyalty to us is as eternal as their pure, magnificent spirits.

And again, never since that experience have I wondered how a client could miss the obvious signs of a visiting departed pet. If I of all people can miss a bull mastiff barking for hours on end, who am I to throw stones?

Like children, who live more in the spirit world than in ours for years, animals are the most naturally gifted psychics on earth. If you don't know that from their uncanny intuitive survival and communication skills, watch them around your own home when a deceased loved one comes to visit. They'll bark and wag at "thin air," they'll arch their backs with their fur standing on end or suddenly begin purring "for no reason," they'll spread their wings to their widest span and begin shrieking at "nothing." If we're not paying attention, we'll scold them and tell them to calm down instead of the far more appropriate response of thanking them for telling us someone we love has shown up to say hello.

Dear Sylvia,

You told me that my mother would be coming to visit soon from the Other Side, and she'd give me a sign by doing "something with a picture or photograph."

If I'd thought someone would be in your office at 2:00 this morning I'm sure I would have picked up the phone and called, I was so excited to tell you this. I was sound asleep when my little Bichon, Spanky, woke me out of a sound sleep, barking like crazy in the living room. He's not much of a barker unless something's really going on, so I got up to see what the problem was. Spanky was dancing around in a gleeful circle all by himself, tail wagging a mile a minute (you said you have a Bichon too, so I know you can picture this), happily barking away. I told him to be quiet, but he ignored me completely (I repeat, he's a Bichon) and kept right on with this solo dance, and then, still wagging, he pranced to the front door, looking up and to his left as if he was following a tall imaginary friend. After just a moment or two at the door he calmed down, like the excitement was over, and he went back to his bed, curled up and went to sleep.

I know this dog very well. He's six years old, he was four months old when I got him, and since I work at home, he and I are constant companions. When I say he's never done anything like this before, I mean he's never done anything even a little like this before. It was peculiar enough that for reasons I'm still not sure of I walked over and checked to make sure the front door was securely locked, and then since Spanky was sound asleep and content I headed back toward the bedroom.

That's when I looked over and noticed that one of the six framed photos on the piano beside the hallway door had fallen over. I'm sure it won't surprise you, but it surprised me so much I gasped when I stood it up again and saw that it was a framed photo of my mother. Yes, maybe someone bumped into the piano on the way past and it accidentally fell over. But six identical frames, and only one, with the picture of my mother, fell over, while the five pictures of other family members were still standing? Also, there were four birthday cards on the piano, all of which would fall down every time someone even walked past the piano, and they were still standing too. I'm sorry, I can only go so far with the "logical explanation" approach. When it starts to defy the laws of physics and gravity, I'm done.

What I know is, you said my mother would come to see me soon, and she would let me know with a picture or photograph. Spanky was definitely having a grand old time with someone in the living room and followed them to the door, and the only thing disturbed in the whole room or house after they left was a photograph of my mother.

No one will ever convince me, or Spanky, that we weren't blessed with a visit this morning, and I thank you, Sylvia, for keeping me "on alert" in the right direction.

from Glennis

I was devastated when one of my twin Golden Retrievers passed away suddenly. Sylvia told me to watch the other one carefully, because Sheba would see her twin brother's spirit running and playing all over the yard as if he'd never left. I thought, "Sheba gets to see him but I don't? That's no fair."

Two days later I was in the kitchen beside the window making dinner and saw a golden blur sprint by in the backyard out of the corner of my eye. I thought no more of it than that Sheba was out there chasing squirrels, as usual (she's never come close to catching one) until I walked in a minute later and found Sheba sound asleep in the dining room.

I think it's times like those that the term "tears of joy" was coined for. I went straight to Sheba and woke her up and said, "Let's go outside. Your brother's here."

What a beautiful thing to have happen. I haven't seen him again. Yet. But I know I will. I know he's here for his sister, too, and that makes me even happier.

from Sydney

Dear Sylvia,

I know what an animal lover you are, and that you have many dogs of your own. So when I had an emergency medical decision to make about my new puppy Coach and my regular vet was being so dire in his prognosis, your office was the first place I thought to call.

To refresh your memory, Coach had been jumped on by my neighbor's Rottweiler. In all fairness, the Rottweiler was genuinely trying to play, but it was a 130-pound dog pouncing on a 7-pound puppy, and Coach ended up with his hind legs paralyzed. My vet recommended putting him to sleep, and the thought was unbearable unless it would be the only humane thing to do.

A member of your staff returned my call in less than an hour and passed along your advice: rush Coach to an orthopedic surgeon in Los Angeles (I live in the Los Angeles area) whose name and number your staff had on hand, because he had a disc injury that could be fixed! Assuming the surgeon agreed with your prognosis and the surgery, if necessary, was successful, you even gave me the name and number of a canine rehabilitation facility called Two Hands, Four Paws in L.A. where we could get postoperative physical therapy. I didn't even know such a thing existed!

Coach had a herniated disc. His prognosis was excellent provided we proceed with the surgery within twenty-four hours. Needless to say, we did. The surgeon was familiar with Leslie at Two Hands, Four Paws and couldn't recommend her highly enough to help Coach with his recovery.

I just wanted you to know that the four-month-old puppy I called about is now a frisky, funny, thriving eleven-month-old puppy who is the delight of my life. I owe it all to you, your compassion, your incredible gift and your staff. I can only imagine how many emergency calls pour into your office every day, and

I'm in your debt, all of you, for making Coach and me such a priority.

from Cara

My dear Sylvia,

I can't imagine what I've done to deserve such kindness from you—maybe in a past life I carried you across the Alps on my shoulders to escape the Nazis or something. But you gave me more comfort and relief about my adored cat's last night on earth than I can ever repay. As I told you, he was a two-month-old kitten when I adopted him, and he was almost eighteen years old when he passed away, so he had a long, happy life, and I had all those years to be spoiled by his beautiful presence and to be enriched by loving him and being loved by him.

He was always affectionate from the time he was no bigger than my hand. But never before, until his last night, had he stretched out across my pillow to touch my head, or laid across my chest to put his cold little nose on my face. There was such a constant, unprecedented deluge of affection in the hours before he died that I was afraid he was in pain and imploring me to help him.

Your assuring me that he was simply giving me all his love and receiving all of mine for him in preparation for his joyful trip Home to God didn't just make me feel better for the moment because it was what I wanted to hear. While I've never been an openly spiritual person, I heard your words and knew they were the truth, and thanks to you there's a deep peace at the heart of my grief. I'm blessed and amazed to know you, and I'm in your debt.

from Marion

Chapter 5

DECEASED LOVED ONES

There's no doubt about it, the number one issue among my clients is the need to know that a loved one who's passed away hasn't really ceased to exist but is really very much alive on the Other Side, happy and healthy and still visiting them.

They are all those things, of course, although even the absolute certainty of that fact can only go so far to ease the bottomless ache of grief. I know grief all too well. No other pain can hold a candle to it. I also know, beyond all doubt, that we can let go of whatever part of our grief is anchored in worry for our loved ones' well-being. With the very rarest of exceptions, they've returned to busy, thriving, blissful lives in paradise, dropping in to visit us more often than we're ever aware. We can safely focus our tears, our pain and our prayers for comfort on ourselves and everyone else who's struggling to survive the loss and make productive peace with the truth that we're still here, and because we are, we obviously have more things to accomplish before it's time for us to go Home.

As for those rare exceptions, I want to mention them, not to give you more things to worry about but just to clear up some frequent areas of confusion.

ORIENTATION, COCOONING AND THE TOWERS

The Other Side, as you know, is a very real place, not an endless landscape of clouds but an impossibly beautiful mirror image of earth's topography and architecture at its most perfect and just three feet above its surface. I describe it in exhaustive detail in my book *Life on the Other Side*, so I'm not about to belabor it here at the risk of bodily harm from my editor.

Obviously we all hope for a peaceful, happy transition to the Other Side from the moment we arrive, and we can certainly all count on living busy, productive lives in the blissful joy of God's safe arms at Home once we're there. The fact that the peace of the transition doesn't always occur instantly is a circumstance the spirit world is prepared for and more than equipped to handle, and the transition process can sometimes explain the delay in a deceased loved one coming to visit.

Spirits whose deaths were very sudden *occasionally* (I can't stress enough that this only happens in a small fraction of unexpected deaths) arrive on the Other Side either confused or annoyed by this jarring change of scenery and circumstance. They're aware that they're dead, and they're aware of where they are, they just weren't prepared for it and are too unsettled to find immediate peace. Those spirits are eased with supreme compassion and expertise through an Orientation process that includes intensive counseling and, very often, time to enjoy activities that brought them relaxation on earth, from sports to concerts to crafts to gardening—yes, all of which exist on the Other Side, and infinitely more.

Spirits who possibly had time to prepare for death but still arrive agitated, restless or somehow disconsolate and need more extraordinary care than Orientation provides—again, a tiny minority of arrivals, I promise you—are often Cocooned, to help them safely through the painful "bends" of the transition from earth to Home. When a spirit is Cocooned, they're simply put into a quiet, healing twilight sleep, during which they're constantly watched over and infused with God's peace and infinite, empowering love. They remain Cocooned for as long as it takes from them to feel whole again, and to awake with the full force of the joy we all ultimately experience at finding ourselves Home again.

And then there is the extreme cleansing deprogramming necessary for those who arrive deeply disoriented or deranged. This deprogramming takes place in two stunning twin facades of white marble and blue glass called the Towers that glisten with waterfalls and etched golden doors in the jasmine-scented air around them. Spirits in need of deprogramming in the Towers can't truly experience the bliss of the Other Side until they've been lovingly guided back to the sanity and identities that circumstances beyond their control robbed them of on earth. Victims of torture, brainwashing, the Holocaust, Alzheimer's, schizophrenia—anyone deprived through no fault of their own of their ability to understand who and where they were when they died is taken immediately to the Towers and guaranteed to be fully healed and reunited with their spirit's eternal, blessed journey.

Again, Orientation, Cocooning and deprogramming in the Towers can postpone visits from a deceased loved one, but they're purely temporary delays. I know—they feel like an eternity to us when we're so desperate for a sign from a beloved spirit. But they feel like no time at all to our loved ones on the Other Side. My father, who was Cocooned, took eight months to visit me for the first time. I was frantic by then and asked where he'd been for so long. His reply was, "What do you mean? I just left!"

THE NATURE OF SPIRITS

Frustrating as it sometimes is, we can't always summon the loved one we're hoping for at the moment we want or need them. Sometimes we'll ask for an appearance, or just a sign of their presence, and get nothing. Other times we'll ask for a loved one and get someone else entirely. And I have to admit, it does make me laugh, even if I hide it, when a client wants to talk to their father, let's say, but I give a detailed description of what turns out to be their aunt Rosemary who's appeared right behind them instead. More often than not, rather than being in awe that anyone from the Other Side is suddenly in the room with us, the client will say, "Aunt Rosemary? Who cares? Where's Dad?"

The fact is, there are several reasons why spirits might not always "come when we call them." (I hate making them sound like pets—you know what I mean.)

For one thing, believe it or not, they're perpetually, joyfully busy at Home, far busier than we are here on earth. (Again, read *Life on the Other Side* for details.) That's not to say they're too busy to be bothered with their loved ones, but they can sometimes be selective about what calls to answer. Even my Spirit Guide, Francine, who's essentially in charge of me, takes her time occasionally, depending on why I'm summoning her. If it's anything urgent, she's there in the blink of an eye without fail. But if I just want to ask her some research question out of curiosity, or I need her to help me find my car keys (I'm psychic—I can find everyone's keys but my own), she'll join me when she gets around to it and not a moment sooner.

For another thing, no matter how many lifetimes we go through on earth and at Home, some of our most basic natures remain consistent wherever we are, in a human body or in the spirit world. Both here and on the Other Side, there are the extroverts and the introverts, the speakers and the listeners, those who prefer the front row and those who are more comfortable toward the back of the room. Chances are if you summon a loved one for some non-urgent reason, and they were an introvert when you knew them, an extroverted substitute might respond instead.

Similarly, those who tended to occasionally need their solitude here on earth will most probably need it occasionally on the Other Side as well. It's nothing personal, and it certainly doesn't mean they've stopped loving you now that they're gone. It's no different from those days some of us have (I include myself, by the way) when, even if the person we love more than anyone else on this planet might be calling, you couldn't force us at gunpoint to answer the phone until we've had some private time. It never means, "Good-bye forever." It only means, "Don't worry, I love you, I'm just regrouping, I'll be with you any minute now."

Like I said, it can be frustrating, knowing that the spirit world isn't going to answer to our agendas each and every time. But I promise you, we're all going to breathe a sigh of relief about it when we're back in the spirit world where we belong and our loved ones are tugging at us twenty-four hours a day.

GHOSTS

We discussed ghosts in the second chapter, so I won't belabor the subject here. I do want to stress, though, that for all the ghost stories we hear, because they're usually interesting and occasionally sensational, ghosts are pretty rare. I doubt if even one client in a thousand has a deceased loved one who's earthbound. It's safe to say that if that's one of your concerns, you can rest assured that the odds are against it.

And in the highly unlikely event that a loved one has remained earthbound, you can still rest assured that they're not lost forever. Compassionate humans are becoming better informed and more eager every day to help ghosts find the light and go to the Other Side, just as we pray someone would do for us. But if earthbounds persist in ignoring the humans around them, and these ridiculous claims that they're dead, the spirit world tracks them every minute, and at the first opportunity that won't be too shocking or do them harm, the spirit world can be counted on to rescue ghosts and personally take them Home.

THE LEFT DOOR

You also won't hear from a deceased loved one if, when they leave their body, they don't make the trip to the Other Side as the vast majority of us do, but instead go through the Left Door, a site strictly reserved for the Dark Side.

The Dark Side (also known as dark entities) is made up of the true sociopaths among us, those without a conscience or any capacity for remorse. Dark entities use love exclusively as a means of manipulation and as a reliable prop. And no matter what rhetoric they've adopted to gain your trust, sympathy or admiration, dark entities are defined by the fact that by their own choice, they've turned away from God. God doesn't turn away from them, nor would he ever turn away from any of us. Count on it, if someone's life is devoid of God, it's *always* their choice, not His.

There is an actual place called the Other Side, but the closest thing to an actual "hell" is this tough boot camp called earth we voluntarily come to from time to time for progress along the eternal journey of our souls. That being true—and it is—it's fair to wonder what happens to the spirits of dark entities when their lifetime ends. The answer isn't pretty, but again, they have no one to thank but themselves.

When a person on the Dark Side dies, their spirit never experiences the tunnel and the sacred light at its end. Instead, they're propelled straight through the Other Side's Left Door. They've pre-chosen the Left Door through a lifetime of physically, emotionally and/or spiritually abusing God's children without remorse. And beyond the Left Door is an abyss of Godless, joyless, all-encompassing nothingness.

The only permanent residents of this abyss are faceless beings in hooded cloaks, who've become the artistic and literary archetype for the persona of Death. These beings don't act as dark spirit guides or avenging angels. They function more as a Council, overseeing the paths of the Godless spirits who make a brief appearance in their presence.

Those on the Dark Side spend a brief, terrifying time in the void behind the Left Door. And then, unlike spirits on the Other Side who choose when and whether to return to earth, dark entities travel straight from their bodies, through the Godlessness of the Left Door and right back in utero again, on a self-inflicted horseshoe-shaped journey that leaves them as dark at birth as they were at death in their previous life.

In other words, if there's someone in your life from the Dark Side whom you're convinced you can change for the better with enough love and patience, please remember that you're fighting a perpetual soul cycle that makes spiritual progress impossible, and that's a fight you can't win.

I happen to think there's great spiritual comfort in the truth of the Left Door and the journey of the Dark Side. On one hand, I know that the perfect God I believe in could never be vindictive enough to banish any of His children from His sacred presence for eternity. On the other hand, I've never cared much for the thought that Adolf Hitler, Ted Bundy and I could end up in God's same embrace of the Other Side between incarnations, as if there is no significant difference between our spirits.

And yet, to prove that our Creator really does love each of His children eternally and unconditionally, not even the Dark Side is doomed to horseshoe from the Left Door into the womb again and again and again forever. The spirits and Angels on the Other Side are well aware of these lost spirits, and sooner or later they literally catch them in their transit from one dimension to another and bring them Home to be embraced by God and infused with love by the healing white light of the Holy Spirit, the only Force powerful enough to reunite them with the sanctity of their soul.

If you know in your heart that a deceased loved one was/is a dark entity, you're not likely to hear from them, because they're probably already back on earth again. Try to be grateful for that, and patient for that eventual day when you'll be together on the Other Side. When that day comes, at long last, they'll be the healed, God-centered spirit you spent all that time and effort pretending they were when you knew them on earth.

THE HOLDING PLACE

The Holding Place is kind of an anteroom to the Left Door, a netherworld of confused despair that many religions refer to as purgatory.

I first learned about the Holding Place when I astrally traveled there in my sleep. I had no idea where I was, I just knew I was surrounded by an endless sea of lost spirits who'd been separated from their faith by the bottomless ache of true and complete hopelessness. They never said a word, to me or to each other. They just shuffled aimlessly, heads down, eyes lifeless. There were no small children. There were only young adolescents and older, moving through a thick, desolate silence.

I had no idea who these tragic people were, but purely on impulse I began rushing around in a panic, hugging them and saying, "Say you love God. Please, just say you love God and you can get out of here." No one responded, or even looked at me.

In the distance I could vaguely make out a vast entrance of some kind. I couldn't see beyond it, but I didn't want to. It terrified me. My soul became aware that it was the Left Door, and that those tragic spirits around me were too close to it to be safe and too confused to understand the danger they were in.

Francine explained the next morning that I'd traveled to the Holding Place, which, again, was a new one on me. The spirits there are torn between the sacred joy of the Other Side and the darkness of the Left Door, victims of tormented, often destructive hopelessness, many of them suicide victims.

I can't repeat this often enough: it's a cruel myth that everyone who commits suicide is eternally doomed. No one writes suicide into their chart, so it can constitute a broken contract with God. And suicides motivated by revenge, self-pity or cowardice, especially if there are children involved, guarantee themselves a trip through the Left Door.

But suicides caused by mental illness, or physiological chemical imbalances and depression can hardly be compared with acts that are methodically calculated for their effect on everyone left behind. So yes, there are absolutely suicide victims who proceed just as quickly as the rest of us to God's unconditional love and forgiveness on the Other Side.

And some languish in the Holding Place, in need of rescue by the spirits at Home and equally in need of our prayers to rekindle the light inside them that will reconnect them to the Light that's waiting to embrace them, that they simply lost track of somewhere along the way.

If you think a loved one might be in the Holding Place, be patient about hearing from them and send them your prayers.

If not, pray for those lost spirits in the Holding Place anyway. Whatever hope you have to spare is all they need to get them safely to the Other Side.

The truth is that most of us are hearing from our deceased loved ones now, and will continue to until we join them. They give us countless signals, countless hints and nudges and winks, and far too often our earthly conditioning sends us leaping to earthly, "logical" explanations, rather than letting us take a breath, open our minds to other, more divine possibilities and say to our visitors, "I love you too."

In almost every book I've written I've enumerated the many ways in which the spirit world lets us know they're around.

In this book, I'm delighted to step aside and let my clients tell you, every bit as eloquently as I ever could.

Through mutual friends, I had the great good fortune to be able to reach Sylvia directly during the most devastating loss in my life. My mother Mildred and I lived 3000 miles apart, but we were very close. We talked on the phone several times a week, and we visited each other as often as we could. When Mom was diagnosed with cancer, I remember wishing it had been me instead of her, because I couldn't stand the thought of her being in pain and afraid.

I called Sylvia, who told me where the tumors were located in Mom's body, which turned out to be so accurate you would have thought she had the doctors' reports in her hand. She also told me what to expect, and for how long, as the cancer progressed, and she helped prepare me for the inevitable by telling me the date when Mom would go to the Other Side. Again, she was exactly right.

On the night my mother died I had left her resting comfortably in the hospital and returned to my parents' home to change clothes and get a quick bite to eat. While I was there I put in a call to Sylvia, who told me that Mom was gone. The hospital called moments later to tell me the very same thing.

During my brief conversation with Sylvia she assured me that Mom had made it to the Other Side instantly, and that she was greeted there by a tall, dark-eyed man named Joe, with dark wavy hair. I had no idea who "Joe" was, and in the days that followed I started asking all my relatives. It almost defied the odds that in my very large Italian family, not one person could think of a deceased "Joe." But then, the day my mom's oldest living brother arrived, we had a meeting with the funeral director. He was filling out the death certificate and needed the names of Mom's parents.

We'd always known my grandfather, Mom's dad, as Jessie. But my uncle informed the funeral director, and the rest of us in the room for the first time, that his real name, his birth name, was Joe.

Thanks to my talks with Sylvia, I can't say I expected to see my mom after she passed, but I was open to the possibility and not as frightened as I might have been if Sylvia hadn't prepared me for it. And one day, several months after she died, there was Mom, standing in my kitchen, very briefly, accompanied by the comforting smell of her homemade spaghetti sauce. A few weeks later I was driving to work when she appeared in the passenger seat of my car, just long enough to tell me to take a different route than usual. I did, and when I arrived at work everyone was talking about the huge accident involving several cars and an overturned truck on the freeway I always took, that had traffic backed up for miles.

I still grieve for my mom, but Sylvia pointed out something I think of every day that eases my pain a little. I know Mom is alive and well on the Other Side, so my grief really isn't about her. It's just about me, and how much I miss her. What a blessing to be able to make that distinction and find comfort in my certainty that I'll see her again.

from Nancy

I had a reading with Sylvia a few weeks after my father died. My mother and I had both had sightings of him since he passed away, and we wondered if he was trying to tell us something. The first time I saw him was when I was flying home to attend his funeral. The plane wasn't very full, and I was sitting quietly in my seat staring absentmindedly out the window, preoccupied with my sadness, when I got the feeling someone had just sat down near me. I turned and looked and, just for a couple of moments, I saw my father in the seat directly across the aisle, dressed in a tuxedo and raising a martini glass in a toast. Wishful thinking? Maybe. Although if it had been wishful thinking I believe he would have stayed longer than a moment or two, and he would have looked back at me, or better yet, talked to me. Sylvia said it was just his way of assuring me that he was happy and celebrating all the reunions he was enjoying at Home. The martini glass was his way of making sure I knew it was him—martinis were his favorite.

My mother and I were together at my parents' home several weeks later when we saw the double doors to my father's study suddenly slam shut, even though the air in the house was perfectly still, and we both felt it was him without ever actually seeing him. My mother caught a brief glimpse of him soon after that. He was stepping through his study door into the garage.

Again, I wondered if both of us were just imagining him to be around because we missed him so much. But what I definitely didn't imagine is that Sylvia said he wanted my mother to look in a cabinet in his study, where he'd left some papers she needed. She had been trying to find a missing deed and some insurance papers, and she thought she'd searched his study thoroughly. But thanks to Sylvia she searched again, and there were the papers, in the back of a locked cabinet, exactly where my father told Sylvia to direct my mother to look.

from Corrine

My late husband David didn't want to leave any doubt in my mind that he was the one who was communicating from the Other Side through Sylvia. So the first thing he did was have her pass along two things that only he and I knew: that he wanted his grandson to have his valuable watch and ring, and that he'd really missed "Philip," our former son-in-law whom we loved very much, even after he and our daughter divorced.

Sylvia then told me there was a man standing right behind me who had salt-and-pepper hair that used to be very dark, a mouth with a natural smile, a prominent nose and a broad chest. A perfect description of David. She said he'd died from an ongoing lung problem, when he'd aspirated and his lungs filled with water. Again, exactly right. And he was met on the Other Side by a short woman named Mary. David's mother Mary, who died soon after we were married, was just under 5' tall.

It especially made me happy when Sylvia said David lets me know he's around by making our chandelier bulbs flicker. We had a huge chandelier in our dining room with thirty-two bulbs in it, and David had a habit of passing through the dining room several times a week to check on those bulbs and almost getting excited if he found one that was flickering and needed to be replaced. Playing with that chandelier from the Other Side is just what he would do, and now when I see one of the bulbs flickering I smile and say, "Hi, David."

from Lorraine

Dear Sylvia,

The tape of my reading arrived today. Knowing absolutely nothing about who I was trying to reach on the Other Side, the circumstances of his death, etc., you were one hundred percent correct in everything you told me. And it struck me right between the eyes as I listened to the tape that I certainly made sure you accomplished it with no help from me at all. Looking back, I wish I hadn't been so determined to give you zero information or affirmations of any kind. I thought I was being so shrewd in making you prove you were for real, but you proved it from the minute I sat down. You must have felt like you were pulling teeth for the whole half hour, and I could kick myself for all the questions I didn't ask from being so "cagey."

Obviously nothing will ever ease the heartache of losing my son, especially under the tragic circumstances that you spelled out as if you'd witnessed the accident yourself. But now I'll tell you (better late than never) that there's yet another thing you were right about—I did have a near death experience a few years ago. It was a powerful, loving event, just as you described, and your reminding me of it and pointing out that it's exactly what my son went through has been an enormous source of comfort to me since the time you and I spent together.

I've promised myself the marvelous experience of seeing you again someday, and next time I'll look forward to participating instead of being the stubborn, skeptical fool with a chip on his shoulder you met the first time around.

from Matt

I'll never forget this, or have any more doubts about the ability of our departed loved ones to communicate from the Other Side. My sons Mark and Roger were very good friends in addition to being brothers, and they were in the construction business together. Roger was killed in a motorcycle accident, and the grief nearly tore our family apart, especially Mark. My wife and I went to Sylvia for any peace of mind she could give us, and through her we asked if Roger could maybe give Mark a sign of some kind that he was around and watching over him.

Roger's response was, "Tell him I'll put a cross in the dirt." We couldn't imagine what that meant, and neither could Sylvia. But Mark gasped and then really laughed for the first time since Roger died when we passed along the message. Mark knew what Sylvia and we didn't, that the next day Mark was starting work on an old church site where there really was a fallen cross in the dirt.

Roger knew too, and that obscure message was proof to Mark, to us and to our whole family that he's still right here with us.

from Frank

I wouldn't have believed this if my husband hadn't been there to witness it right along with me. I'm sure everyone who comes to Sylvia after losing a loved one wants some kind of sign that their loved one is okay on the Other Side. I was no different, grieving for my mother who'd died six months earlier and ready to give up hope that she would ever come to me as other people's loved ones seem to come to them. Sylvia gave a very detailed description of a picture that was hanging on our bedroom wall and told me to keep an eye on it, because my mother would be using that picture to send me a sign of some kind.

Not long after the reading my husband and I were standing several feet away from the picture, staring at it to see if maybe there was something different about it that we were missing, when suddenly, my hand to God, it jumped right off the wall toward us. It startled us so much that we both jumped away from it at the same time, and then, after we calmed down a little, we went over and picked it up off the bed where it had fallen. The wire on the back of the frame was perfectly in place, strong as ever, and the wall hook it had been hanging from for years was strong as ever too. There's no practical reason why that picture jumped off the wall that day, and it's never happened again. The skeptics can laugh all they want, but no one will ever convince me, or my husband, or our families, who know what down-to-earth people we are, that it wasn't my mother, giving me the sign she promised through Sylvia that I needed so much. It's been a great comfort to me, and I'm very grateful.

from Bari

My goal for my reading with Sylvia was to find some peace of mind for myself and my family about my mother's passing. When she died ten months ago, we felt she had been terribly wronged. Her funeral service was conducted by our family rabbi, who chose this crucial time to demonstrate his inability to conduct services any longer. My mother's funeral took all of seven minutes, and never did he mention a word about her personally. He might as well have been conducting a service for my pet. I tried to correct his ineptitude at the cemetery that day by speaking directly to Mom myself, but I was too unprepared. So since that day I'd felt like she was denied the parting respect she so richly deserved.

On Mother's Day, we held the unveiling at her gravesite, and I had my heart set on using that occasion to make amends for the injustice of her funeral. I'd written a personal letter to her that I wanted to share with my family at the ceremony, but I dreaded everything about it—the ceremony, the emptiness of Mother's Day without my mother, the impossibility of making it through the letter without sobbing . . . that is, until I spoke to Sylvia.

Sylvia gave me a gift that no one else could have given me. She gave me peace. She gave me comfort. Through her, I now KNOW that Mom is with Daddy. I KNOW that she is happy. I KNOW that she will always be with me. I KNOW that we will be together someday. And I KNOW that it was only those of us here on earth, not her, who were offended by that ridiculous funeral service. Mom is in the bliss of Home. She couldn't have cared less what that rabbi said or didn't say. For the rest of my time here on earth I'll miss her, think of her and keep right on talking to her. But I'll never be sad again.

And the nicest surprise came as a result of my reading with Sylvia. The tape of my reading arrived, and I shared it with my brother and sister, who were very comforted by it too. I was hesitant to tell my uncle, Mom's 81-year-old brother, that I'd even talked to Sylvia, or any psychic, because I wasn't sure how he would feel about it. In fact, he and I had never even discussed death or the afterlife before. I felt a whole new closeness to him when I learned that he's an avid believer in the afterlife, and angels, and the fact that Mom is watching over all of us. And even before I played the tape for him, he openly admitted that he's a great admirer of Sylvia Browne. He and I have had many talks since that day that I'll cherish all my life, none of which would have been possible without Sylvia and her ability to touch such a wide variety of people of all walks of life and all ages.

from Irene

Dear Sylvia,

I just wanted to thank you for helping me resolve a 26-year heartache.

During my time with you my sister Linda communicated from the Other Side after you accurately identified the cause of her death 26 years ago. She told me through you that she was blissfully happy in her life at Home, playing music, doing research work and spending time in the library. Her two favorite things here on earth were playing the violin and reading.

She also told me that she wanted me to light a candle for her, and that she wanted me to find and enjoy two photographs she remembered. One she described as "the three of us," our arms linked, in which she was making a face of some kind. In the other she was doing something funny with her hand, like making bunny ears or something. I honestly had no idea what photographs she was talking about, and I wasn't sure I could bring myself to look for them. My parents had put together a family photo album for me years earlier as a Christmas gift, and I'd never admitted it to anyone, but I'd never even opened it because I was afraid it would still be too painful.

I didn't tell you during my reading how completely it con-firmed Linda's presence that she wanted me to light a candle for her. But it was something our mother used to say to us *verbatim* whenever it was time to let go of someone. I could hear my mother's voice as I lit a candle for Linda that night.

And then I called my brother to tell him about my reading, which I guess is what gave me the courage to finally reach for and open that family photo album from my parents. A couple of pages into it I gasped when I found myself looking at a picture I know I'd never seen before. It was a shot of my foster sister holding me, Linda and my sister Nancy on her lap ("the three of us"). Her arms were around us, and we had locked arms to keep from falling off her lap ("our arms linked"). The sun was stream-ing onto the patio right into Linda's eyes, so that while the rest of us in the shot were smiling and looking normal, she was squinting ("making a face of some kind"). One page away was a shot in which Linda was waving at the camera in such a way that her fingers were parted, forming a one-sided bunny ear ("doing something funny with her hand, like making a bunny ear or something").

I can't say for sure what I expected from my reading before I went, but I can say what I got from it. I got messages from a sister who's still very much alive about healing and letting go. Lighting a candle was about letting go. Those two particular pictures were to let me know that the sun is shining on her face now as it was 26 years ago, and her sweet wave of the hand was telling me it was time to move on. My life has been different since our meeting, Sylvia. I'm finally at peace with my sister so that she can be at peace. A great burden has been lifted from my heart due to the teamwork of you and Linda. Thank you, from the bottom of my heart, for your beautiful gift.

from Pamela

The main issue I was concerned about when I had my phone reading with Sylvia was the violent death of my nephew. I didn't doubt that he was at peace on the Other Side. But there were troubling details about the circumstances of his death, and I knew I wouldn't be at peace until I learned the truth. Not only did Sylvia simplify things for me, but she also confirmed who was with him at the time he was shot and the name of the person who shot him.

Everything she told me, including the name of his companion and the name of the shooter, was subsequently validated by police reports. I'm sure my nephew was so relieved to find me on the phone with Sylvia so that he could finally tell me, through her, what really happened and put my mind at ease.

from Jennifer

My brother David died a few years ago. I kept hoping he was coming around our family from the Other Side for a visit, but I was getting discouraged, because I never sensed his presence or saw or heard any strange sights or noises. Finally I had the opportunity to ask Sylvia, in a letter, what sign David was giving us that he was here, if he was here at all.

We had a good laugh at ourselves when we got Sylvia's reply. Talk about overlooking the obvious! Sylvia said that David lets us know he's visiting by clicking off the TV. Our television turns off "by itself" a few times a week, and we keep saying that if it gets any worse we're going to call a repairman. The thing is, it's such "classic David." He's the only person I've ever known who hated TV. He never watched it as a child, and he never owned one as an adult until he finally broke down and bought one for his daughter when she was old enough. So of course it's David who's been turning off our TV, and please thank Sylvia for the "wake-up call"!

from Lola

I wrote Sylvia a letter to ask who the presence was that I could feel around me so strongly, particularly when I'm in my car. A member of Sylvia's staff called to tell me that according to Sylvia, it was a woman named Mary. It took my breath away. My mother Mary passed away two years ago, and in the last years of her life we made it a tradition for me to pick her up at the nursing home where she lived and go for long drives every Sunday afternoon, to visit relatives, or go shopping, or go nowhere in particular just to spend time together. It gives me the greatest peace to know that Mother is still with me, carrying on the tradition.

from Elizabeth

I did a phone reading with Sylvia. I was interested in my family history, and particularly in finding the home of my third great grandfather. Beyond his name, no one on either side of the family seemed to know anything about him, and I'd been running down false leads for years. I gave Sylvia his name, and she told me to look near Monticello, the Thomas Jefferson mansion in Virginia. I did, and found his childhood home and a wealth of information about him in Charlottesville, less than twenty miles from Monticello.

from Brad

Dear Sylvia,

You told me during my reading that I would lose both my parents within the next two years. Fair enough, I asked, and I know your reputation for "telling it like it is." But then you said my mother would die first, and I frankly didn't listen to anything else you had to say for the rest of the reading. My father was very ill, but my mother was in fairly good health, and it was so obvious you were wrong that it put me off.

My mother died suddenly, six months after my reading. My father outlived her by almost a year.

I'm so glad I kept my tape of the reading, which I finally listened to. You were as accurate in everything else as you turned out to be about my parents, and I definitely won't doubt you again.

from Vanessa

Dear Sylvia,

My boyfriend George and I were in a six year relationship. The last two years were stormy because of a brief affair on his part, and I finally moved out in September. He was very remorseful and wanted to reconcile. I never stopped loving him, but I was afraid to trust him again, for obvious reasons. As a token of his commitment to me and our relationship, he bought me a beautiful ring. I refused it and told him I would only accept it when the time was right, if and when I knew in my heart that his love for me was real. He left my house with the ring and put it in the duffel bag he always kept in his truck.

A week after he offered me the ring, George was killed in a violent accident in that same truck. He managed to pull himself from the truck before it burst into flames, but he didn't survive his injuries.

Several days after the funeral I got an urgent message. I don't know how to describe how I got it, because there wasn't an audible voice involved. I just suddenly knew that the ring was still in the truck, and George wanted me to find it and keep it. The police told me that everything salvageable had already been retrieved from the burned-out truck and there was no ring.

Days later I got a call from George's sister, saying that she and her husband were on their way to the police compound to take pictures of the truck for insurance purposes. I asked if I could go along, convinced that I had to find that ring if only because it had been so important to George that I have it. The three of us searched the charred hull of the truck for over an hour. I even reached under the back seat with a police night stick, but it was too long to be useful. I felt completely disheartened when we finally gave up and left with nothing but the photos George's sister needed.

The next morning I woke with even stronger, more urgent feelings than ever that I had to go back to the truck, because the ring was definitely there, we had just missed it. I didn't know if that meant it was there in the form of melted metal and I hadn't recognized it, or exactly what that meant, but I knew I would never forgive myself if I didn't look one more time.

The police officer at the compound recognized me from the day before and let me in. I examined every square inch of that truck, looking for a ring or even some melted lump of metal that might have been a ring once upon a time. I'd brought some tongs this time, and I moved and poked every lump of anything whether it looked like melted metal or not. No luck. After several hours I sadly resigned myself to the fact that I was wrong, these supposed messages were nothing but my own grief making things up. I picked up my jacket to leave and took several steps toward the compound gate when that same non-voice yelled in my head one more time and said, "Look under the back seat again."

I went back to the truck and took out the tongs, which were easier to manipulate than the night stick I'd used the day before. I reached as far under the back seat as I could with the tongs and raked them across the floor, and my heart stopped when I felt them touch something. Slowly and carefully I eased the object out from under the seat. It was the ring box, singed and covered with ashes but completely intact. Inside was the velvet box, as perfect as if it hadn't been near a fire. And inside the velvet box was the ring, gleaming and beautiful like new.

I had told George I would accept the ring when I was sure his love for me was real. I accepted it that day, and I haven't taken it off since. It will always be a reminder not just of that wonderful man but also of the inaudible voice that I know was him from the Other Side, urging me to keep looking. I look at this ring and see a miracle.

from Will

Dear Ms. Browne:

I had to write to thank you for literally saving my life. I lost my son last year, and I was at the lowest point in my life. I had frankly given up on God—religion portrayed such a cruel God that it just made no sense to me. And the more I sank into despair over losing my son and a God I could believe in, the more often I frankly thought about suicide.

During my most awful emptiness I happened across one of your books. From the minute I opened it it was like buried memories, hope and faith opened up in me again. I've now read all your books, and you've truly saved my life and my soul.

Thanks to your help in opening my eyes, I'm aware of and can embrace my son's visits to me in dreams, knowing they're real and not just my grief playing tricks on my mind. We also have photos of his funeral that clearly show him among the crowd, attending his own service.

According to your books, everyone has psychic ability, and the ability to tune in to the spirit world, we just forget how as earthly life gets in the way. More out of curiosity than anything, I started meditating, for the first time in my life, to see if I could re-train my brain and start tuning in again. I got my first validation this weekend, and I was ecstatic.

My oldest son doesn't believe in God or psychics, so when I told him I was on the waiting list for a reading with you, he tried to talk me into cancelling it because it was a ridiculous waste of time and money. When I refused, he came up with an idea that I'm sure he thought was going to prove to me that all this psychic and Other Side stuff was nothing but talk—he told me to ask you how the bumper on his truck got dented. It was something only he knew, so if you got the answer right then he'd know you didn't get it from my telling you or you reading my mind.

As I said, I've read all your books, and I got curious about putting everything I'd read to the test by seeing if I could find out for myself what happened to the truck bumper. In addition to some meditating and spiritual "exercises" in your books, I had a talk with my deceased son that night before I went to sleep and asked him to give me the information in a dream.

To my joy, that's exactly what he did. He and I met in a room full of people I didn't know. All I remember about them is that some of them were sitting and some of them were standing. He told me it's beautiful where he is, and that he's busy with classes. Then he told me about my eldest son's truck bumper. He said he had connected a chain to the back of the truck to pull a signpost out of the ground, and the sign pulled free and dented the bumper.

My eldest son confirmed the next day that that's exactly what happened. He's so determined to be right about his point of view that he came up with all sorts of silly explanations for how I came up with it—I "imagined" the answer, or he'd told me and just forgot, or someone else told me (even though he said himself no one else knew). But I know where it came from. I was blessed with 100% validation that my son is alive and happy on the Other Side, and answers are available if we just ask and listen.

Without your books I would never have tried to reach my deceased son. You have given me back my belief in God and taken away my fear of death, and I'm grateful beyond words.

from Kate

I can honestly say I didn't want to be on earth anymore after my husband passed away, I wanted to be with him, because life seemed unbearable without him. Sylvia kept telling me over and over during my reading that I'm not without him at all if I'll just communicate with him and pay attention to all the ways he communicates with me. I hate to admit it, but I was pretty abrupt with her and kind of snapped when I said, "Like what?"

She told me that one thing he does is move things around the house, even though I know exactly where I put them, and I spend a lot of time looking for them and feeling frustrated because I assume I'm just preoccupied and it's making me absentminded. Sylvia said no, it's not me, it's my late husband trying to get my attention. And I could prove it to myself. Next time something wasn't in the place where I knew I had put it, I should acknowledge my husband and tell him I appreciate his letting me know he's there, and then I should simply ask him to put the item back where I'd put it so I wouldn't have to search for it. Then I should forget about it for a few minutes and go back and look, and chances are I would find the item in its original spot.

I didn't believe it until I saw it with my own eyes, but about three weeks after my reading my car keys were suddenly missing from the place I always keep them, in a little basket on the kitchen counter, where I knew I had put them. No one else was home but me. Instead of tearing the house apart like I would have done in the past and driving myself crazy, I made myself calm down, said hi to my husband and asked if he would please put my keys back where they belonged while I changed my clothes, because I was in kind of a hurry.

I changed my clothes and came back into the kitchen a few minutes later, and there were my keys, right there in the basket on the counter, where they absolutely were not when I left the kitchen.

The same kind of thing has happened several times since. (And I do know the difference between when I misplace something and when it's been moved.) It might not sound like a very big deal to anyone else, but it's a very big deal to me. It proves that my husband is around me, it proves that he hears me when I talk to him and that's nothing short of a miracle as far as I'm concerned.

from Charlene

Dear Sylvia,

I read and love all your books. They've made God so much more personal to me. My faith is so much deeper now because of you, and I needed it more than ever before when my mother died suddenly of congestive heart failure four months ago. It helped so much to know that it was only her body that died, but *she* was alive and better than ever. I didn't expect a visit from her, because things like that don't happen to me, but I knew she'd be the first one to hug me when it was my turn to go Home.

After the graveside service I asked to be left alone there for a while, just to talk to her. I know she wasn't really there, it was just comforting. I was standing there by myself when a dove flew past, close to my head, and landed on the lowest branch of an oak tree several yards away. I looked over at it, and it just sat there, looking right back at me. We stared at each other for a good minute or two, and then I decided it was time to leave, so

I started walking to the car where a friend was waiting to drive me home.

While I was walking I suddenly remembered that when I was a child and my father died, my mother told me he had gone to a beautiful place where God lived, and it was so peaceful there that everywhere you went, there were white doves watching over you.

I know my mother sent that dove to me when I was standing by her grave. I haven't told anyone else this story. It's not that I care if they believe me, or if they think I'm crazy. I just know some people would try to argue about it and tell me there are doves all over the place, so why make such a big deal about one of them sitting in a tree where I could see it? I don't understand what they get out of not believing in anything past what's right in front of them, but that's their problem, not mine. I get joy out of knowing the dove was a gift from my mother, and I thank her and thank God.

from Molly

I had a phone reading with Sylvia, and there were two ways that she validated for me beyond question that my son is alive and that he was giving her information from the Other Side, because the information definitely didn't come from me—in fact, I was so close-mouthed during the reading that I still get frustrated with myself when I listen to the tape of the reading. I was telling her about an incident at my son's funeral when she suddenly asked why he was holding his head. I hadn't even hinted at what he died from, let alone that he was shot in the head during a robbery. Then she wanted to make sure I remembered that he'd told me on several occasions that he was going to die very young. Of course I remembered, but I hadn't shared those conversations with anyone, including Sylvia. It was the greatest comfort, exactly when I needed it, and now that I know my son is around I enjoy making passing comments to him throughout the day, like giving him a hug of acknowledgment.

from Stephanie

This is difficult and painful to write, but it's the truth. My husband committed suicide. And for all intents and purposes, when he killed himself, he killed me too. I had no desire to be alive without him. I became agoraphobic and clinically depressed, and I wasn't interested in seeing a psychiatrist and hearing a lot of textbook clichés and pep talks. Frankly, I came to the conclusion that the only relief available to me was suicide. I even researched the best and least painful ways to kill myself.

I also came across a couple of Sylvia's books. I've never been a spiritual person, but as I read them I felt I was being given straight, logical answers from someone who was convinced without a doubt that God is in me and around me and never leaves me. I found some peace in what she had to say, and I decided to call for a private reading with her. It was an 8-month wait, and I remember having the conscious thought that I would wait until after the reading to kill myself.

It's just a fact that Sylvia saved my life.

First, she urged me to get help with my depression, by getting a complete physical from my regular doctor and asking him to prescribe the right anti-depressant based on the results of the physical.

Then she addressed my husband's suicide and my thoughts of suicide, and she was so kind and caring and, most of all, made sense! She explained that my husband was manic depressive, which was true. It was an illness he'd never been able to face, or agree to get treatment for, and it was hardly something he'd brought on himself. God would never blame us for our illnesses, so despite his suicide, my husband was immediately welcomed to the Other Side when he passed away.

Sylvia pointed out that if I chose to commit suicide to be with him, it would be pure selfishness and self-pity, which is a whole different thing. Instead of being with my husband on the Other Side, I would have to come right back to earth before I'd see him again and delay the one thing I'd be trying to accomplish.

My husband's illness clouded his judgment and made him believe that the only cure for his emotional pain was to end his life. Thanks to Sylvia's honest, straightforward talk, I know that my situation is different than his was. I can get better here on earth. I have options here. I have hope here, even if it's hard to find. I need to finish my life in its own time, and my reward will be a reunion with my husband on the Other Side when God and I decide I'm ready to be there, where I'll be able to tell him that in the long run, I didn't give up, as much as I wanted to.

I'll say it again: Sylvia saved my life. Not by telling me what I wanted to hear, but by telling me what I just knew was the truth when I heard it. My friends can't get over the difference in me since the day of my reading. They see me smiling again, they see me willingly leaving my house again, and they say it's like a light turned on inside me that had been turned off for a long time.

from Judy

I had an experience in the late 1960s that I'll remember until the day I leave this earth, and that no one believed until I talked to Sylvia about it thirty-some years later. I'm a sane, rational, practical woman, so I've always understood the disbelief, but I've also been a little resentful of the suggestion that I would or could make something like this up.

It was the middle of the night, and I woke up out of a sound sleep to find my deceased father-in-law standing at the foot of our bed. I'd never met him, but I instantly recognized him from my husband's photo albums. He was dressed in a cowboy hat, a white shirt and jeans. He didn't say a word, he just looked at me, smiled and nodded his head and then walked out of the bedroom.

I'm not sure if I was too shaken to think of waking up my husband or if I thought I was dreaming and decided not to bother him. But I felt compelled to follow my father-in-law, so I slipped out of bed and hurried out the bedroom door after him. I'm sure I expected him to be gone, but I got to the hallway just in time to see him step into my children's room. That panicked me. I raced to their doorway, but there he was, gently and lovingly just pulling their blankets up around them, without disturbing them.

Next I followed him to the kitchen. We never used our back kitchen door, so it was locked and the clothes dryer was in front of it. I noticed him looking at it, and I remember registering the thought, "Now where are you going to go?" But my memory of the event ends there. The next thing I knew I was waking up in bed with the sun streaming in through the window and a feeling of peace and normalcy, and I did what I'm sure any other sane, rational, practical person would do: I assumed it was just one of those incredibly real dreams that happen to all of us from time to time, got out of bed and headed to the kitchen to make coffee.

I froze in place and maybe even let out a little scream when I walked into the kitchen and saw that the dryer was moved aside and the locked back door was standing wide open.

My husband naturally wanted to know what happened to the dryer and the back door. I finally told him what went on during the night while he slept, and he didn't give it a second thought, he simply assured me that I was either dreaming or crazy. Neither of those possibilities explained the moved dryer and the open back door, so his logical conclusions were that either someone broke in (even though nothing else in the house was disturbed and that door was hidden behind bushes on the out-side) or I did it myself. He never did come up with an answer when I asked, "And I would move the dryer and leave the back door wide open because . . . ?"

It didn't surprise me or my husband when, all those years later, Sylvia believed me and confirmed that what happened that night wasn't a dream at all, and I wasn't crazy, either. She said my father-in-law had come from the Other Side to say hello and check up on us, and he left the moved dryer and the open door as a physical sign that he'd been there. Again, no surprise that she would say that. I've read all her books, and I know and love her philosophies on these things.

What was a surprise, and what I think has convinced my husband that his father really is visiting and communicating, was when Sylvia described him *perfectly* and then, to confirm that she knew what she was talking about, told me my father-in-law's middle name. No way could she have known it ahead of time or guessed it on her first try.

For thirty-plus years this has been an uncomfortable memory that I've been able to do nothing about but wonder. Now, thanks to Sylvia and her accuracy, it's an experience my hus-band and I look back on *with* wonder.

from Monica

Chapter 6

CAREER, FINANCES AND HOUSING

Career, finances and housing. The nuts and bolts of our charts, and therefore of our lives on earth. They're probably the three most challenging aspects of the transition from the Other Side to here, because they're non-issues back Home. We all have careers there, but they're exhilarating, stimulating, what we love and what we wouldn't dream of *not* doing. Money on the Other Side doesn't exist at all, and if it did the spirit world would simply stare at it and say, "What are we supposed to do with *this*?" As for housing, we simply project whatever kind of home we want where we want it to be and it's there. So it's small wonder that when it comes to these three necessities of life in this world, we often feel like an involuntary "it" in a perpetual game of dodgeball.

When a reading involves any one of these subjects, it usually ends up spilling over into one if not both of the other two, for the most obvious reason—all three are so intertwined with one another that it's hard to separate them. I can tell clients exactly what their chart says they had in mind when they came here and where they're likely to find themselves at some point, but the saying is true, "Many people are too busy earning a living to have a career." And we all know there's not a mortgage company or bill collector in the world who's going to put up with an excuse like "I'm sorry, I won't be paying you this month, my chart says I'm supposed to give up my waitressing job and form my own charter airline company."

It won't surprise you that the occasional blank stares I get from people in the audience about possible upcoming changes in any of these areas are identical to the ones I occasionally get from clients during readings. "You're going into counseling," I'll say, or "You're going to be working with children," or "You'll be getting an unexpected court settlement in three years," or "You're moving to New Mexico." And they don't just seem a little confused, they seem as if they've never heard the words "counseling," "children," "settlement" or "New Mexico" before. (Not that that doesn't really happen from time to time—I told a man in my office one day that he'd be going into something to do with horticulture, and he dejectedly told me he'd had his heart set on becoming a gardener.) If you've ever wondered why I dig in my heels in the face of those blank stares, it's because, again, I'm just getting the information from the charts they wrote, and sooner or later the ones who are following their charts will drop a note to my office saying, "You're not going to believe this, but you were right!"

It's not me. You just got back in sync with your chart, that's all.

I was doing a past-life regression one day on a woman named Helena. She'd finished experiencing her previous life as an Alabama blacksmith in the early 1900s and her death from congestive heart failure in that life, and she was in breathless awe as she recounted her trip through the tunnel to God's brilliant white light following that death. Most clients relive one or more of their returns to the Other Side during regressions. Far fewer of them linger there as long as Helena did. She began describing the stunning landscape of Home, the breathtaking love-charged atmosphere, the magnificent buildings, a massive white marble stairway, a glittering dome and infinite aisles of infinite shelves filled with countless parchment scrolls. I knew she was in the Hall of Records, but I didn't say a word. I didn't need to. She knew exactly where she was, and she began exploring, vast aisle after aisle, searching, stepping up her pace as she realized she was getting closer and closer to what she was looking for, describing it all in a hushed, reverent voice.

Suddenly she let out a gasp.

"What is it?" I asked her.

"My chart," she whispered. "My chart, of this life I'm living now. My hands are shaking. Can I open it?"

"Go ahead."

There was silence. Then she began to cry.

I asked what was wrong.

"It's blank. There's nothing written here. Not one word."

"I know," I said.

I waited until she was awake to explain it to her.

I'd taken many astral trips to the Hall of Records myself, and I'd found my chart once too. I can still feel how hard my heart was pounding when I carefully unrolled the ivory parchment to read every detail of what I'd planned for myself on this particular strange, thrilling, heartbreaking trip to earth.

The scroll was blank. Just like Helena's.

I was confused and oddly devastated when it happened, just as Helena had been. And as always in situations like that, I'd turned to Francine.

The explanation was as obvious as it was frustrating: none of us are allowed to read our own charts while we're living them. It would be kind of the cosmic version of cheating on a very big test, or fast-forwarding to the ending of a great mystery movie and missing its significance because you skipped all the people, events, plots, subplots, twists and turns along the way.

So there it was, and there it is. None of us can read our own charts, even when we're standing in the Hall of Records holding them in our hands and staring right at them. Which explains why I'm a psychic without a clue about my life: I can read your chart, but mine is off-limits to me.

This "triumverate" of career, finances and housing is a perfect opportunity to clear up a common area of confusion about our charts—in no way does the fact that we arrive on earth with a life we've already designed eliminate the concept of free will. The circumstances, events, population, etc., of our lives are important, obviously. But how we respond to them, what we do about them, whether we overcome them or wallow in them are all ours to choose as we go along, and the real yardsticks of our growth in this lifetime. Not only is free will alive and well within the structure of our charts, it's the biggest daily test we all face.

An obvious example: We've all read about people who charted themselves to win vast amounts of money in the lottery. It's free will that makes the difference between those who handle their sudden wealth responsibly so that it makes a positive difference in their lives and those who've ended up homeless, jobless, bankrupt, in vicious disputes with their families and friends, in jail (for everything from DUIs to assault to murder), and even dead from a self-inflicted shotgun blast to the chest.

There are stories upon stories of those who charted themselves to be born with every possible disadvantage, or to suffer unspeakable tragedies in their lifetimes. It's free will that makes the difference between those who use their circumstances as an excuse to become bitter, cruel and self-pitying and those who use them as an impetus to excel, inspire and leave the world better than they found it.

There are those who charted themselves to be born with every possible advantage, whose free will allows some to become greedy, abusive and discompassionate, while others become kind, generous philanthropic humanitarians.

All of which boils down to: it's not your chart that determines your earthly success, it's what you do with it.

Dear Sylvia,

You told me at my reading in May that I would become the founder of a holistic center within the next four years. I couldn't imagine what you were talking about—I'm a clinical hypnotherapist, so a holistic center didn't exactly sound like something that would be "right up my alley," so to speak.

But now it's December, seven months later. Thanks to your piquing my curiosity and/or seeing some potential untapped resources in me, I began exploring and attending some "beginner" seminars on all things holistic. Through those seminars I met some of the most stimulating, humanitarian-driven people I've run across in a long time, which only deepened my interest and convinced me that I was only scratching the surface of my desire to make a meaningful contribution to society. Every day became an exciting new adventure, and I went from taking the baby steps of the seminars to making leaps and strides into every relevant course and conference I could find. On the rare occasions when I'd find self-doubt creeping in, I'd remember my reading with you, and the words of one of my instructors, who told me I was "born to do this work" and I'd be re-engergized all over again.

I'm now both a clinical hypnotherapist and a metaphysical minister. Five like-minded professionals and I have started meeting regularly to discuss the exciting possibility of forming an alternative therapy center, aka a holistic center. And I've given you every bit of credit to everyone around me for opening this thrilling new door I would never have found without you.

from Linda

Dear Sylvia,

My nephew and I attended your lecture a little over a year ago. He'd been very depressed for a long time, stuck in a dead-end job but afraid to make a move with no positive sense of direction. The only career that sounded like something he could get excited about was real estate, but his depression had eroded his self-confidence so much that he'd convinced himself there was no point in trying because he would probably just fail. I thought seeing you in person might cheer him up and inspire him, since he never misses your television appearances and loves you.

To be honest, and admittedly a little selfish, I was really hoping to be called to the microphone to ask Sylvia a question, because I had a few things on my mind besides my nephew's problems, believe me. But out of the more than 3000 people who were there, it wasn't meant to be—my nephew was called to the microphone instead! You might remember him. He's the one who stepped out into the aisle, jumped up and clicked his heels together before he raced up front to get in line.

When his turn came he asked you if you saw him changing careers. You answered "real estate" almost before he got the whole question out of his mouth. Neither of us could believe it.

The change in him since that night has been a joy to watch. As far as he was concerned, you confirmed what he was meant to do and promised he would be successful at it, and that was more than enough of the self-confidence boost he needed. He has his real estate license, he's quit his dead-end job and he told me the other day that he looks forward to waking up every morning. None of us who know and love him ever thought we'd hear those words from him, and they're music to our ears.

I just wanted to be sure you're aware of the difference you make in people's lives even in the briefest encounters. What a blessing it is for all of us that you've chosen to share your extraordinary gifts so generously.

from Rae Carol

I was in the audience for a television appearance of Sylvia's, and I was able to ask her about my job search, which had been very discouraging. She told me I would hear something positive and significant on the following Friday that would lead to a new career in marketing.

The following Friday I was interviewed by a firm that had a position available in their client relations/marketing department. Two interviews later I was hired, and on Monday I start work in marketing, which is indeed a whole new career for me, not to mention a very exciting one.

Because there were a few hundred people in the studio audience and more than a few million people watching, I didn't want to take up more than my share of Sylvia's time by telling her this, but her prediction was even more amazing than she might have known. I studied marketing in college, was good at it and loved it, but my parents convinced me I'd have a more stable future in finance. I focused on that instead, and I was good at it, but I was also getting burned out on it and kept trying to ignore the fact that my heart just wasn't in it the way it was, and will be, in marketing.

So I guess Sylvia can think of this as my validating her to thank her for your validating me.

from Bernie

I had a phone reading with Sylvia after three years of depression and confusion, hoping for some kind of clear direction to get me back on track.

Here's what I didn't tell her when the reading started:

- I'd completed my bachelor's degree in psychology.
- The same year I graduated, my husband was diagnosed with and died from leukemia.

- I'd finally pulled myself together enough to be certified in an area called "Addiction Studies."
- What I really wanted was to apply to graduate school. Unfortunately, I'd taken the "Graduate Record Exam" too soon after my husband died, when I was barely coherent, and I did very poorly on it. With such low grades on that exam, I was sure that applying to graduate school would be an exercise in futility.

All I did say to Sylvia at the beginning of the reading was "Should I apply to graduate school?" Her reply was "Yes, absolutely. And keep an eye out for a man named Bill who's going to be important, not romantically, but as some sort of mentor or instructor."

Two months later I was in one of my Addiction Studies classes when a man I'd never seen before walked into the room, looked around and then asked if he could sit with me. His named was Bill, and he was a retired school administrator. Somehow as we chatted we got around to the subject of graduate school, and I confessed that my scores on the Graduate Record Exam were so pathetic I couldn't imagine any graduate school accepting me.

He told me, after reminding me that he was qualified to know these things, that G.R.E. scores were a very minimal consideration in the eyes of most graduate schools. I shouldn't give those test results a second thought according to him, I should go right ahead and apply anywhere I wanted and prepare to be pleasantly surprised.

I never saw him again after that one class. I never even learned his last name. But I did take *Bill*'s advice and apply to graduate school. I was accepted, I'm getting straight A's and I'll graduate with a master's degree in counseling this summer.

Just like Sylvia said, as usual.

from Gayle

Dear Ms. Browne,

I just had to write and thank you for being so gracious, not to mention accurate, to a stranger who couldn't resist taking advantage of finding himself in close proximity to you.

I was your skycap in the American Airlines terminal at the San Jose Airport, and I asked you if you saw a career change in my future. You told me I was wasting my talents and that it was time for me to devote all my energy to my music career.

I took your advice, Ms. Browne. And I'm now a successful music producer, with names like Mariah Carey and T.L.C. on my resume.

Someday I'll find a way to repay you. Until then, thanks is inadequate but it comes from the bottom of my heart.

from Keith

I wrote to Sylvia at a time in my life when I was completely lost. I'd started college with such enthusiasm for the career I thought I always wanted, but during my freshman year it became painfully clear that I wasn't even interested enough in that field of study to continue until I graduated, let alone for the rest of my life. It was discouraging, even a shock to my system, to find myself with no direction after growing up with such confidence and certainty. Suddenly I was second-guessing every thought, every effort, every decision I tried to make, and my self-confidence sank to such a low level that I was starting to think maybe I'd just been nothing but a phony and a loser until that point in my life. I begged Sylvia for any direction she could give me, knowing from seeing her on TV that she would "give it to me straight" whether it was what I wanted to hear or not.

Several weeks went by before a member of Sylvia's staff called with her response to my letter. Sylvia said I was correct to give up on my previous career plans, because what I was really meant to do was become a social worker. All I could do was laugh when I heard that. It wasn't that she was wrong. It was that she was so right, and she had no way of knowing that I'd already come to that exact same conclusion "out of nowhere" and was starting school toward that goal the week after Sylvia's office called. I guess you could say Sylvia and I kind of validated each other, and her "thumbs up" on my decision has turned the emptiest time of my life into the most exciting yet."

from Sonia

Dear Sylvia,

I was concerned about a legal matter when I came to you for a reading. You told me the case would never go to a jury trial, that it would be settled "on the courtroom steps." We went through two sets of negotiations with no success, and jury selection was about to begin.

I was beside myself and called your office to ask if you might want to revise your prediction. Your message back to me was "no"—you knew you were right, and we should just go back into negotiations one more time with a slightly more modest settlement offer. You emphasized the word "slightly." I took your word for it, we went back with an offer that can only be described as a minimal concession, and what do you know, they accepted the offer and we narrowly avoided a jury trial after all.

Maybe I should keep you on retainer instead of my lawyer from now on!

from Rick

Dearest Sylvia,

Just wanted to let you know that the information you gave me in my reading was right on the money, if you'll excuse the pun. Just as you promised, moving to Hawaii brought my husband and me all the success we'd prayed for, and there's no doubt that your very specific guidance saved us five or ten years of fumbling around trying to find the direction on our own that you provided so clearly.

Friends of mine gave me a hard time about spending so much money on a psychic reading, even if the psychic was Sylvia Browne. But I have two answers for them. For one thing, you recommend only coming to see you once, because if you give an accurate life reading, once should be enough. Less expensive psychics I've been to encouraged me to come back over and over again, and their fees added up to a lot more than yours, believe me. For another thing, like I said, who knows how much money you saved us by giving me a "direct hit" that kept us from wandering all over the place for all those years.

In other words, Sylvia, the simple fact is, you're a bargain!

from Lee

Please tell Sylvia that not only did I win the lawsuit we discussed in my reading a month ago, just as she said I would, but I was awarded the exact amount she predicted. Many thanks, and bravo!

from Devon

Dearest Sylvia,

You wouldn't remember me, but I had a reading with you six years ago, and as far as I'm concerned you saved my life and the life of my young son.

I came to you about what seemed like the most pressing problem in my life at the time. My husband had lost yet another job, and I was sure if I could pass along good news from you about when he'd be working again, it would pick up his spirits and he wouldn't be so angry and depressed.

It shocked me like a splash of cold water in my face when you said, "I'm not worried about his next job. I'm worried about yours. When are you going to stop being his crutch and start making a life of your own? And by the way, have you taken a good look at how depressed *you* are?"

I had never confided in anyone about what was really going on in my life, my husband's cruelty and abuse, his insistence that I stay home and take care of "his son" and take care of "his house," how frightened I was that it wouldn't be long before he started hitting our child, since he thought nothing of hitting me in front of him, and overall just how trapped I felt. I was ashamed of my weakness. I was ashamed that this innocent little boy was growing up in a house full of anger and fear. I was ashamed that I didn't know where to start to find a way out. My only family was 3000 miles away. I had no friends where we lived, and I had nothing but a high school diploma to offer a potential employer.

I can't even put into words how compassionate you were, as a psychic and as a woman who was so open about sharing how many things her life had in common with mine when she was my age. And here you were, this powerful, successful woman. I'll never forget saying, "It almost makes me feel like I can make it too," and you saying back, "You *will* make it. I know. I'm psychic." It was like feeling a door opening up inside me, letting in fresh air and light for the first time in years.

Anyway, I did everything you suggested, starting with seeing my doctor, who agreed with your recommendation of an antidepressant. That by itself helped clear my mind a lot. The online classes in the area you said I'd charted for myself, excellent day care for my son so he'd have a happy place to spend much of his time (you were right, my husband agreed to it when I said it was so he and I could have more privacy, and I didn't feel one bit guilty about lying for the sake of my child), finding inconspicuous ways to start setting aside a little money of my own, the whole list I left your office with.

Like I said, that was six years ago. I'm now divorced, with full custody of my son, living in our own apartment, and I'm a licensed cosmetologist with a clientele of thirty-two regulars and growing. As for my ex-husband, his live-in girlfriend after he and I broke up had the courage to do what I never did and pressed charges on him for assaulting her. He was convicted and is serving three years.

It wasn't a figure of speech, Sylvia, I really do believe you probably saved our lives. Please keep my number on hand. If there's ever anything I can do for you in return, you've got a devoted friend for life who loves you.

from Camille

I had a phone reading with Sylvia to ask if I was going to get a promotion I was in line for. Imagine my surprise when she told me she saw the company I hadn't even told her the name of being in deep trouble within the next two years. She advised me not to worry about the promotion but look for a position with another company instead.

I did a lot of soul-searching about it. On one hand, I didn't have any hint that the company I worked for was in any kind of trouble. On the other hand, if I trusted Sylvia Browne enough to schedule a reading with her, wouldn't it be foolish not to listen to her?

My wife, who thankfully believes in both me and Sylvia, said she knew I'd be a success no matter what choice I made, so why not look around and see what else was out there?

Three friends and I actually ended up starting our own business, custom-designing and installing video, audio and phone systems. We're making money and having a great time, and it's the most gratifying work I could have imagined.

The company I was working for? I'm afraid Sylvia was wrong on that one. It wasn't in deep trouble two years later. It took two and a half years, and an all-out war within the family that owned it forced it to close its doors forever. If I'd stayed, with or without that promotion, I'd be writing to Sylvia from the unemployment line.

from Bryan

The minute I sat down in Sylvia's office, she said, "What's this about a move?" I nearly fainted. I moved to Oregon from southern California six months ago, and for a lot of reasons having nothing to do with Oregon, it wasn't working for me. I'd been preoccupied with moving again, and where to go from here, for weeks. Before I could say any of that, Sylvia added, "To the Prescott area. Get back into your love of seamstress work, maybe working with specialty clothing or wardrobes."

I was dialing my daughter on my cell phone before I was even out of Sylvia's building. My daughter produces theater in Prescott, Arizona, and she'd been trying to talk me into moving there for five years. I kept telling her it sounded great, but I couldn't imagine what I'd do when I got there.

For the record, I made my living for thirty-eight years in California as a custom dressmaker before my ill-conceived retirement and move to Oregon.

from Lucy

When Sylvia told me that my family and I would be moving soon, I blurted right out, "No, we're not." It didn't faze her a bit, she just said, "Yes, you are." I was on the phone with her, so I kind of scribbled down her description of this house she thought we were moving to but not paying much attention, since she was wrong. I felt much better when she told me there were two women at my work who were making my life miserable, and I should go ahead and take the job offer that had just dropped in my lap in the last couple of weeks. That was all 100% true! And I love my new job, I should add!

My phone reading was in October. In late November, on my birthday, my husband told me to get in the car, we were going for a drive because he had a surprise for me. He took me to a big vacant lot a few miles from town, on a hill overlooking the ocean, helped me out of the car, waved his hand across the lot and said, "Well? What do you think?" I said, "What do I think about what?" and he said, "The land. It's your birthday present."

I still can't quite believe it, but the following summer we moved into our dream house that we designed ourselves. When it was almost finished I couldn't resist getting out that list from Sylvia of the house description that I'd scribbled down out of boredom. It read:

- gorgeous ocean view (definitely)
- circular driveway (my husband's favorite)
- several fireplaces (we have four), one of them stone (master bedroom)
- ideal neighborhood (spacious homes spread out from each other, in a gated community with its own security patrol)
- close to work (a ten-minute drive to my new job)

I don't know when I've been so glad to be so wrong, but I'll never doubt Sylvia Browne again, that's for sure. (You'll be hearing from my husband—he wants a reading too!)

from Beth

Dear Sylvia,

I just had to share this story with you.

My husband had a phone reading with you. He had me sit in the room with him while he talked to you. He'd been a nervous wreck for weeks, waiting to hear if he'd passed the bar exam, and all I was hoping was that you'd do a better job than I'd been doing of calming him down.

I could tell from his end of the conversation that you were doing most of the talking for a while and that you were covering a lot of subjects, and he was all over the room, very interested but pacing and doing deep knee bends and doing everything but bouncing off the walls.

Finally he took a deep breath and said, "Do you think I passed the bar exam?" Then he started jumping up and down, pumping his fist in the air, cheering and whooping, and he even ran over and gave me a high five. I was staring at him. He didn't get that excited when he played high school football.

When he hung up he said, "I passed!"

I told him I'd gathered that, and I didn't want to be a party pooper, but wouldn't it be a good idea not to get this carried away until it was official?

He said, "It is official! Sylvia Browne told me!"

I just thought you'd like to know how much weight you carry in this family. And of course you were right, he did pass the bar exam, and he's now an assistant district attorney.

from Stella

Dear Sylvia,

I'm the woman who argued with you about how wrong you were about the future of my two grown sons.

You said they'd start a successful personal training business together in our small town, where they were born and raised, and then when it was up and running with the right people managing it they'd each move to separate towns in the state and expand their "franchise," which would be every bit as successful if not more so.

I said they were looking into some spaces locally to start a gym or personal training business, but there was no way they'd move, let alone separately, since they've always been inseparable and even married two women who were best friends of each other's.

My reading was five years ago. My sons' local business is thriving. One of them now lives 90 miles north of here, and his "branch" of the "franchise" is a huge success. The other one lives about two hours east, and his is doing even better.

Fair is fair—you're more than welcome to call and say "I told you so," because you've certainly earned the right to do just that.

from Susan

Dear Sylvia,

Do your other clients hate listening to themselves on tape as much as I do? All you said was, "You know, if you'll talk to your doctor about helping you with your depression, you'll finally start feeling good enough about yourself to make that move to California." Those were practically your first words after "Hello, I'm Sylvia."

The rest of the tape is you telling me all sorts of amazing things and me sitting there blubbering.

Now that I've collected myself, I'll tell you that the only person I had talked to about my depression was my minister, who doesn't believe in medication, so he never suggested seeing my doctor. You did, and I went, and I'm on a very low dosage of an anti-depressant, just enough to make all the difference in the world.

And, it's always been my dream to move to California, close to friends who live in Carmel. Once the depression "fog" had lifted I started putting out actual feelers instead of just dreaming, and on October 1, I officially take occupancy of the house I'm leasing in Carmel, which should be just enough time to settle in before I start my new paralegal job on October 20.

I hope all this great news expresses my thanks and makes it worth all that blubbering I put you through!

from Carla

I was really self-conscious about going to see Sylvia for career insight, since my chosen profession is spiritual reading. For obvious reasons I was afraid she might laugh me right out of the room. But I always think, when you need help, don't bother with the rest, it saves all sorts of time and money to go straight to the best.

I tried to sound as confident as I could manage when I told Sylvia I was a spiritual reader. I was so surprised when she immediately added, "And a healer," that I had to ask her to repeat it because I couldn't imagine getting this kind of validation from her of all people.

She went on to compliment me on how gifted I am and gave me her cell phone number in case I need any advice along the way in getting my practice up and running.

She has to be the most generous person I've ever met.

from Billy

Chapter 7

THE DIVERSITY OF LIVING
ON EARTH

A friend of mine calls it, usually with chagrin, "life's rich pageant," those large and small issues that weave the basic fabric of our day-to-day lives. And very often, those issues, in all their diversity, are what clients bring to me, lists in hand for us to sort through and make sense of together through the perfect clarity of God's loving eyes. Instead of one concern, they have three, or five, or ten, unique and common at the same time—as much as the details might vary, and as impossible as they are to narrow down to a specific category, these issues resonate with familiarity to all of us who are trying to slog our way through another grade of this rough school on earth and return Home wiser than when we left.

A critic who neither believes in psychics nor seems to know much about us recently scoffed at me and two of my colleagues on national television for not devoting ourselves to major natural disasters (tsunamis, hurricanes, earthquakes, etc.) and/or somehow alerting all soldiers in Iraq who are about to die that their lives are in imminent danger. As if they're not already painfully aware of that. Or maybe the point was that we psychics aren't doing our jobs if we're not on the front lines in Iraq yelling, "Duck!" at the appropriate times to the appropriate people, or racing up and down the American Gulf Coast yelling, "Run inland, everybody!" when hurricanes are bearing down.

One of many truths the critic either refused to acknowledge or simply didn't care to is that every person on earth faces real, important, difficult and complicated problems that deserve attention, whether they involve natural disasters and war or not. They count, their problems count, and more often than not, I can help, thanks to this gift God gave me. It's what He meant for me to do with it, and it's my commitment and my heart. I make no apologies for the fact that the vast majority of my work is focused on communicating one on one with people—one problem, one issue, one fear, one worry, one loss, one sorrow at a time.

As you read in the first chapter, when I was a child trying to make sense of this gift and learn to manage it somehow, I asked God to only give me information I could do something about. That's what He's done, and that's what I honor. If it registers as trivia to the critics and professional skeptics, that's frankly of no interest to me. I can honestly say that to the best of my memory, not once in this half decade of readings has a client shared a problem with me that I thought of as trivial. Some more pressing or significant than others? Absolutely. My clients would be the first to agree with that. In fact, they're often the first to say it. But trivial? Never.

In these pages you'll read excerpts of affidavits from clients who had a variety of issues to cover in their time with me. When you come across passages in which I accurately described someone's house, or their children, or their future office, or some other detail that might inspire you to think, "So what?" remember this and you'll know why I refuse to regard anything between me and my clients as trivia:

None of those descriptions and details comes from me. How could they, really? By definition, that means they come from someone and somewhere else. And if they didn't come from my clients, or from Google, who/where does that leave?

It leaves the spirit world, on the Other Side, taking every opportunity to assure us that they're with us and they're watching us. They know our homes and our children and our grandchildren and our latest furniture arrangement and our new cars and our upcoming moves and vacations and our charts in general. With every one of those details they pass along through me, they're saying, "I'm alive. I survived death. And so will you. Eternity isn't just a comforting myth after all. God kept His promise."

When you realize that every bit of information I couldn't possibly know is more proof of our souls' God-given eternity, it makes the word "trivia" look like the ultimate oxymoron, don't you think?

I'm sure the fact that I take every reading seriously has contributed enormously to my clients' complete confidence that they can tell me *everything*. And they do. I'm not complaining, I'm bragging. I take it as nothing short of an honor that my reputation inspires so much unedited openness and bare-bones honesty among my clients. The biggest challenge on my end is simply to be ready for anything from one reading to the next.

One of the best examples also happens to be one of my favorite stories. I've told it before. If you've already heard it, please bear with me for the benefit of those who haven't.

A psychiatrist friend and colleague called to ask if I could see a patient of his ASAP. He'd been working with her for quite some time and didn't seem to be making as much significant progress as he'd hoped, and at his session with her that morning she'd been particularly distraught. She wouldn't listen to him. Would I be willing to see if maybe she'd listen to me?

"Of course," I told him. "I'll clear an hour for her as quickly as she can get here. Was she able to give you any idea of what she's distraught about?"

"Absolutely," he said. "She's convinced she's got a snake wrapped around her waist, and she's terrified of it."

Just when you think you've heard everything.

I spent the half hour between hanging up the phone and the woman's arrival trying to figure out how on earth I was going to handle this. I came up with absolutely nothing.

So I was as shocked as the woman was when she stepped into my office and, on pure instinct, I screamed, "Oh, my God, you've got a snake around your waist!" I lunged at her, grabbed the imaginary snake, and, while the woman watched in mesmerized silence, wrestled around with it all over my office. I banged into walls with it, I rolled on the floor with it, I let it pin me to my desk for a moment, I grunted, I cursed, I even broke out into a very real sweat. That was one strong imaginary snake, let me tell you. But finally I managed to get a good grip on its tail, swung it around and beat it to death against the window molding.

Then I sank down into my chair, not having to pretend to be exhausted, looked at the woman and said, "It's gone. Now. Hi, I'm Sylvia Browne."

And I spent an hour with a perfectly calm, perfectly content, perfectly relaxed woman who was so relieved that someone had taken action against something that was terrifying her instead of putting all their energy into trying to convince her she was nuts. Mind you, I recommended a full battery of tests at an excellent psychiatric facility where I knew and trusted many of the doctors, and because I'd established credibility with her the instant she arrived, she agreed to go. She was accurately diagnosed and treated, and she and her family still check in from time to time to let me know that, thanks to ongoing therapy and the right medications, she's doing beautifully.

There was the week my staff and I still refer to as Disrobing Week. One woman walked into my office and immediately unbuttoned her blouse. (To my relief, her intention was simply to show me her crucifix, since she knew I always wear one.) Two days later another woman rushed in, said, "Dr. Browne, take a look at this!" and lifted her dress and pulled her panties down to her knees. To this day I have no idea what she wanted me to look at, nor did I look at anything. In my least welcoming voice I informed her that I'm not a doctor, never have been, never will be, I'd refer her to one if she needed one, but in the meantime, put your clothes on!

There was the woman who couldn't wait to share the news that her parrot was possessed with the spirit of her deceased husband. Her parrot, Sinbad, had begun sleeping on her late husband's pillow, perching on the frame of her late husband's favorite picture of himself, even enjoying exactly the same TV shows her late husband used to watch, including channel surfing on the remote with his beak "just like Jim always did." She was furious with me when I explained that spirits can certainly manipulate animal behavior to let us know they're around, and the incredibly psychic animal world is always happy to cooperate. But they can't and wouldn't possess another living being, or an inanimate object either, for that matter. She wasn't hearing a word of it. Why she wasn't satisfied to know that her husband was visiting on a regular basis but had not actually turned into a parrot I have no idea, but because nothing will make me play along with a spiritual lie, I'll never be able to list her as a happy client.

In case you're wondering why I mentioned the idea of spirits possessing inanimate objects—a client once asked for help with exorcizing his vacuum cleaner, and then there was the woman who thought I'd be fascinated to know that she and her husband owned a haunted sponge. This sponge, she said, "sits on the windowsill listening to music." She was right. I *am* fascinated. How do you discern that a household sponge is listening to something, as opposed to just sitting there like a . . . well, like a sponge?

In sharp contrast, there was the woman who'd been arrested for trying to fill forged prescriptions, not for herself but for her addicted boyfriend. She might have been even more terrified than the woman with the snake around her waist. I knew from her chart that she wasn't going to jail but that she had a long legal ordeal ahead of her, and we spent her reading discussing what she needed to talk about most—lawyer recommendations, the importance of letting this experience inform and expand her spirit by taking responsibility so that she would never have to repeat this mistake, and the many reasons she charted it in the first place. I promised her that if she stepped up to this very difficult plate and handled it with integrity, she would look back someday and actually be grateful it happened. She's stayed in touch, and these several years later, she's made so many positive changes as a direct result of that low point in her life that she now says, "If that's what it took to get me where I am today, then you were right, I am grateful."

It's hard to know where to start, Sylvia and I covered so many things during my reading.

One of the most helpful, believe it or not, was her bringing up my sister, telling me my sister is a "dark entity" and explaining that means she was born this way and I can let go of my lifelong feeling that I can somehow rescue her from being such an awful person if I try hard enough. It's so liberating to know how and why she is the way she is and to have confirmation that she's her own problem, not mine.

The medical information was a Godsend. My energy level has quadrupled since I eliminated wheat from my diet. I had no idea I was allergic to wheat, but the improvement in my overall health since I started carefully avoiding it makes it clear that Sylvia was exactly right about that.

Sylvia had no way of knowing that the minute my husband and I met, we weren't just attracted to each other, we both felt like we were sharing a reunion. Sylvia described it perfectly, as if she'd been there the day we met, and then she explained that it's because he and I had been together in several past lives.

She also said that my mother, who died two years ago, visits me when I'm in my kitchen and that she calls a lot. I've smelled my mother's perfume a hundred times, but only when I'm in my kitchen, and I assumed it was just my imagination. As for the phone calls, I can't count the number of times I've answered the phone and nobody's there, although the line is "open," as if someone actually called and then won't say anything. I've complained about it to the phone company, but they can't find anything wrong with the lines or with our equipment.

Everything else about the reading was so "right on" that my husband and I are already planning ahead for the move Sylvia says we have to look forward to a year from now. We've been talking about relocating to the southwest for years, and now that Sylvia has confirmed it's going to happen we're "going with it" and excited about it.

There's no doubt about it, my reading with Sylvia changed my life.

from Courtney

My phone reading with Sylvia happened on April 3. I was very worried about money at the time I talked to her, and she promised that financial help would arrive by the end of May. I thought she was just telling me what I wanted to hear, because I couldn't imagine where that help would come from in such a short time. But on May 28 I received an unexpected check from a distant family member that more than got me through the temporary crisis.

Even more fascinating to me was when Sylvia asked me about the near death experience I had when I was a young child, when I left my body during surgery for an upper respiratory problem. I nearly fell out of my chair. I had never told anyone about it, not even my parents. But when I was five years old, while I was in surgery to have my tonsils removed, I have the clearest memory of finding myself levitating above the operating table. I still remember how interesting it was to notice that my legs were in midair at the same level as the nurses' heads. Sylvia described it to me before I even confirmed to her that it happened.

A friend of mine who's never believed in psychics thought that Sylvia's staff probably researches everyone ahead of time who comes in for readings. But she had to admit that they couldn't have researched something that no one knew about but me, and there's no way they could have found out about that unexpected check, either.

My friend who's never believed in psychics, after hearing the tape of my reading, has now booked her own appointment with Sylvia.

from Bonita

I had the pleasure of attending one of Sylvia's salons at a time when my life was in transition, with my living situation and with my work. Sylvia said we'd get the house we wanted, even though it was in escrow with another buyer, and that I would give up truck driving because of my back and be successful at investing in houses to "fix and flip." I didn't know anything about "fixing and flipping," I didn't know anyone who did that, I didn't know any more about real estate than the basics everyone knows who's ever bought a house, and from everything I'd heard everything was going fine with the other buyer's escrow on the house I was hoping to buy.

Well, that buyer's escrow fell out after all, and we got the house we wanted after only a six-day escrow. Our new neighbor has several rentals and all sorts of contacts with workers who can fix up houses to "flip," so I've started taking real estate classes and am excited about this new career that will keep me off the road and probably save me from back surgery someday.

All of which is to say that everything Sylvia said seemed impossible at the time, but six months later it's all a reality, and it's nothing less than amazing.

from Aaron

The initial reason I made an appointment with Sylvia was because I discovered my fiancée was being unfaithful to me. I was distraught, to say the least, and of course I broke up with her, but I was having a hard time getting over it. Sylvia described my fiancée perfectly and then pointed out what a blessing in disguise it was that this weak, selfish woman never became my wife. The marriage would have only dragged me down. Sylvia said my fiancée knows she made a terrible mistake, has turned to drugs and will be getting in touch with me wanting me to give her another chance, but I have to be strong and say no or I'll regret it the rest of my life. I know that's true, and hearing a warning like that from Sylvia of all people has made me start celebrating being free of the wrong person instead of mourning a supposed loss.

Then she asked me what was wrong with my right shoulder, neck and lower back. I was stunned. This was a phone reading, so no way did she get any physical hints from me that anything was wrong with me anywhere in my body. I dislocated my right shoulder three years earlier, and it was still painful, as were my neck and lower back. I was afraid to see a doctor because I was sure they would say I needed surgery. I'm a drummer, and I'd go broke during however long it would take to recover from an operation. Sylvia said the pain in my shoulder was just a calcium build-up that would be helped with lecithin, not surgery, and all I needed for my neck and lower back was an adjustment from a licensed chiropractor or physical therapist. Thanks to her I worked up the courage to go to a doctor, and every word of that was exactly true—the calcium build-up, the lecithin, everything.

Most uncanny of all was when she said that around June of that year my band's success would reach a whole new level and there would be contracts offered. The band is very successful in our area, so this was beyond anything I had imagined. But two weeks after my reading in May we played in a showcase held by some major record labels, and while all the other bands were rejected, we're now in negotiations on our first CD.

from Terrance

There were three separate issues Sylvia addressed in my reading that caught me off guard. I wasn't expecting them. Sylvia brought them up, not me. And she was right on target on all three of them.

First, she didn't ask me, she told me that I'd been struggling with low energy for several months. I had been, but I kept either trying to ignore it or scolding myself about it. She recommended some over-the-counter vitamins and supplements, and they've made all the difference in the world.

Second, she said I'd be moving soon. I thought she was crazy. I'd been in the same apartment for years, and I had no intention of going anywhere. Three weeks after my reading I received notice that the new owner of the building was converting the apartments to condominiums, and all of us would have to buy our places if we intended to stay. I was out of there a month later, in another apartment that's more convenient to my work and that I like even more than my previous one.

Third, she said I'd be accepted in medical school. I was pretty skeptical about that, because my entrance exam scores were lower than I was comfortable with. But sure enough, I was accepted, and I'm so excited to discover that Sylvia wasn't just telling me what I wanted to hear, she was telling me the truth.

And I have to add that through her straight-forward, no-nonsense, no-double-talk approach during my reading and in her books, Sylvia Browne has reunited me with my faith in God and my personal relationship with Him. I can't imagine a greater gift that one person could give to another, and I thank her with all my heart.

from Matias

It's taken me more than twenty years to get around to writing this report on the aftermath of my partner's reading with Sylvia Browne in 1984. But I remember it as if it happened yesterday.

My partner John, a medical doctor, had the reading in Sylvia's private office while I sat in the outer office wanting desperately to put my ear against the door and eavesdrop. As it turned out, I didn't need to, since Sylvia taped it and we listened to it on the drive home. And we laughed until our sides ached. Sylvia said we'd be moving "farther west," and I'd be working with poor people. Hilarious. We lived in Napa, California, and we were moving farther west? That pretty much left us moving to the Pacific Ocean. And I won't go into my exact corporate title at the time, but let's just say it didn't bring me into contact with a lot of poor people. We howled and joked all the way back to our house.

Three months later John was offered a once-in-a-lifetime opportunity on Kauai, Hawaii. Definitely farther west than California. I immediately called a friend who worked for the state of Hawaii to put out feelers for a job for myself. It turned out there was one position open in my area and level of expertise—they were looking for an executive director to initiate a new AIDS service project. For the poor and underprivileged. So much for our howling and joking.

Two other things Sylvia told John that day were that John needed to pay close attention to his stomach, and I should be very wary of the medication I was taking. That was just silly. I was only taking one medication. A prescription diet "cocktail" called Fen-Phen. Everyone knew how safe that was, until a few years later, when it was pulled off the market and started destroying people's health. Including mine.

Six years ago John, who was warned to pay close attention to his stomach, was diagnosed with stomach cancer. He went Home to God three months later, in a hospice, with our three dogs and me lying in bed beside him watching *Larry King*. His guest that night, unbeknownst to us until she was introduced: Sylvia Browne.

I now have an irreparable broken hip, but using a walker is nothing new to me, thanks to all my heart and lung problems typical of previous Fen-Phen users. I can't even participate in the class action lawsuits against the manufacturer of Fen-Phen. John was a doctor, don't forget, and he bought it for me directly from a drug company. I never had an actual prescription for it, so there's no record of my ever having taken it.

I love Sylvia Browne, and I'm writing this simply to memorialize how right she was twenty years ago and how I wish John and I had listened more closely.

from Isaac

Sylvia started with my ongoing stomach problem. She instantly told me I had a spastic colon. I followed up the reading with a colonoscopy. The diagnosis was a spastic colon. The medication my doctor prescribed has made me feel 100% better.

She told me I'd be getting divorced that year, and that if I was really honest with myself it would be a relief. I put up quite a fight when she told me that, too. My husband was my first love. He'd been the center of my life since I was fifteen years old. He had a bad temper, he would disappear for two or three days at a time when he got depressed and refuse to tell me where he'd been, and he had trouble holding onto jobs because he wasn't always very good at getting along with his co-workers. But I'd convinced myself, or he'd convinced me, that no one else would ever understand him like I did, and that no one else would ever love me like he did. Then one day he hit me, for the first and only time, and broke my nose. I left him that same day, filed charges against him and also filed for divorce. It was eleven months to the day after my reading with Sylvia, and as hard and painful as it is, I have to say it, the relief of not living my life walking on eggshells is overwhelming. For the first time in years I wake up every morning looking forward to what the day might bring, and I feel good about myself again.

She also said I'd be going to graduate school to further my counseling education. I'm now a full-time graduate student, working toward my master's degree in counseling.

Just amazing.

from Annette

After describing my house in such detail you'd have thought she lived there, Sylvia asked how my husband's back was doing. I hadn't mentioned that he'd hurt it the week before.

Then she asked if I was aware that our 14-year-old daughter was lactose intolerant. It was news to me. I immediately eliminated all dairy products from our daughter's diet, and the psoriasis she's suffered with since she was a baby, which I also hadn't mentioned to Sylvia, has cleared up by about 85%.

Before Sylvia called for my phone reading I was having a talk with my Spirit Guide about some very personal issues I was hoping Sylvia could help me with. Sylvia specifically addressed every one of them as if she'd been sitting in the room with me, eavesdropping on everything I'd said to my Spirit Guide.

from Robin

Sylvia made all the difference in the world by recommending niacin and ferrous sulfate for my headaches and lack of energy. I feel like a new person.

She said I was hesitant about an upcoming trip, which I certainly was. But she recommended I follow the instinct that was telling me I really should go. I went, and it turned out to be a trip I'll treasure for the rest of my life—my last chance to spend time with an aunt I was very close to, who passed away suddenly two days after I returned home.

Then, out of nowhere, she asked if my son's two hip surgeries were behind him yet. I hadn't even mentioned that I had a son, so I definitely hadn't said anything about his two hip surgeries. He had just finished his second one. Sylvia said he would be up and around by November. On October 29 he walked without his crutches and with no sign of a limp for the first time in almost three years.

from Edie

Dear Sylvia,

I originally scheduled a reading with you because I was suffering from severe headaches. My doctors couldn't find anything physically wrong with me, but I was afraid they were missing a warning sign of something serious, and I was at my wit's end. When you told me that stress and anxiety were the cause, I was relieved that it was nothing physiological, but I also wasn't sure I believed you. I thought of my life as busy, and full, but I'd never allowed myself to think of it as stressful. The more you and I talked, the more I realized that there were many things I was anxious about that I was simply managing to stay too busy to address. Your help with unraveling them, and with easy dietary recommendations I've continued to follow, were a Godsend. I'm writing this letter more than a year after my reading, and I honestly don't remember my last headache, it was so long ago.

If I'd written you immediately after my reading, I'm sure I would have said you missed the mark about the move you saw for me and my husband within a year and a half. We were very happy where we were, and we had no plans to move. I frankly didn't give your prediction another thought for many months. Even the fact that I was suddenly meeting people in the real estate field didn't trigger anything beyond a flash out of the blue one day on what you'd said. I finally mentioned it to my husband, knowing he'd think it was ludicrous—he loved our house, and his "stuff" fit into it perfectly.

Shock of shocks—he thought the idea of moving was exciting.

One rainy Sunday he and I went for a drive and came across a brand new house in a brand new housing development on the other side of town from where we lived. We walked in to take a look, and I instantly knew that was "it."

I went from being sure you couldn't have been farther off about a move to finding myself unpacking boxes in a new house across town that couldn't be more perfect for us. All in just over a year and a half.

Even if all you did was plant an idea that I finally acted on, it was exactly the right seed to plant, especially when, thanks to you, there were no headaches in my way to keep me from paying attention.

from Janie

Sylvia made the unexpected prediction that my youngest son will be hired by the Los Angeles fire department. That would be great, but of course only time will tell.

I won't be shocked if it happens, though, considering Sylvia's accuracy on everything else. This was a phone reading, and I have a nondescript voice, so I don't know how she knew I'm African American, or how she knew I have a good marriage, or how she so quickly and easily recognized me as a "family person." I suppose maybe those could have been good guesses.

But she also told me that one of my sons is a graphic artist, and that my mother-in-law is jealous of my niece. Those two facts are much too specific to be just good guesses.

I'll keep you posted on when—not *if*—my youngest son joins the L.A. fire department!

from Maxine

I only had a couple of questions for Sylvia, so I requested a letter reading from her. I'd been told that she was just as accurate on letter readings as she is in person, and I can now verify it.

I'd been taking care of my chronically ill aunt for more than thirty years. She's the one who'd raised me, so I felt I owed it to her. But living with a very sick, negative, self-centered, demanding woman was taking its toll on me and preventing me from having any life of my own. There was no question that my aunt needed full-time care, and my fantasy was to find a first-class nursing home for her where she'd have qualified medical attention twenty-four hours a day and maybe even meet people her own age and (in my dreams) make a friend or two. The fantasy continued that once she was happily settled in somewhere, I would move to a new house, a house where I hadn't felt so trapped for so long.

I asked Sylvia in my letter if I'd find a place for my aunt to live where she'd be content and well cared for, and if I'd ever be able to move.

Her answer really surprised me. She said my aunt would pass away within the next eight months, and I would then relocate to Rhode Island. I was living in Reno, Nevada at the time, so there was no obvious logic on her end in that response. I hadn't said a word to her about the hundreds of conversations with my identical twin sister about moving near her if it ever became possible, where we could see each other every day and I could get to know my nieces and nephews. My twin lives in a beautiful lakeside community near Newport, Rhode Island.

Five months later my aunt died of heart failure. I never found a suitable nursing home for her (or had the nerve to tell her I was looking for one), so she was still living in my home until those last two days she spent in the hospital where she passed away.

Two months after that I moved into a perfect little house in Rhode Island less than ten miles from my sister's house.

Last but not least, I asked Sylvia in my letter if there was anything about my health I should be paying attention to. She said I should have my hormones checked ASAP. You can't imagine my surprise when my gynecologist informed me that, at the age of 42, I was in the early stages of menopause. It explained a lot of physical symptoms I'd been going through that I just wrote off to depression and exhaustion.

So much for worrying about Sylvia's accuracy on letter readings!

from Jean

Dear Sylvia,

Two quick follow-ups to last month's phone reading. First, the minute I hung up the phone I went straight to where you told me to go, and there was my missing driver's license, exactly where you said it would be, although I will never understand how it got there! (Not that it matters, and I won't waste your precious time asking.)

Second, you saw me doing hands-on work with animals, which are the love of my life, as you know. Yesterday I received a job offer that will lead to my training and caring for dolphins. It's a dream come true that I never saw coming, but you saw it coming, and just knowing it was "out there" for me undoubtedly helped me draw it to me.

From one animal lover to another, I thank you, and I'll cherish every minute with these precious dolphins on my behalf and yours.

from Leslie

Dear Sylvia,

The information you gave me about the perpetrators of the travel scam my husband and I fell victim to was incredibly accurate, according to the law enforcement authorities we've talked to. While no arrests have been made, I'm happy to announce you were also right when you said we'd get all but a small percentage of our money back. (We got back all but about 10% of it, to be exact, and the rest we'll gladly write off to a good education to keep us from being so gullible next time.)

from Aurora

I attended a lecture of Sylvia's and was shocked to be one of the people chosen to ask her a question. I thought of a hundred more important questions later that I should have asked instead. But what I did ask was if she could help me find a savings bond that had been missing for four years. She said it was in a red book. The minute I got home I went through all the red books in my bookcases, with no luck. I gave up on it yet again.

Last week I was rushing around preparing for dinner guests and pulled out a microwave cookbook I'd never used. Inside the unused cookbook, between two bright red pages, was that savings bond.

What more can I say but "good call!" and "thanks!"

from LaVerne

The night before my phone reading with Sylvia, my car was stolen. It was my first "new" car, after getting by with a second-hand ancient Toyota for years while I saved up for a Jeep Wrangler right off the showroom floor. I'd had it for less than a month when it was stolen, and it's an understatement to say I was upset. Not what I had envisioned for the subject of my reading, but at the moment it was all I could think about.

Sylvia felt sure I would get my Jeep back within a week to ten days and that it would have only minor damage. I thought at the time that it was nice of her to say, but I imagined it either torched or in a "chop shop" somewhere, providing free parts for other people's Jeeps.

The police called six days later to say they'd found my car. I had to replace one tire and get the upholstery cleaned. Other than that it was good as new.

Of all the things Sylvia told me that day, that's the one I just plain didn't believe. It makes me that much more excited about everything else she had to say, knowing I don't have to doubt a word of it.

from Oneida

I still haven't recovered from Sylvia's accuracy throughout my reading.

She described my children in extraordinary detail—most specifically, that my daughter is extremely opinionated and my son is disabled.

She told me without my mentioning a thing about it that my injuries from the fall I took shortly before the reading will heal with no long-range effects.

And last but definitely not least, she described the house my husband and I would be buying. Not just generalities like the number of bedrooms and bathrooms, or the style, but the exact area, the fact that there would be a lot of land around it and, the thing I couldn't imagine but turned out to be absolutely true, the "small detail" that we would have a view of geysers.

It only confirmed the credibility of the far more difficult emotional issues I was struggling with that she helped me with more than I can ever express. Sylvia changed my life, it's that simple.

from Dawn

Dear Sylvia,

As you requested, here's what happened in the months after my reading:

- Just as you predicted, I was accepted to Sonoma State University, to start this coming fall. And just as you predicted, it's not going to be a problem after all that my math courses aren't completed yet.
- Just as you predicted, an older tiny (4'11", to be exact) blonde woman with a heart-shaped face and a widow's peak appeared out of nowhere to help me. She turned out to be the realtor who found the house I ended up buying.

She's also eased my mind a lot by helping my parents sell their home.

- Just as you predicted, a tall, thin, sandy-haired, very honest man named Ray with light blue eyes and a soft voice came into my life. So far it's just a friendship, but since you were right about everything else, I'm taking your advice and not pushing, even a little, because I definitely don't want to blow your prediction that this could grow into a significant romantic relationship.

I'll keep you posted, I promise.

from Bette

When I had my reading with Sylvia I was concerned about whether or not to go forward with expanding my business. She said I should, and that I'd be moving offices to a much bigger building. My office in the bigger building would have lots of glass, she told me, and there would be one wall with four colors—red, white, blue and yellow.

Thanks to her encouragement, I started checking out potential new office space. I knew immediately I'd found the right place when I walked into a large corner suite with lots of glass and stopped in my tracks when I saw that one wall had been painted with a huge geometric design of red, white, blue and yellow.

It's turned out to be a great move all the way around, and I thank Sylvia for the great advice and the unmistakable signal that I was exactly where I was supposed to be.

from Walter

Chapter 8

PAST LIVES

God promised us eternal lives at the moment He created us, and God doesn't break His promises. That means that all of us have been blessed with the sacred truth of eternity. And eternity doesn't just mean "from now on and forever after." It means "always was and always will be." That's just a fact. Our promise from God includes the past as well as the future, which means that the idea of reincarnation, or past lives, isn't just a theory embraced by us weird, spiritualistic goofballs, it's simple God-centered logic.

I swear to you, this life you're currently living is just one more step along an unending path you and God designed together toward your own greatest potential. Your life this time around, like the lives before it, won't end in your extinction. It will end with your eternal spirit simply freeing itself from your body and continuing its gorgeous, unbreakable continuum between here and your Home on the Other Side. You've lived in both places an eternal number of times. Your trips to earth, wildly varied as they're likely to be depending on your spirit's unique path, aren't separate lives at all, as the term "past lives" sometimes implies. They're woven into the history of that singular essence that is *you*. You will forever be, on whichever dimension you choose to occupy, the same being you are now, who thinks and feels and laughs and grows and changes and learns and loves and is loved by God every moment of your endless life. Your past lives are simply threads in a tapestry, phases of the one eternal life that belongs to you, *and your spirit remembers them all.*

An easy analogy to how past lives weave into this one can be found in the life you're living now. However much or little of it you consciously remember, it's safe to say that since you were born you've been an infant, not even two feet long, weighing about the same as a full-grown Yorkshire terrier; a toddler taking its first awkward steps with no clue what a toilet is used for; a five-year-old who can't yet reliably spell both your first and last name; a thirteen-year-old whose ambition begins and ends with the concept of getting a driver's license; a twenty-year-old, emerging into adulthood with more bravado than wisdom. In other words, in this one lifetime you've taken many physical forms, gone through many levels of physical and emotional maturity and learned an incalculable number of lessons, many of them in the hardest way possible. Those forms and levels and lessons don't just happen and then vanish as if they never occurred. That infant, that toddler, that five- or thirteen- or twenty-year-old you once were didn't magically appear out of nowhere and then cease to exist. Every step of the way, you've been *you,* a complex, sacred work in progress unlike any other spirit ever created. You and I, in other words, are designed to be the miraculous sum total of every instant we've experienced, no matter how dramatic or how trivial, and we'll keep right on changing and evolving, learning and growing with every instant we experience from this moment on.

Now, look at your life, with all its forms and phases, and understand that it's nothing but a smaller version of the eternal life you're living as God designed it. Whatever you've looked like in previous centuries, whatever stages of learning and growing you've struggled through, whatever lessons and changes lie ahead, they're simply steps along your path toward the most perfect *you* you can be. Your past lives, here and on the Other Side, are no different from the stages of this life, pieces of the same puzzle, parts of the same whole and, like every other moment of your past, affecting your life today in more ways than you might imagine.

READINGS AND PAST LIVES

I began studying hypnosis as a part of my psychology courses in Kansas City, and I continued those studies in California until I achieved my goal of becoming a certified master hypnotist. I wish I could tell you that I had a brilliant plan in mind to use that skill as a tool to help clients unlock the stumbling blocks buried in their past lives.

But no. Frankly, all those decades ago, before I understood the continuity of the same eternal spirit occupying a variety of bodies, what little thought I'd given to past lives had led me to the misconception that from time to time throughout history we'd all been a variety of completely different people. That seemed pretty random to me, not to mention pointless. And beyond that, let's say someone was able to actually prove that once upon a time I was a member of the very first British Parliament. That didn't change the fact that I was still a young single mother whose reality was tied up in diapers, work and scrambling to make my mortgage payment every month. Unless the bank was handing out free housing to all former members of the very first British Parliament, my position on past lives boiled down to "Who cares?"

And so my plan was to use my master hypnotist certification to help my clients with problems they were struggling with in their current lives. I could help them lose weight, quit smoking, overcome any number of phobias, conquer insomnia—you name it, I was trained for it and ready to tackle it. Hear me roar.

Enter one of my first hypnosis clients, a man whose compulsive overeating was hurtling him toward obesity and diabetes. I skillfully "took him under," and then sat gaping like a novice as he began talking about his difficult life as a pyramid builder and then lapsed into what sounded to me like several minutes of incomprehensible nonsense. The one thing I did right from that session was to send a tape of it to a friend who was a professor at Stanford at the time, wanting a second opinion on whether or not I should rush this poor client to the nearest psychiatric hospital. My friend shared the tape with several colleagues who, after a lot of research, were amazed to conclude that the man's incomprehensible nonsense was actually a very fluent monologue in an ancient Assyrian dialect common among the civilizations who participated in building the pyramids of Giza.

I admit it, I was shaken. Either this client, this unassuming northern California hardware store clerk, had taken it upon himself to become fluent in ancient Assyrian, or being under hypnosis had opened some floodgate of information in him that came spilling out in my office. And in response, all I'd had to offer him was a slack-jawed stare and variations on the word "Huh?"

I started intensely researching past lives and their potential connection to present lives. I did a lot of soul-searching (if you'll pardon the expression). And I had a lot of long talks with my Spirit Guide, Francine, who gently led me to the inescapable conclusion that our past lives are as relevant to our present lives as our childhood is to our adulthood, separate but essential pieces of the same complex puzzle that is our eternal spirit's identity.

Of all the words Francine has ever said to me, one of the most life-altering was her reply to my question "If I do use hypnosis to help my clients explore their past lives, will there be some point to it besides just proving that they've lived before? What's in it for them?"

"Healing," was all she said. And it was enough. I couldn't imagine a more worthwhile, gratifying purpose than that.

Not long after that pronouncement from Francine, a group of

friends from the medical and psychiatric communities invited me to participate in a seminar addressing the issues of reincarnation and the soul's eternal survival. I suggested letting me try a past-life healing regression on a random volunteer from the audience. My colleagues weren't what you'd call enthusiastic, concerned as they were that under the watchful, curious gazes of a packed auditorium, healing regression and I would fall flat on our faces.

My question back to them, that settled the issue once and for all, was "How will we know if we don't try?"

A mortgage broker named Neil was the least enthusiastic of the many volunteers, so I perversely chose him to join me onstage and be my guinea pig. I briefly explained the hypnosis process to him and the huge audience. Then, just before we started, I asked him if he had any physical or emotional issues he'd like to tackle while he was "under." There were two: a recurring pain in his right foot that had never been successfully diagnosed or treated, and a lifelong fear that no matter how hard he tried or how well he provided for his family, he would always be a disappointment to those he loved.

He was in many ways an ideal subject—bright, responsive and so guilelessly honest that it was obvious he would tell the truth, even if the truth turned out to be that healing regression was the most worthless waste of time he'd ever endured. I easily relaxed him into a hypnotic state and gently walked him back through this life, his death in a previous life and then into whatever he chose to tell me about that lifetime.

Without a hint of fanfare or change of pace, this attractive, self-confident man seemed literally to wither, drawing into himself as if he didn't even want to take up his own share of space on his chair. His voice became small and apologetic, and his right foot twisted under on its side at an angle to his leg.

He told me his name was Calvin, that he was twelve years old, that he lived on a farm in Virginia, and that it was currently the year 1821. He was born with a clubbed right foot, which made him an embarrassment and a burden to his parents, as opposed to the healthy son they'd counted on for added help with the crops and the livestock. He was an outcast at school, an easy target for bullies, and he took solace in the farm animals he tended as best he could, who either didn't notice or didn't care that he was crippled, they just loved him unconditionally. By the time I eased him back into this life, on that night, in that auditorium, even my fellow panelists were fighting back tears.

And then, urged by Francine, I added something before I "woke" him: "Neil, whatever pain or fear or negativity you've carried over from a past life, let it be released and resolved into the white light of the Holy Spirit."

His right foot immediately returned to normal, his posture self-consciously corrected itself, and he seemed dazed and preoccupied as he muttered a quiet "thank you" and left the stage.

Weeks later he called my office to report that his foot pain seemed to have completely disappeared and that he was already noticing a difference in his attitude about himself and his right to be appreciated for the loving, responsible, generously reliable provider he was.

The obvious, fair question is, "How do we know these supposed past lives aren't simply fantasies the mind creates to relieve pain?" I have lots of answers for that, including how invariably detailed and mundane these "fantasies" turn out to be. (Thousands upon thousands of regressions later, the one historic "celebrity" I ever came up with was an apparently well-known eighteenth-century British economist I'd never heard of. I guess all the Cleopatras, Napoleons, Joan of Arcs and Julius Caesars are taking their business to other past-life regressionists.) But the one question that matters most to me is, "Who cares, as long as it helps?" The fact that past-life regressions can heal, and solve present-life physical and emotional pain, and just help relieve some undeserved unconscious obstacles, gives them all the validity they need as far as I'm concerned.

Hypnosis isn't always necessary for putting clients in touch with information they're holding from previous incarnations. Francine always says, "The soul knows the truth when it hears it." And that's demonstrated over and over again during regressions, or simply readings when I give a client some relevant highlights from their past lives. It's not like they're hearing news, it's much more like long-buried memories have suddenly rushed to the surface and made any number of question marks disappear.

An affidavit from C. illustrates the point beautifully:

Sylvia mentioned toward the end of my reading that I was carrying over a past life memory of being burned at the stake as a witch in Salem in the late 1600s. I was shocked at how immediately it made sense. I've always had an irrational fear of fire. I can't be near bonfires or "natural" fireplaces because I can't stand the smell of burning wood. I've always felt an extreme empathy for burn victims, and when I was a child I was so drawn to everything about St. Joan of Arc, who was burned at the stake, that I took her name as my confirmation name. When I reached adolescence I developed a fascination with the Salem witch trials and a deep distrust of the court system. And there's nothing in this lifetime that could possibly explain where any of these fears and fascinations came from. I know Sylvia was right about that past life, and it's such a strange relief to know that things about myself that never made sense to me really make all the sense in the world.

Dear Sylvia,

I came to you for help with a career decision, but almost immediately after I sat down with you, you told me that the son I have now is also the son I had in a past life, who was killed in battle in the Civil War. You were adamant that I separate that past life tragedy from this life, in which my son will live well into his 80s. You couldn't possibly have known the terror I've had since the day he was born, that I would lose him when he was young and there was nothing I could do to prevent it. I know all parents worry about their children, but this was a serious problem for me, and for my son too. I've always been overprotective of him, even now when he's a newlywed and starting a successful new career.

Without my even asking, you "cured" me of a phobia I've been struggling with for more than twenty years but could never understand."

from Bennedetta

When I came to Sylvia for a hypnosis session, I was as lost as I could be. I'm ashamed to say I was in the grip of an overwhelming three-year drug addiction. Not something I ever thought could happen to me, but I guess all addicts say that. I probably hoped Sylvia could give me a post-hypnotic suggestion that would make me not want drugs any more. I'm not really sure what I pictured when I walked into her office, but I could never have pictured what happened.

While I was under hypnosis I started telling her about six of my past lives, which I didn't even believe in before then, but there's not a doubt in my mind now. The more I talked about them the more obvious it was that my addiction problem wasn't new, that it was carried over from several of those past lives. I was just repeating old, irrelevant behavior, and I could let go of it now. One life was in England in the 1800s, when I was a woman, and I was married to a doctor who kept me under his control by keeping me on morphine all the time. I was a spoiled, arrogant, overindulgent member of Spanish royalty in one life, who spent all my time drunk because nobody stopped me, I damned well felt like it and nothing was expected of me but partying and womanizing. There was another life in Argentina where I was very sick from the day I was born and died at an early age, but I was on some kind of strong medication the whole time I was alive.

Anyway, that day, thanks to that experience with Sylvia, I was able to find the strength and conviction to overcome my drug addiction and reclaim my goals in this life. I went in lost and walked out with direction and hope.

Whenever I find myself straying off course, I think back to that day in August and everything falls back into place again. "Thanks" just doesn't say enough.

from Eli

After three years of visiting various doctors, therapists, chiropractors and psychiatrists, Martha Grace finally had a complete mental breakdown. Her symptoms included hallucinations, delusions, occasional panic and disembodied voices talking to her. Two separate psychiatrists diagnosed her as schizophrenic, but when she refused medication they gave up on her. There seemed to be some hope with a third psychiatrist, but when he couldn't accomplish the real breakthrough they were both expecting, her other problems were added to by an acute case of agoraphobia.

One day out of nowhere a friend suggested a visit to Sylvia Browne. It was the first time in weeks that Martha Grace had left the house, but she willingly went to see Sylvia.

To this day I don't know much about what went on in that room. I know Sylvia took Martha Grace through regressive hypnosis, but Martha wouldn't discuss the specifics. All she said was that Sylvia told her she would leave the house within seven days and the disembodied voices would never come back.

On the 8th day Martha Grace walked confidently out of the house to play tennis. She never heard the voices again, and she steadily improved without medication from that day on.

We were nervous about the expense of ongoing treatments from Sylvia, but since she gave us the first concrete results we'd seen in years, we were ready to do whatever we needed to find a way to afford it. We were so relieved and surprised when the follow-up turned out to be one more visit and one phone call a few months later to fill Sylvia in on how Martha Grace was doing. No charge. We couldn't believe it.

Martha Grace is currently living in Berkeley, studying computer programming at Cal State. She's a happy, successful young woman with a limitless future, and there's not a doubt in our minds that it's Sylvia Browne's regressive hypnosis that made this dream come true.

from Jana

Dear Sylvia,

As much as my regressive hypnosis session with you helped me with all sorts of health and personal issues, I think you helped my wife even more. You had no way of knowing that she's spent our whole marriage suffering from a deep fear of losing me. I reassure her, I take great care of myself, I'm healthy, and we have a good, strong marriage, but this idea that she was going to lose me was always there, to the point where she had recurring dreams about it several times a week.

Thanks to you and regressive hypnosis, I found out that my wife and I were married before, in the 1800s, and she lost me to the Civil War. The minute I told her that it was like I was reminding her of something she already knew, and she was afraid of something that had actually already happened in another life. Her fear just dissolved, her recurring dreams stopped and she's been at peace about this ever since. Thanks so much from both of us.

from John

I wasn't sure how I felt about past lives when I went to Sylvia for help with severe neck pain. My doctor and a few doctors he referred me to couldn't find what was causing it and just kept offering me muscle relaxers and pain pills I wasn't comfortable with. When Sylvia offered to do past-life regression, I decided I didn't have anything to lose and I trusted her, so I agreed.

I don't remember much that happened while I was under hypnosis, but I have the tape from the session, and there's my voice, with no coaching from Sylvia, talking about a lifetime in France in the 1700s that ended with my being guillotined. I described my death in detail without being upset or frightened by it, and I also described going right to the Other Side after it happened, as if it was the most normal thing in the world.

I can honestly say that my neck pain hasn't returned since that past life regression. And thanks to Sylvia I know that if it starts to come back, all I have to do is say it doesn't belong in this life, it's an old pain from another time, and give it to God.

My doctor said he's glad it worked, but he doubts the past life connection. He thinks it's more likely that Sylvia eased the pain by giving me some kind of post-hypnotic suggestion. My question about that, which he didn't have an answer for, was, if all I needed was a post-hypnotic suggestion to help with this pain, why didn't the hypnotherapist he sent me to think of that?

Thank you and God bless you, Sylvia.

from Rosemary

I'd been having constant severe pain in my hands that made it impossible for me to do the most minor chores, hold a brush or comb or on some days even dress myself. I went to my doctor, expecting to hear that I had arthritis. He ran tests, sent me to a specialist who ran more tests, that specialist sent me to another specialist, and in the end I was devastated when I was told they'd found cancer in the bone marrow of my hands.

I called for a reading with Sylvia because I'd read her books and just wanted her spiritual help with this news and how to cope with it.

Instead, when I sat down with her and started to cry and told her what was going on, she said she'd like to do a past-life regression on me if I wouldn't mind. I knew about it from her books, and it was fine with me. Whatever, at that point.

I won't go into the whole thing, but I remember a lot of the session and I remember telling her about living in poverty in Persia, being caught stealing and getting my hands cut off as punishment.

I can't put it any more simply than this: My regression with Sylvia was on March 29. On April 7, the pain was completely gone and my doctor advised me that I no longer had any cancer present anywhere in my body.

If I were reading this, I wouldn't believe it. All I can say is, it happened, and I'd swear to it.

from Lynn Marie

MORPHIC RESONANCE

Morphic resonance is a relative of cell memory and déjà vu. My Spirit Guide, Francine, describes it as déjà vu multiplied by the number of stars in the universe. It occurs when the spirit mind finds itself in a place so familiar from a past life that it experiences almost total recall. The recall resonates so powerfully that all the factual and emotional information the spirit mind is holding about that place is infused into the conscious mind, to the point where the whole body knows and feels that same information. You're in a city or country you've never been to before in this lifetime, and suddenly you don't just have the strange sensation that this place is not new to you, you're pretty sure that you could find your way around with no help from guides or road maps. And to thoroughly make your head spin, you realize that being in this place you've never been before is creating waves of an emotion that you'd almost swear was homesickness, or maybe having found your way back to a little corner of the world where you'll always belong, if you didn't know better.

That's morphic resonance.

I don't know anyone who's experienced it, including me, who saw it coming. In the blink of an eye a trip is transformed from "sightseeing" to "life-altering." Mine happened on my first trip to Kenya, where I found myself telling the driver where to turn and how to get to various landmarks without the benefit of a map, and also found myself fighting back tears over how much I'd "missed" it.

But it has nothing to do with being psychic. Clients have shared stories of the same phenomenon, with no cues from me and not a single mention of the term "morphic resonance." As many of you know, I occasionally take groups on wonderful overseas trips, kind of spiritual and geographical explorations, and especially in Egypt one or two members of the group will confide in me that they had "the oddest experience" while we were touring the pyramids.

Hi, Sylvia!

Sending an overdue update, as promised, and a bit breathless from all that's happened since my hypnosis session with you. Sorry for the delay, but I know you'll understand.

I'm the software designer who had a reading for your help with recovering from a painful divorce. Within minutes after I sat down with you, after you correctly told me I was struggling with carpal tunnel syndrome, you said, "What's this about Paris?" I said maybe you were picking up that it was the one place I'd always dreamed of visiting, but I certainly had no plans of going there.

We did a past-life regression, theoretically about my past relationships with my ex-husband. (Notice how unimportant he's become.) When I started talking about a life in Paris in the early 1700s, even though I was definitely hypnotized, I was still "conscious" enough to think it was probably because we'd been talking about Paris when I first got there.

So now, here it is, two years later. Notice the postmark on the envelope. Paris, France. Through a series of "coincidences" and "chance meetings" (I've been reading your books, so I know you don't believe in those, and I don't believe in them anymore either), I got one of those job offers only a fool would turn down and moved to Paris eight months ago.

But there's more to the story. When the job came through and I was telling my friends about the whole connection between Paris and my reading with you, I was always the first to say I was sure I'd just become hyper-conscious of that particular place because you and I talked about it. It's like when I was first diagnosed with carpal tunnel syndrome, and all of a sudden it seemed like I was hearing those words every time I turned around.

On my first trip over I was in the rental car, headed from Orly Airport into the city, with maps and written directions spread all over the passenger seat. I was preoccupied with how thrilled I was to be there, and how beautiful it was, so it took a while for me to realize that for several miles I'd been heading straight for the hotel without even glancing at the maps or directions. To see if maybe I was imagining this, I deliberately kept my eyes focused straight ahead for the rest of the drive, and my heart was pounding when I came to a stop at the entrance to the hotel twenty minutes later without one wrong turn, one hesitation or one instant of confusion. *I knew the way exactly!*

I've continued to feel like I'm at home ever since I moved here, and Paris and I definitely belong together. I'm so happy. That first day of "knowing" will always rank as one of the most extraordinary experiences of my life, along with meeting you.

Please excuse my corniness, but I can't resist—*merci,* Sylvia!

from Annie Laurie

Chapter 9

HEALTH

Let me start this chapter with my usual critically important warning about health-related readings: don't ever use me or any other psychic as a substitute for a fully trained and educated, board certified, thoroughly qualified professional when it comes to your physical and emotional well-being!

I'm remarkably tuned in to my clients' health issues. That would sound like an outrageously immodest thing to say if I thought I could take one bit of credit for it, but all it means is that I'm good at faithfully repeating the information I'm given from Sources who obviously have impressive expertise. Thanks to them, I can "read" a problem, an inaccurate diagnosis, a nutritional deficiency, an undetected allergy or the need for a specific battery of tests from exactly the right specialist. But on my best day I'll only offer suggestions (sometimes strongly), and I'll still never reach the 100 percent accuracy that belongs exclusively to God. I have no formal medical training, no certification (except as a master hypnotist) and no license to practice medicine or prescribe medication. I'm enormously proud of the reciprocal referral relationships I've enjoyed for decades with more than three hundred medical and psychiatric doctors around the world, and believe me, when I get sick, I head straight to a doctor, not to a fellow psychic, no matter how much I respect their gifts.

In fact, the health area probably makes me more aware than any other that my psychic information comes *through* me, not *from* me, because I've often been every bit as surprised as my clients at what comes out of my mouth. I can't swear that the story I'm about to tell was my first health-related psychic reading, but I can swear that, looking back, it seems to be the one that hurtled me into the center of the medical arena whether I was ready to go there or not.

It was around thirty years ago, in the middle of a normal day of readings (if you'll forgive the oxymoron). A client walked into my office, a well-dressed, attractive woman with a pleasant smile who was there to talk about a career dilemma. I completely startled us both when, before she even got to her chair, I shrieked, "No! Don't sit down! We've got to get you to a urologist!"

As it turned out, she had a severe bladder infection. The urologist I urgently sent her to told me if she'd waited any longer for treatment, she would have been in serious trouble.

To this day I don't know if that experience unconsciously expanded my focus or if it simply tuned me in to a whole new Source of information. It definitely triggered a hyper-awareness of and passion for my clients' health concerns that haven't wavered for a moment ever since.

I can't resist sharing a very long-running joke between me and my office staff, by the way, which only slightly amuses me. Most of the people who work in my office have been with me for twenty, thirty, even forty years. They've seen people fly in from every corner of the world for readings on their health problems. They've read, sorted and filed literally thousands of affidavits validating my accuracy on countless medical issues. Some of them have even witnessed a healing or two (more about those later in their own chapter). And yet—and Lindsay, who's witnessed it with her own eyes, will back me up on this—you've never seen a group more apathetic in your life than my staff when I try to get one of them to see a doctor about some illness I see developing, or some medication I know has been misprescribed, or something they've become allergic to that I know they can easily avoid. They have total faith in me when it comes to everyone else on earth. When it comes to themselves, they stop just short of yawning in my face. And if any of them deny it, they're lying, trying to be polite.

To be fair, it might have something to do with the fact that throughout all these years of focusing on my clients' health issues, I've faithfully shared what information I was given with absolute precision and then, after the client left, had to dive into a medical dictionary to look up the terms I'd just been talking about when they were brand-new to me.

A perfect example was Mary Beth, who'd been suffering for years from severe pressure in the back of her head, at the base of her skull. It was so debilitating that it led to her inability to work, or sometimes even to get out of bed. And it's not as if Mary Beth had let herself be victimized by it. From the first day the dull, relentless pain started, she'd seen doctor after doctor, had test after test and scan after scan, tried medication after medication and still found no relief. She was told so often by so many doctors that everything seemed to be normal that she even saw a psychiatrist, to explore the possibility that this was some psychosomatic condition her mind had created and could make go away. But several months and hundreds of dollars later it became apparent that no, that wasn't it either.

She was embarrassed when she blurted out that she'd turned to me as "a last resort," and she couldn't stop apologizing. It didn't, and doesn't, offend me in the least. As I said earlier, when something goes wrong with my body, I call doctors instead of psychics too.

The affidavit Mary Beth sent several weeks after her reading says, in part:

> Sylvia told me the problem was rooted in my C3 and I needed to see an orthopedist ASAP. If the first orthopedist said my C3 was fine, go to another one, and keep going until I found one who could

see the injury and treat it. I didn't need to go beyond the first one, who confirmed that it was my C3 that was causing all these years of pain. He began treatments immediately, and it's like I've been given a miracle. That awful pressure is completely gone, and I never thought it would happen, but I'm starting to live a normal life again and look forward to every new day. All this and, to be honest, when Sylvia started talking about a C3, I didn't even know what it was, let alone that I had one. I thank her from the bottom of my heart for giving me back my life.

I don't mind admitting that when I started talking about the problem being rooted in Mary Beth's C3, I didn't know what a C3 was at the time either. I looked it up as soon as she walked out the door. It turns out to be the third vertebra of the cervical part of the spinal column, i.e., the part of the spinal column that starts at the base of the skull. Who knew?

I've actually developed a very impressive medical vocabulary over all these years, thanks to my clients, the spirit world, the hundreds of doctors I work with and again, my passionate belief in the importance of this area of my work. We forget all too often—and I'm sometimes as guilty of it myself as everyone else—that no matter how much money we've got, or what awards are sitting on our trophy shelves, or how grand and impressive our houses might be, or how brilliantly our social lives and/or love lives are going, they all count for nothing if our physical or emotional health is in trouble.

I was also happy to discover early on that I could tune in to my clients' health concerns whether I was in the room with them or not, whether they'd mentioned a single physical problem or not, or whether or not the problem had even cropped up yet.

Edgar was a phone reading, more years ago than either he or I would probably care to admit to. He was adorable, a sweet, funny, articulate man who wanted help with his love life. Or, more precisely, his lack of one. It seems Edgar had an unfortunate tendency to become exclusively smitten with women who'd invariably end up giving him the "I think of you as a friend" speech. (What is it with us women and our tendency to pass up nice guys in favor of trying to reform the ones who seem to have been raised by wolves? We really need to rethink that. And a note to Edgar—Please do write and let me know if you met and married the "Diane" I promised would come along. As I told you at the time, she was and is a woman who would genuinely appreciate you.)

Edgar and I were about to hang up after a truly delightful half hour when I was suddenly compelled to ask what was wrong with his tooth.

"My tooth? What tooth?" he asked.

"Your lower right molar," I told him.

"Sorry," he said, "but I don't know what you're talking about. There's nothing wrong with that tooth, or any of my teeth."

There would be. I knew that. But I decided against telling him. Why plant a suggestion in case I was wrong?

Two months later a note arrived in my office from his home back east:

> *Dear Sylvia, Just thought you'd like to know that I had to make an emergency trip to my dentist last week. One minute I was fine, the next minute I was in excruciating pain, and he ended up having to remove my lower right molar. My dentist is a little worried that you're apparently more reliable than his x-ray machine.*

Not really, Edgar. I just have a more reliable Source.

Several of the doctors I work with on a regular basis have suggested that it might be to my advantage that I *don't* have a vast amount of medical training. It allows me to view my clients and their problems objectively, simplistically and without the doctors' occasional disadvantage of being so incredibly knowledgeable that they "can't see the forest for the trees." I think there's some truth to that. I can definitely miss the forest for the trees in my own areas of expertise from time to time, so why wouldn't they? And you'll never hear me complain about being too knowledgeable about the infinitely complex worlds of medical and psychiatric health. As I'll keep repeating every time the subject comes up, all I do is pass along the information I'm given and stay out of the way.

It didn't take a psychic to know that Dorothy wasn't feeling well when she walked into my office—she was pale, and she was moving too slowly for a woman as young as she was. It wasn't as if she was sore or arthritic, it was more as if her body was in pain and depleted while she tried to appear to be moving normally.

She blurted it out before I even had a chance to say hello: she'd been suffering for years with chronic respiratory and gastrointestinal problems, and despite countless examinations and tests by her family internist and a few specialists, she still had no idea what was wrong, let alone why she seemed to be getting worse, not better.

"Because you haven't seen an allergist, that's why," I told her.

"What?"

"You haven't seen an allergist, have you?"

"No," she said, "it never occurred to me. What good would an allergist do?"

"An allergist would confirm that you're very allergic to wheat, and that these problems you're having are really nothing more than strong allergic reactions that will disappear as soon as you eliminate every trace of wheat from your diet."

After all these years, I can instantly spot the difference between a client who believes me and a client who doesn't but is just desperate enough to humor me. Dorothy definitely fell into that second category. She looked at me as if I'd told her that any minute now she was going to turn into a Lexus convertible. But she was clearly sick and tired of being sick and tired, so I can't say it came as a huge surprise when, a few months later, a letter from her arrived in my office:

> *You told me on July 3 that I'm allergic to wheat and that it was causing my respiratory and gastrointestinal problems. I made an appointment with an allergist on August 13. He told me that while he couldn't specifically test me for that food allergy, he could give me a more general grass allergy test. Most people who test positive for allergies to all seven grasses in this particular series are usually allergic to wheat in their diet as well. We went ahead with the grass allergy test, and it turned out I was highly allergic to each and every one of those seven grasses. Needless to say, I'm going off wheat immediately! Thank you for coming up with a solution my internist admits he would never have thought of.*

For what it's worth, I've come to believe that food allergies are underrated, by many doctors and by most of us "ordinary people" as well, as a cause of seemingly unrelated, supposedly undiagnosable physical ailments. Let's face it, if some allergies are powerful enough to show up externally as hives and swelling and red, itchy eyes, imagine what damage they can do to our bodies when they direct themselves inward.

Thank you, Dorothy, for humoring me and asking a licensed physician to validate what I told you. I hope all the clients who'll be coming to me with health concerns for the next fifty years will follow your example.

And then there was Nikki, who wrote to me out of sheer frustration after any number of doctors had scratched their heads, given up and passed her on to yet another colleague. Nikki, who was accustomed to being very healthy and full of energy, was suffering from exhaustion, general achiness and a low-grade fever that had been going on for seven months. Three of her doctors, understandably assuming that low-grade fever must mean a low-grade infection somewhere in the body, prescribed a variety of antibiotics. They didn't make a bit of difference, except to possibly make her feel worse.

My notes in the margin of Nikki's letter read, "You have *Candida*. Yeast infection. You'll have to have a fecal matter test to find it. Antibiotics feed it, exacerbate it. High-protein diet will starve it out."

One of my staff relayed the information to Nikki on the phone. We got a note from her several weeks later.

> *I went back to my regular internist and told him I needed a fecal matter test. He said he'd never had a patient ask him for one of those before. I was tempted to tell him a psychic told me to get one, but I wanted him to take me seriously, so I didn't. (Good choice, by the way.) He couldn't believe it when the test came back positive for a yeast infection because the antibiotic he gave me was a form of penicillin that can promote growth in yeast infections. He apologized for that and said* Candida, *which is what I have, is hard to get rid of, but now that he knows what's going on with me he can treat me for the right problem. In the meantime, he said a high protein diet is a good idea and wondered what I've been reading to be so well informed. I still didn't tell him it all came from a psychic. Maybe someday I will. The main thing is, it's been five weeks since the correct diagnosis, and since I started on the high protein diet and medications for my specific problem, and I'm starting to feel like my old self again.*

Some of you may be surprised, or even a little disturbed, to hear that the spirit world would pass along information about a topic as indelicate as fecal matter. But one of countless fascinating things about the residents of the Other Side is that they don't trouble themselves with petty judgments about whether something's tasteful or indelicate, polite or rude, chic or unfashionable, or even good or bad. Those are strictly things we humans seem to trouble ourselves with when we don't have enough to do. The spirit world can't be bothered—when they have a message to communicate that someone needs to hear, no subject matter is off limits.

Dear Sylvia,

This note is to confirm for anyone who might be wondering that it is a very good idea to listen to your words of advice.

I was very pregnant when I had my private reading with you. You told me it was a girl (which I didn't know), you said she'd arrive early, and then you really urged me to race to the hospital the instant my water broke.

Well, that's exactly what I did, with your words echoing so loudly in my head it was as if you were in the car with my husband and me cheering us on. We made the twenty-minute drive to the hospital in twelve minutes, and we got there in the nick of time, it turned out. I began having seizures and had to have an emergency C-section.

Our beautiful daughter was born six days early. And thanks to my arriving at the hospital not one minute later than I did—in other words, thanks to your warning—she and I are two happy, healthy girls.

from Dusty

Dear Sylvia,

I was in the Montel Williams audience and asked you about my stomach problems. You told me that my doctors hadn't been able to find the cause, and you said I needed to go back to them and tell them the problem was in my bile duct.

You were 100% correct. Unfortunately, it's terrible news—I have incurable biliary cancer, which you probably know is cancer of the bile duct. But I thank you so much for your amazing accuracy. While my prognosis couldn't be worse, I am getting treatments that are improving my quality of life for the time I have left, and it would never have happened without you.

from Joi

For as long as I can remember I've had breathing problems. Doctors insist I don't have asthma. The best they can come up with is "possibly some kind of allergy." Not very helpful. Some days I would be fine, but on other days it would feel like all my air passages were constricted so that I couldn't breathe, and I'd have painful coughing spells. It was dramatically interfering with my lifestyle, which I prefer to be as active as possible. I love to play sports, and I work out at the gym five or six days a week if my breathing allows.

Sylvia told me to do three simple things. 1) increase my protein intake and reduce my carbohydrate intake; 2) supplement my diet with lecithin and amino acids; and 3) avoid dairy products, because I was lactose intolerant (that was news to me).

I could always count on two or three days a week of straining to breathe. It's been three months since I had my reading with Sylvia and followed her advice, and I haven't had a single episode of breathing problems in these three months.

from Sharon

Dear Sylvia,

During my reading you described my oldest son with incredible accuracy, right down to his "sea-green eyes," and then told me that initial diagnoses had been wrong—he does not have a brain tumor after all, he has a virus that creates neurological problems when he's under severe stress.

A week after the reading my son called to tell me he'd been

hospitalized with viral meningitis, a virus that's in his blood and flares up at times of nervous or physical fatigue.

Thorough testing at the hospital confirmed that his two previous doctors were wrong, there was no brain tumor, just the inflammation of his brain and spinal cord that defines what viral meningitis is.

Thank you for your words of assurance and support at a time that was so frightening, and thank you even more for being so accurate yet again.

from Cindy

Dear Sylvia,

I just had to write a quick note to thank you for your simple, life-changing advice. I'd never had the slightest idea that I have any food allergies, and certainly not dairy products. But you told me to avoid them like the plague and see if it didn't make a difference. Well, it did, in a big way. For the first time in three years I've stopped taking heartburn medication three times a day, and I'm finding I have more energy than I did when I was twenty (a long time ago, we'll leave it at that). I even gave my doctor, who's also a friend, a good-natured but sincere scolding thanks to you. I suggested that instead of just handing out prescriptions for whatever problem comes up, he try your approach and find out what's causing the problem in the first place and get rid of it. He actually said it was a great piece of advice and I was right!

Thank you again for my renewed good health and for helping me give my doctor something to think about.

from Janis

Sylvia and her staff made it clear after my reading that Sylvia wanted feedback, good or bad. I'd been having a very hard time getting pregnant, and Sylvia told me that I needed to have my thyroid checked. I'd get pregnant about eight months after getting the thyroid treatment I needed.

I called the office a few weeks later to say that Sylvia was wrong. According to my doctor, there was nothing wrong with my thyroid, and my only hope of getting pregnant would be in vitro fertilization.

After several months of no success with that doctor, a pregnant friend referred me to the fertility specialist who helped her. He ran a series of tests and informed me that I had a thyroid problem, but once the problem was corrected he was sure I could look forward to getting pregnant in about eight months.

I called Sylvia's office again to apologize for the first call and change my feedback from "wrong" to "exactly right."

from Renatta

I had a private reading with Sylvia more than a year ago. I flew 2000 miles just to meet her, and it was worth every minute and every dime. My husband and I were eager to start a family but were having no luck. Three different doctors/fertility specialists had finally told me I would never be able to have children. My heart kept telling me they were wrong, but they were the experts and their sad pronouncements of doom were final as far as they were concerned.

Sylvia calmly confirmed what I believed—the doctors and specialists were wrong, and not only was I able to have a child, I *would* have a child.

Enclosed please find a picture of our beautiful three-week-old son, conceived three months after my reading. Our only regret is that no matter how hard we tried, we couldn't convince ourselves that it would be fair to a boy to name him "Sylvia."

from Shanna

I had a personal reading with Sylvia on a Monday. She addressed some health issues some of my family members were going through, but she expressed no concern at all for my daughter, whom we discussed in passing.

Three days later my daughter broke the news to me that she had breast cancer and was scheduled for surgery. She'd postponed telling me until two days before the surgery because she knew I'd be frantic and saw no point in upsetting me until the last possible moment.

I was frantic, to say the least, and I also couldn't imagine how Sylvia missed something so horrible during my reading. I called the office to complain about it, reminding Sylvia that I'd just been there days earlier and she hadn't said a word about my daughter's breast cancer. I got a message from Sylvia on my answering machine a couple of hours later: "Your daughter doesn't have breast cancer. She's going to be perfectly fine."

I played the message for my daughter, hoping she would find it reassuring. Instead she burst into tears and said, "I've been told by a doctor, an oncologist and a surgeon that I have breast cancer. I think they know more about it than some psychic who's never even met me. And there's nothing perfectly fine about it!"

The biopsy showed beyond all doubt that all those nodes in my daughter's breast were benign and harmless as could be. There was no cancer. She was, and is, perfectly fine. The first thing she did when she got the "all clear" report from the doctor was call Sylvia's office to apologize for the skepticism Sylvia never even heard and to schedule a reading for herself.

from Amanda

I repeat: my respect for the vast majority of the medical profession is boundless and indelible. But as we all know, and members of that profession would admit it themselves, there are exceptions to the typical dedicated physician whose life is sincerely devoted to our physical and mental vitality.

Few things make me crazier than the occasional stories I hear from clients who've been passed along from one lazy, careless doctor to another to another, usually with no apparent game plan in mind whatsoever, when each of them runs out of ideas or patience. And in the meantime the client's pain goes on and on while they wait for the next appointment with the next new doctor, essentially held hostage by the lack of hope, the lack of reliable answers and the lack of a remedy once and for all.

Yet another reason why I take no offense when a client blurts out that I'm their "last resort." In some cases, if their doctors had done their jobs, these clients wouldn't need me, and invariably, in those same cases, I'd happily forfeit the clients for just one doctor along the way who'd paid attention.

I suffered from Panic Disorder for three years. It was a terrible way to live, and I finally went to my doctor for help. He referred me to a psychiatrist, and between the two of them—they were consulting with each other, so they were both aware of this—they had me on three different medications every day (Xanax, Prozac and BuSpar). I told them both I have a low tolerance for drugs, but they insisted they knew what they were doing. Very soon, instead of choking, loss of air, heart palpitations and a general feeling I was going to die, I was either in a foggy stupor or I was asleep. I tried adjusting the medications myself, but I gave up completely when they tried to add Valium to the mix.

I already had a phone reading scheduled with Sylvia a long time in advance, and by the time she called I had reached a point where I was completely confined to my house, the panic attacks had become so severe. Just hearing her voice made me feel as if I was finally talking to someone who might really listen and understand.

Sylvia told me my pancreas wasn't functioning correctly. She said my blood sugar was much too low and that I needed to start right away adding protein like fish and chicken to the fruits and vegetables my diet mostly consisted of. She encouraged me to see a doctor about my pancreas, which I admit I haven't done yet. But I did change my diet immediately according to her recommendations, and slowly but surely I felt the anxious tightness in my chest, the heart palpitations and the shortness of breath starting to ease.

After a couple of weeks I started making myself step outside the house at least once or twice a day, and within maybe two months I ventured out on a few errands I hadn't been able to handle in three years.

Six months after my phone reading with Sylvia I not only felt like a whole new person, but I was so ready to face the world again that my husband and I took a 2000-mile cross-country trip on our Harley Davidsons and had a wonderful time.

from Michelle

(Note from Sylvia: Michelle, I'm thrilled with your letter, but I still hope you'll get your pancreas checked. You have benign cysts, and you'll feel even better once they're removed. Keep me posted, will you?)

Dear Sylvia,

When I had my telephone reading with you, my doctors had given up on me, but I was still so sick I honestly prayed you would tell me I would die soon.

Well, you didn't tell me I was going to die, you told me what was wrong with me and what to do about it. In the eight months since the reading I have lost 77 lbs. without dieting, cravings or going hungry, I just did what you told me to do. My blood pressure has stabilized so much that I went off my blood pressure medication with my internist's blessing, and he also gave me permission to go off my diabetes medicine. (All of a sudden he was interested in me again, I guess because he could see such amazing improvement without having to come up with it himself.) I'm enclosing the lab work to prove to you that, even without medication, my blood sugars have become normal! The neuropathy in my legs and feet has stopped spreading and even reversed to a point. My lower legs are no longer "wooden," and I now have muscle and feeling under the skin and no more of the swelling that made my feet and ankles look like two big bloated dead fish. I was also able to go off the Lasix I was prescribed by my cardiologist.

For the first time in over three years I can shop while pushing a cart instead of riding in one. My weight loss, my general health improvement and my ability to walk around like a normal person are so incredible that people who haven't seen me for a while say, "What happened to you?" I just answer, "Sylvia Browne."

from Felicia

If you're waiting for me to tell you what it was I told Felicia to do, you have a long wait ahead, by the way. The information I was given for her might be completely different from the information I would get for you, even if your symptoms sound identical, and I'm not about to have you experimenting with someone else's "prescription" when my name is attached.

READINGS AND CELL MEMORY

As I discuss at length in the "Past Lives" chapter, it was my Spirit Guide, Francine, who introduced me to the idea that regressive hypnosis into clients' past lives could result in healing. And it was also my Spirit Guide, Francine, who introduced me to the concept that many areas of our current lives, including and especially health, can be traced directly to something called "cell memory." Cell memory is a real, potentially powerful and often negative physiological connection to our past lives that we're rarely aware of until we acknowledge its existence and then release it into God's Hands where it belongs.

Francine knows that biology and the sciences in general were never my best subjects, so when she explained cell memory to me she walked me through it step by step:

- Our bodies are made up of billions of cells, all of which interact with each other.
- Each one of those cells is alive, a breathing, thinking, feeling organism that receives, retains and reacts very literally to the information the subconscious mind transmits. You've heard the example, I'm sure, that under hypnosis, for example, when the conscious mind is out of the way and the subconscious mind is in charge, the hypnotist can plant the suggestion that his finger is actually a lit match. If that finger touches our arm, the cells in that spot will react exactly as they're programmed to when they're burned and form a perfectly real blister.
- It's in the subconscious that our spirit minds live, safe, sound and always intact, no matter how healthy or unhealthy our conscious minds might be.
- Our spirit minds remember everything our souls have experienced, in every life we've lived since we were created, both here and on the Other Side.

- At the moment our spirit minds enter our physical bodies, they infuse the cells of our bodies with all the information and memories they possess, and our cells respond accordingly until our spirits leave our bodies again and head Home.
- Our cells react in utterly real, literal ways to all the memories they're infused with, whether our conscious minds are aware of those memories or not.
- By accessing and releasing those *cell memories,* we can rid ourselves of long-buried illness, phobias, pain and trauma and also re-create the greatest emotional and physical health our spirits have ever enjoyed.

Cell memory, then, is all the knowledge our billions of cells contain and act on, instilled by the spirit minds that enter them when a new lifetime on earth begins. It's the tangible rush of familiarity that our spirits experience when they find themselves in a human body again, after years or decades or centuries in the perfection of the Other Side. The lines between past and present blur as every cell of the body is inundated with the reality of other times and places when our spirits occupied other human bodies and, alive and sentient as they are, our cells begin responding to anything and everything they perceive to be the truth.

POINTS OF ENTRY

A small, fascinating detail of doing cell memory work with clients is the concept of "Points of Entry." Francine first introduced me to Points of Entry years ago, during a regressive hypnosis session with a man who'd flown almost three thousand miles for his regression. He was as sweet as he could be. He was also without a doubt the most long-winded person I've ever met in my life. We were there to help him with what he described as his "sheer terror of being alone," which had led him into some pretty hideous relationships, let me tell you. He was so enchanted with experiencing his past lives firsthand that he decided to linger and explore every detail of each and every one of them—the names of four wives and ten children in Egypt, every town and village he visited when he was an itinerant Romanian laborer, you name it, he covered it. Almost an hour later he was still contentedly chattering away, and I was getting a little wild-eyed knowing we hadn't covered a single moment of a single life that could have triggered a sheer terror of being alone, when suddenly I heard Francine's voice chirping in my ear, "Point of Entry. Go to your Point of Entry."

I didn't have a clue what it meant, but she's not big on gratuitous blather, so I just went with it and repeated out loud, "Point of Entry. Go to your Point of Entry."

It was like hitting a fast-forward button. Or, from what computer people tell me, opening a file and selecting "find." Zoom! He was in Peru, alone in a self-imposed exile on top of a mountain and dying there of exposure, punishing himself for causing the death of his wife and children. In less than two minutes after hearing the words Point of Entry, he revealed and released the cell memory that isolation and solitude were synonymous with guilt, punishment and death of loved ones.

As Francine explained later, the Point of Entry is simply the moment at which the event or events happened that created the painful cell memory to begin with. It was spirit world shorthand, essentially, a way for clients struggling with a specific issue to jump to its cause, without wading through past lives that weren't relevant to the problem at hand.

I just had one question. "What are the odds of my clients even knowing what 'Point of Entry' means? I didn't."

She simply replied, "It's not for you. It's for them. They'll know."

That was twenty years ago. And without exception, every regressive hypnosis client I've directed to their Point of Entry has known exactly what I was talking about and jumped straight to the relevant event in the relevant lifetime.

What's been equally helpful, maybe even more so, is that once I learned about Points of Entry, I was able to jump to them myself on my clients' behalf during readings, whether we were doing a regression or not, and clients still received the same healing benefit from them. Francine always says, "The soul knows the truth when it hears it," and there's just no doubt about it, she's right. It doesn't matter if it's my voice or the voice of a client, the truth is the truth, and when it heals, thank God.

I wrote an entire book about the potential impact on our health and daily lives of Points of Entry and cell memory in general. It's called *Past Lives, Future Healing,* and it gives one illustration after another of the potentially immediate results of exposing a Point of Entry and releasing the damaging cell memories around it. But here's an excerpt from a letter a recent client sent that beautifully sums it up:

Dear Sylvia,

I wrote you about my panic attacks, and you were kind enough to respond within three weeks. You told me my panic attacks didn't come from this life, they came from a past life when I was imprisoned for a crime I didn't commit. You also made some suggestions, including talking to my doctor about an antidepressant, and starting a high protein, low carbohydrate diet. I admit I didn't see the doctor, because I don't like taking medication. But I've increased my protein and reduced my carbohydrates significantly. And most of all, I felt *free,* the instant your office called and told me what you said about that past-life memory.

I've done everything, except medicate myself, that my doctors told me to do about my panic attacks for the last ten years. I mastered relaxation and bio-feedback. I reviewed my life and recognized every event that could have caused this to happen to me.

But in ten years no doctor was able to do for me what you, through your staff, were able to accomplish in a three-minute phone call. You've eased an agony I've been dealing with for over a decade, I ask God every day as you suggested to let this past-life trauma be released and resolved in the white light of the Holy Spirit and I know I'm on the road to full recovery. I'm sure people in the sciences would claim I've fallen into the proverbial mind trap. It doesn't matter. I don't care what people think, I care what works. You "work," and I truly hope the universe gives back to you as much as you give.

from Mindy

One thought I'll happily repeat from *Past Lives, Future Healing* as a personal note to every doctor in the medical and psychiatric communities:

I don't ask you or anyone to take a word I say at face value, including and maybe especially the cell memory approach to healing.

But if you have patients who seem to be immune to every other form of "traditional" treatment you've tried, please don't dismiss the possibility of trying a cell memory/past-life healing before you give up. By definition, you know it's safe, and incapable of doing any harm, so there's no risk to you or your patients.

Wouldn't it be sad to turn your back on something that might provide permanent relief to those who need it, for no other reason than that it came from a psychic?

I also find myself doing spontaneous readings, on occasions when I honestly can't help myself (or, some might say, when I can't keep my mouth shut).

One of my "targets" was a guest at a very small dinner party given by my friend and collaborator Lindsay Harrison. This guest was the ultimate gentleman and would never have dreamed of taking advantage of having a psychic in the room, which I deeply appreciated. He's also an enormously gifted actor whose work I've admired for years, so I don't mind admitting that I did more than a casual "scan" of him because, selfishly, I want him around for a long time.

Shortly after we settled into the living room for after-dinner coffee, I blurted out, "I want you to completely eliminate carbohydrates and alcohol from your diet for the next three months, and then have your blood sugar tested. I'm worried that you're in danger of becoming diabetic."

Hilariously, instead of gaping at me as if I might sprout antennae at any moment, he whirled around and glared at Lindsay.

"Did you tell her that?" he demanded.

Lindsay, with the calm that comes with innocence, answered his question with a question: "How could I tell her something I didn't know?"

He thought about it for a second and then apologized to her before turning to me. "My doctor said those exact words to me two weeks ago," he said. "But Lindsay's right, I didn't tell her because I didn't want her to worry. So, uh, I guess that's why you're known as a psychic, isn't it?"

Now, here's the part that fascinated me. He and I have become friends since then, and he told me that hearing the identical advice from me and his doctor had much more impact coming from me. I asked him why, considering the fact that I have no medical training whatsoever.

He replied, "Maybe that's exactly why. My doctor telling me something is one thing, but getting it confirmed by Whoever you're tuned into makes me think I'd *really* better listen!"

Sylvia, I owe you one. I met you for one brief moment at one of your book signings in Florida. The line was so long you couldn't see the end of it, so you didn't have more than an instant with any of us. But in my instant with you, you told me there was a problem with my immune system and I needed to see a doctor.

I did, and it turns out I'm HIV positive. Obviously I'm frightened and worried about my future, but I'm so thankful that you sent me to a doctor so that I could start getting treatment. It never entered my mind until you spoke up.

from Victor

Spontaneous readings have also been known to happen during the lectures I do throughout the United States and Canada. I'm as invariably surprised as the audience member I find myself drawn to. You'll read more examples in the "Healings" chapter, but here's a letter from Rickie I've kept and continue to appreciate:

Dear Sylvia,

My sister and I attended your September seminar in San Diego. We bought our tickets months in advance, and we were thrilled to find ourselves sitting in the second row. "Thrilled" doesn't begin to describe how we felt when you suddenly called us onto the stage because you knew we were both suffering from migraine headaches. I have been tortured by migraines since I was ten years old, and I'm now 45. I was in the middle of a cluster of them at your seminar when you insisted my sister and I come up and join you.

You put me in a chair, asked me to sit back and put your hands on me, and I have to confess I felt so safe and loved by you, a complete stranger to me. I put all my trust in you, as I believe you are truly a messenger from God. When you prayed to God to help you help me get rid of my headaches, not just for the moment but always, the pain left me immediately. I told you I felt like crying, as I have lived with pain my entire life, and you kissed my forehead.

I have not had another migraine since that day, and I'm learning how to live without that constant blinding pain.

My sister has been migraine-free as well. You also told her to see an endocrinologist about her thyroid problems, which she didn't know she had. She followed your advice, and had tests run. You were right, they found a hyperthyroid condition that she's getting treatment for now. So thank you from both of us.

Many people approached me as we left the seminar and asked if what you did was real, or if I knew you, or if I was lying about my headache being gone. I was stunned! Why would people come to your seminar, pay to hear you speak, and then question your ability to work through God's hands? I just had a miracle performed on me and they wanted to question the authenticity of it. People are amazing.

from Rickie

(Note to Rickie: Now you know how I feel after being accused for all these years of planting "ringers" in my audiences and on phone-in radio and television shows. If that were true, don't you think at least one of them would have stepped forward by now? Maybe the reason they haven't is that I'd give up my career before I'd stoop to any such thing.)

Dear Sylvia,

I don't know how to thank you for the blessing you gave me at your lecture yesterday. I've had three surgeries in the last year. My spinal cord was damaged in the surgeries, which left me barely able to walk or sometimes even do something as simple as pick up a plate or a fork, and more than one doctor told me there was nothing anyone could do for me. What you told me was that I would be healed.

The friend who brought me to the lecture and took me home belongs to one of your study groups, and while she was very re-assuring too, she said that healings usually don't happen right away. But when I got home I was sitting on the couch hearing your voice say so clearly that I would be healed, and suddenly, I don't know any other way to describe it, I just felt completely well. I got up off the couch, easily, and started walking. Not just around my house. Four blocks down, across the street, back up and home again. The stiffness, pain and weakness were gone. My arms moved freely when I walked. And as you can see, I'm able to hold a pen and write to you.

It's a true miracle, and I'll remember you eternally.

from Jeanette

And one from Donna that made me chuckle, since we share the same pitiful luck when it comes to games of chance:

Dear Sylvia,

I'm a lucky person in my life in general, but I've never been lucky when it comes to games, drawings, playing cards, any-thing involving chance. I can't even win silly gifts at baby and bridal showers unless it's designed so that no one leaves empty-handed.

So when I went to see you speak for the second time, I went into a state of shock when you drew my number as one of the people who got to step up to the microphone and ask you a question. My state of shock was seriously compounded by the fact that I'm not good at speaking in front of large crowds, and this crowd was *huge*.

My turn at the mike came, and my mind went completely blank. I thought of a thousand questions on the way home that

I would love to have asked, but at the time I couldn't think of a single question, or even my own name. Something dumb came out of my mouth, and we all had a good laugh, but it wasn't a question. Instead, you used my time to say, "Have your gallbladder and bile ducts checked, and stop eating dairy products." I said you were exactly right about the dairy products, and you said, "Of course I'm right, I'm psychic."

Ten days later I was at a doctor's appointment for my regular blood pressure check-up, and I told my doctor about this experience and what you said. Possibly just to humor me, he checked my abdomen, and then he sent me for an ultrasound. Guess what—I had an enlarged gallbladder, gallstones and a cyst on my liver.

The laparoscopic surgery on my gallbladder was a complete success. I thank God every day for pointing me toward you, and you for pointing me toward a potentially serious problem that neither my doctor nor I knew I had.

I have a blood disease called Sjögren's Syndrome. I'd been complaining to my doctor about my chronic exhaustion, the general swelling of my body that made me embarrassed to leave my house and my inability to concentrate, which was seriously compromising my job performance. All my doctor kept saying was, "It's the Sjögren's," as if these were all things I was just going to have to learn to put up with.

Three months ago I attended a lecture of Sylvia Browne's. Without my asking her a single question, she looked at me and said, "You need to have your thyroid checked." I thought about correcting her and saying, "No, I have Sjögren's Syndrome," but I kept my mouth shut, and from the Saturday of the lecture until Monday morning when my doctor's office opened I became more and more curious about her remark.

I had my thyroid checked, and it was very low. I started medication to correct it immediately, and the improvement in those symptoms that were dragging me down is miraculous. I feel as if I've gone from just existing to really being *alive*. It was so easy for my doctor, and me, to blame Sjögren's for anything and everything that was wrong with me that we stopped paying attention to the basics, until Sylvia Browne came along, that is. What a difference she's made in every day of my life, and what a Godsend she is!

from Brenda

And then there are those "readings" I'm not even conscious of at the time, until people are kind enough to take the time to write or call and tell me about it after the fact. To all of you who are so generous, I hope you know how much it means to me and how much added motivation it gives me to hear from you. From Roxanne, for example:

I attended a lecture of Sylvia's several weeks ago, and during the lecture she took the whole audience through a beautiful meditation. I don't remember the last time my body and mind have been so relaxed. I felt as if I was in good health that night, so I was very surprised when, during the meditation, I started getting a strong "message" (no actual voice, I just "knew" it) that I needed to go see my doctor, sooner rather than later.

I ignored the message for a few days, thinking maybe I was just reaching for something meaningful to happen to me during Sylvia's lecture, and I'm certainly not one to go to the doctor when I feel perfectly healthy. But it kept nagging at me, so I finally made an appointment.

My doctor found a malignant mass on my breast. I'm writing this from the pre-op room in the hospital, where I'm having a modified radical mastectomy in a few hours. The malignancy has moved into the lymph areas, but it seems it hasn't penetrated other parts of my body.

I don't know what the next weeks and months hold for me, but I'm feeling positive and so grateful for a meditation that I believe ended up saving my life.

I never missed Sylvia's appearances on the *A.M. Northwest Show,* especially when she did her annual New Year's predictions. I paid particular attention to one of her predictions in the early 1990s, when she said that an effective AIDS treatment would be developed soon in France. My brother had AIDS, and I remember praying she was right, that something effective would be developed somewhere soon, for him and the millions of others who need help.

I didn't mention it to my brother, not wanting to give him false hope, and besides, it was "just a prediction." In fact, I didn't think about it again, until my brother called a year or so later to tell me he was leaving for Europe for a series of new cutting-edge AIDS treatments. He'd initially planned on going to Italy, where some good work was being done. But then, through connections in Washington, D.C., particularly at the Pentagon, he'd heard that the real breakthroughs in the treatment of AIDS were happening in France, so he was headed there instead.

My brother's a fan of Sylvia's as well, so it didn't surprise him a bit when I told him she'd predicted that very thing long before it became a reality.

from Merlin

Dear Sylvia,

I still can't quite believe this happened to me of all people, but it did, and my daughter and a local nurse can verify it.

I've been very concerned about my daughter's health. A persistent virus in her system was causing her a lot of problems, and she seemed to be getting worse instead of better. Either the virus was showing up in different ways or a whole new health problem had taken hold on top of it.

The night before a very important doctor's appointment, you came to me in a crystal clear dream and told me exactly what was going on. Like I said, maybe this kind of thing happens to other people, but it definitely doesn't happen to me, and I was so stunned by it that I described every detail of it to my daughter the next morning before she left for her appointment.

My daughter told the nurse who administered all her tests that day that Sylvia Browne had already explained what was wrong. The nurse not only thought that was great, but when she came back with the test results she announced, "Sylvia was right."

What you said to me in the dream was that there was no need to worry, my daughter was going to be fine, she was just going to have a baby.

Because of my daughter's virus, this is a complicated pregnancy requiring lots of appointments and medications to protect both her and the baby. We're naturally very concerned, so any time you want to come visit again while I sleep and fill me in on anything else we need to know, you're more than welcome.

For now, just a thank you for something you might not even be aware of.

from Erin

I went to a lecture of Sylvia's during which she led a healing meditation for the entire audience. I'd found a lump under my arm three weeks earlier that I was frightened about to the point where I kept putting off making a doctor's appointment because I was afraid of what he'd tell me.

The morning after the healing meditation I woke up and the lump under my arm was completely gone! I was so astonished at this miraculous development that I immediately called Sylvia's office and left the news on their voice mail.

I couldn't have been more surprised when a member of Sylvia's staff returned my call a few hours later, which I hadn't even asked them to do. It seems that although Sylvia was very happy to hear about the lump under my arm disappearing, she still wanted me to see my doctor. Not that anything was seriously wrong, but she said I'm prone to developing lumps in my breast and my doctor and I need to be diligent about keeping an eye on them on a regular basis.

I was so impressed, for two reasons. One is that she was exactly right, I am prone to lumps in my breast, that always turn out to be harmless calcium deposits, and I'm so used to them that I've become much too careless about regular check-ups. It would only take one lump that's *not* a calcium deposit to get me in serious trouble, so what a stupid thing to be careless about and take for granted.

The other thing I was impressed with is that instead of just patting herself on the back for how successful her meditation was and going on with her day, Sylvia was responsible enough to recommend a trip to the doctor anyway. I felt so cared for, and cared about after that phone call.

I did make a doctor's appointment for the following week, and all is well, despite a few new very small calcium deposits in my left breast. I've now committed to getting a mammogram every six months instead of every year (or two—like I said, I've been careless), and my doctor adds his thanks to Sylvia as well for inspiring the extra precaution.

from Sandra Jane

I read Sylvia's book *The Other Side and Back* at a time when I'd been suffering for months with severe insomnia. My doctor was ready and willing to prescribe sleeping pills, but a friend of mine became addicted to those and told me the addiction was almost worse than the insomnia. I was really losing my mind and physical stamina from lack of sleep and afraid I might lose my job as a vet tech (veterinary technician) if I didn't do something and do it fast.

There was a "mental exercise" in *The Other Side and Back* called "The Lab." It was also a meditation, but Sylvia offered "mental exercise" for people like me whose eyes glaze over at the mention of the word "meditation." According to her Spirit Guide, if you could visualize, you could do The Lab, and if you'd practice The Lab for a few minutes every day you could heal yourself of whatever ailed you.

Well, like I said, I don't know the first thing about meditation, but I understand exercise, and everybody knows how to visualize. I didn't want to jinx it by telling anyone I was doing it, but I started practicing The Lab one (sleepless) Sunday night in late January. I admit that sometimes I rushed through it in less than five minutes, and sometimes I took my time and spent maybe fifteen minutes on it. I made myself do it every night, which makes it sound like a chore, and that's not really the case. I can honestly say I liked it, and I decided early on that even if it never cured my insomnia, at least it was relaxing and made me feel like I was doing something about it instead of nothing, or taking pills.

By the end of March I was averaging 7–8 hours of sleep a night and feeling better than I felt when I was twenty. (I'm 61.) The Lab works. It's that simple. And now that it's a habit, and an enjoyable one, I don't intend to give it up, to keep myself as healthy as I am now. This is one addiction I'll never complain about.

Thanks, Sylvia! Thanks, Francine!

from Jess

That letter from Jess is one of literally hundreds I've received about the healing success of The Lab. In some cases I don't mind a bit referring you to others of my books for helpful information. But with my publisher's kind permission, rather than insist you buy *The Other Side and Back* to experience The Lab for yourself, I'll repeat it here, with my blessings and prayers for the greatest health you've enjoyed in longer than you can remember.

The Lab

In your mind, create a rectangular room, of whatever size feels ideal and comfortable to you. Leave the far wall open, but color the three remaining walls a soft, calming green.

To the walls, add large windows that allow you a beautiful view of water, clear blue and serene, to lend power to the healing that's about to bless you.

In the center of this room, create a table, large enough for you to lie on, with the most exquisite carvings and designs you can imagine.

Piece by piece, detail by detail, decorate your room with your vision of the furniture, artwork, plants, candles, flowers and other décor you love most. Take your time. Linger over and appreciate every beautiful item. The more personal your room becomes, the more "yours" you make it, the more real it will feel to you and the more you'll find yourself looking forward to returning to it. Let it be perfect, in no one else's definition of perfection but your own.

Turn to the far wall you left open, and, in its center, in midair, suspend a breathtaking stained glass window. Study every inch, every tiny line and curve of its magnificent design as you create it, and let its colors be the most brilliant blues, golds, greens and purples you've ever seen.

In the center of your exquisite stained glass window, place a beautiful depiction of whatever spiritual symbol touches your soul at its deepest and most resonant.

Now slowly move through this beautiful Lab you've created, appreciating every perfect detail you've blessed it with, until you've arrived in front of the stained glass window, which has suddenly become illuminated from behind, so that you can feel the warmth of its soft rainbow glow.

As you stand there, the brilliant colors of the window begin to beam out to you one by one, penetrating your mind and your body, entering deep inside you so that you can feel each ray of your own sacred prism cleansing your soul.

Blue—tranquility and heightened awareness fill your body . . . your heart . . . your spirit . . .

Gold—you embrace your divine dignity, the genetic legacy of your Father, Mother and Creator, who loved you so much that after filling the universe with stars and giving life to the earth from the warm sun, He refused to rest until He created you . . .

Green—a laser of healing reaches to your core, empowering, exhilarating . . . your intellect sharpens . . .

Purple—the color of royalty, your birthright as God's child . . . your spirituality grows deeper, more sacred, more humble, more grateful, more generous, nurtured and nurturing . . . your spirit soars . . .

You're an open, hungry vessel now as you ask the white light of the Holy Spirit to surround and heal you. Feel its pure white, loving glow bathe you in peace, stability, power, control . . .

The top of your head . . .

Each contour of your face . . .

Your neck and shoulders, releasing the tightness and the tension . . .

That beautiful light working its way down your chest, your spine, each bone, each muscle, letting go of every pain, every burden, every sorrow, every worry . . .

Your waist, your abdomen, calming, cleansing, purifying . . .

Slowly down your legs, all strain and tightness leave them, so relaxed they can barely support you . . .

Your feet, cooling, soothing, refreshing . . .

Slowly, effortlessly, you almost glide to the beautiful table you created. The white light of God's love moves with you, stays wrapped around you, an exquisite glowing cloak flowing soft as the finest silk over your body as you lie down on the table.

Its surface is smooth, strong and firm, refreshingly cool to your touch, perfect support. You're safe. You're protected. All fear, all anxiety, all of life's burdens leave you, released and resolved into your perfect aura of God's light.

Wordlessly, you beckon the Other Side to come to you. They've been watching, adoring you, eager to join you in your perfect room. They arrive in an instant and gather around your table . . .

Your Spirit Guide . . .

All your Angels . . .

Your departed loved ones . . .

And with them, the great teachers, doctors and healers from the Other Side, all there to care for you, God's child . . .

Surrounded by perfect health, perfect wisdom, perfect acceptance, and the sacred love of the Angels themselves, your mind clears, relieved of its stress and burdens as these loving spirits lift them from you one by one and absorb them forever.

All sadness, all grief, all depression, all emotional chaos unravel—an angry, churning sea of unspoken pain calmed to clear, quiet water by the Hands of God's Healers, sent by your Father, who's there in every healing breath and every beat of your healthy heart.

Your Father's sacred emissaries move closer now, reaching out. You feel their peace. Their Hands wait above your body, and you silently ask them for the full force of their healing power on the sources of your greatest discomfort and distress. They smile, understanding, promising, loving you.

You close your eyes and feel the cool, sure, skillful touch of those divine Hands, hard at work with blessed certainty, soothing, calming, dissolving your pain forever. You surrender, one with your Creator, one with these Healers, all doubt gone, every cell releasing its memories of illness and trauma and grief and betrayal and loneliness, restored to that moment when it was at its healthiest and most vital.

Healed and at peace while the Hands continue, you fall deeply asleep. A minute, an hour, a day . . . time doesn't matter, time doesn't exist. You're content, knowing you'll awake refreshed and energized, with a renewed sense of well-being, life more manageable, the flame of joy reignited in the core of your soul, nothing to fear any longer because there's nothing you and your Father can't handle together.

You are His child. You are blessed. You are sacred.

It's a new day. A new life.

Thank God.

Chapter 10

HEALINGS

Healings and miracles come from God, and whatever personal name you have for the Christ Consciousness.

They don't come from me, or from anyone else on earth. And anyone who claims the ability to promise them is a fraud.

When the power to heal comes *through* any of us, and miracles happen, it's a sacred honor for us to receive or to witness, but never, ever to take credit for. That I've had that sacred honor more than once over all these years fills me with more gratitude, and more humility, than I can possibly express.

The fact that God is the only true Source of healings and miracles is misinterpreted so often, and I think the real reason for that is how hard it is for us to remember that this earth we cling to in our fear of dying is not our Home at all. The Other Side is Home. We're just here on brief voluntary trips to school for more growth in the eternal journeys of our souls. Death, our means of going Home, is never God's punishment, it's His reward, for reasons that always make perfect sense everywhere but here. When you pray to the core of your spirit that a loved one not die, and it seemingly doesn't work, it doesn't mean that God denied your prayers, that your prayers weren't heard or that you failed in any way. All our prayers for survival are heard, and they're all granted, in the universal, infinite context of eternity. It's hard to accept that the survival we pray for doesn't always result in our loved one staying with us on earth, but that's our innate and very human selfishness talking, it's not God being cruel and saying no.

In a way, healings and miracles are intensely personal phenomena between their recipients and God—almost none of our business, oddly, although we other "cast members" can certainly contribute. Oversimplifying it to a fault, there are five elements that are essential to every healing:

- God, without whom nothing exists.
- Prayer, in whatever form it takes—any open communication between us and God is prayer, after all.
- Belief—and that word transcends rhetoric and dogma, piercing straight to the divine spirit within us and simply acknowledging its genetic connection to its Creator.
- Affirmation, which is simply the conscious or unconscious awareness that the miracle of healing is possible, like all things, through God, if that possibility will serve the greatest purpose.
- The Exit Points we each compose into our charts before we come here, the five options we and God agree on about those times when, for reasons we and He understand perfectly, we'll choose to go Home again. (You'll find a full explanation of Exit Points in the discussion of charts in Chapter 3.)

Knowing that all those factors have to be in perfect synch for a healing to occur, how can we possibly blame God, or ourselves, when it doesn't happen? And how can we be in anything short of awe when it does?

I was on the receiving end of a miracle healing in my life, and I remember every moment of it, so I'm in the position to give a firsthand account of exactly what went on. I've told this story in other books, but it illustrates the point so well that I can't resist repeating a brief version of it here.

I was forty-three, and I'd just had major surgery. Thanks to an unanticipated complication with the anesthesia, I physiologically died—literally flatlined—shortly after I was returned to my hospital bed. I'm always conscious of God's presence, and my belief in Him has never been in short supply, so the first two elements of a healing were already in place. My bed was also surrounded by loving, God-centered family and friends whose prayers for my survival were more than covering the third necessary element.

I have perfect memories of the tunnel rising at an angle from the etheric substance of my body, and of finding myself moving through the tunnel in blissful, joyful awareness of where I was going. I remember that I'd never felt more alive, more loved and more at peace. I remember God's divine white light waiting for me at the end of the tunnel—not a myth at all, I promise you—and my beloved grandma Ada stepping forward through the light to welcome me.

And then, clear as a bell, I heard the voice of a woman beside my hospital bed, saying, "Sylvia, please, you can't leave, you're so needed." Element #4—the affirmation, the reminder that I still had the option of returning to my body, and a purpose for doing it if I chose to.

Which brought me to the fifth element, the Exit Point. This was the third Exit Point I'd experienced in my life and by far the clearest, and for a split second I was aware with crystal clarity that it was up to God and me, and no one else, whether I would keep going into that glorious light of the Other Side or postpone my Homecoming to finish what I'd come to earth to accomplish in the first place.

Next thing I knew I was slamming back into my body on that hospital bed, and I could hear cries of joy around me as my heart monitor blipped back to life. To be honest, I was depressed about it for days afterward, but I can't for a moment claim to regret it.

All of which is to illustrate that when I tell you death is not God's punishment or cruelty but is actually His most thrilling, sacred embrace, and when I assure you that in the end a miracle healing is a personal decision between God and the one spirit facing the choice, I'm not just telling you what I believe, I'm telling you what I *know*.

I have the rare benefit of complete recollection of every step of my healing. Not all the subjects of the stories you're about to read have that same luxury, but that makes them no less powerful and no less affirming of God's grace among us.

I became a huge fan of Sylvia Browne when my dear father died and her books brought me so much comfort. I had never heard her speak in person before, so I was very excited when a friend invited me to see her at the Palladium in Los Angeles where I live. It was a standing-room-only crowd, and you could feel the electricity in the air when Sylvia made us laugh and cry and think for a magical two hours.

At one point she took us through a healing meditation. I remember thinking when it first started how quiet three thousand people can get when they're focused on a voice they trust as much as we all trusted her. Then I became "lost" in the meditation, even though I've never been good at meditating on my own because I'm too easily distracted and it's hard for my mind to slow down.

It was a whole separate issue for me that for the previous month I'd been suffering with terrible neck pain. It was keeping me awake nights and interfering with my career and my activities with my son. I should add that I'm a dentist, and my husband is a doctor. Between the two of us, we have excellent connections in the medical community in Los Angeles, and I saw several specialists and had any number of tests to find out what was causing this severe pain and how to get rid of it. After a month of the best medical attention anyone could ask for, I still had no answers.

When Sylvia's meditation ended that night, I was aware that my pain had subsided and I felt unexpected significant relief. The relief lasted through the rest of the evening, and I appreciated it so much but fully expected the pain to return during the night or certainly the next morning when I was facing a long, full day of patients.

It's been six weeks, and the pain hasn't been back once, not even for a minute or two. I didn't attend Sylvia's lecture that night for a healing, but I got one through her meditation, a healing none of my husband's and my colleagues in the medical profession could accomplish. Thank you, God, for sending your healing words and energy my way and delivering them through such an extraordinary messenger.

from Ruby

Dear Sylvia,

I just had to thank you for what I consider to be a true healing. I'm 25 years old, and I've been suffering from Irritable Bowel Syndrome since I was 12. In fact, I was ranked in the top fifth percentile of sufferers of this syndrome in the U.S. I've lost track of the number of specialists I've been to, and none of them could help me.

Last spring I read your *Book of Dreams*. There was a paragraph that read:

> *For thirty consecutive days, I want you to say the following, in my words or your own, in the quiet moments before you fall asleep: "Dearest God, in these hours while my conscious mind and my body are at rest, please bless my dreams and my astral travels with affirmations of health, strength, and well-being, infuse every cell of this body I inhabit with a surge of Thy loving, compassionate healing, and help me*

*wake with the certainty that as I slept, I was restored and re-
newed by Your divine grace."*

Thirty days didn't sound like a commitment I couldn't keep,
and I certainly had nothing to lose, so I said the prayer, substi-
tuting a few of my own words, and counted the days to make
sure I did thirty in a row.

I have not had an Irritable Bowel Syndrome attack in four
months, the longest I've gone without one since I was 12 years
old. Your simple words of advice have changed my life.

from Dru

I attended a lecture of Sylvia's at Chabot College. During
the lecture she took the large audience through a healing meditation. I've never been a big believer in healings, and I'd never
meditated before or even been curious about it, so I just went
through the motions as directed, eager to get that part over
with so Sylvia could get on with the lecture I was thoroughly
enjoying.

For the previous five years I'd been suffering from a chronic
tightness in my entire left side, centering in the shoulder and
neck area. Doctors couldn't seem to find the cause of it, and
physical therapy, exercise and massages weren't providing me
any relief. I even tried prescribed medications from my doctor
for awhile, but when I took enough to ease the tightness I had
trouble concentrating and finding the energy to keep up with
my accounting job, so I gave up on those.

The morning after seeing Sylvia, about 80% of the tightness
seemed to have disappeared. And now, a week after seeing her,
even more has disappeared, and my energy is back. That healing
meditation was a miracle as far as I'm concerned.

from Kathy

Dear Sylvia,

I sent my friend Steve to you after watching him suffer for many years with a constant, painful ringing in his ears. Doctors weren't able to help him at all. But after just one hypnosis session with you, the ringing has stopped! It may not seem like a miracle to you, but it certainly is to us.

from Nina

Dear Sylvia,

I'm blessed with a wonderful husband and a young son I cherish. But my life in general has not been easy. I grew up abused by a family member and then began abusing myself, primarily with alcohol and an eating disorder, when I reached my late teens. I began receiving treatment for both, and the depression that went with them, with only limited success. And then, shortly after my son was born, I was diagnosed with multiple sclerosis.

I'd lost my health, all sense of self-worth and, most horribly, my faith in God.

While on a summer vacation I happened across your book *Life on the Other Side*. I wasn't one bit prepared for the impact this book had on me. Reading about the beautiful, productive lives we live at Home was inspiring enough. But somehow, learning that I composed my own life chart for this time on earth, and that it is all planned out for me, was a genuine miracle. My alcoholism and eating disorder are gone. Not forced away, not battles I struggle each day to win. They have just left me. I'm sure my Spirit Guide has been an enormous support as well, and someday I hope to find out if it's a he or a she, and a proper name. But not knowing those details doesn't prevent me from communicating with him/her and saying thank you with every breath.

And as if these victories aren't quite enough, *Life on the Other Side* restored my faith in God.

I look forward to the cure for MS, although here in England many medicines are not available due to the cost.

Sylvia, I thank you from the very depths of my heart, body and soul. I pray my body can heal from the abuse and allow me a long life with which to serve God.

from Maryanne

My dear Sylvia,

I e-mailed you more than a year ago, asking to be added to your prayer chain list. It was the morning after I was diagnosed with ALS (Lou Gehrig's Disease). According to my doctors, my prognosis was that I had eighteen months left to live at the very most.

According to God, with the power of your prayer chain as my petition, I'm beating those odds, and then some.

In the past year this illness has taken my voice and made swallowing difficult. It has affected the lateral movement of my left index finger and thumb. Those were the first signs, over a year ago, that something was wrong.

But!—there has been no progression of the illness to other parts of my body. It has been contained to its original locations, which any doctor will tell you is a miracle.

I don't need any confirmation that I have God and your prayer chain to thank. I am my own joyful confirmation, every morning when I open my eyes and every night when I close them again after another productive day in God's service.

from Traci

Dearest Sylvia and All,

I'm writing to report a miracle that you made possible.

My brother has had a rough time in his life. A sweet soul

who wouldn't hurt a living thing, except himself, I'm afraid. One of those people who seemed to have a cloud of bad luck hanging over his head, and nobody could accuse him of not trying, he would just end up with something happening that was completely unfair and wouldn't have happened to anyone else. He was 17 when our parents were killed in a car accident, and that seemed to finish him off. He stopped trying, and he got swept up in a bad group of people who found out that he and I had inherited some money from our parents and were also getting a wrongful death settlement. He disappeared for seven months, and the next time I saw him he was addicted to crack cocaine. He admitted it to me. He wasn't proud of it, but he wasn't sad about it either. He just didn't care.

By the time he was 20 he was broke and on the streets. I'd done a lot of research and joined a support group, so I knew better than to give him money or enable him in any way. I tried to be a good listener for him for a while, but half the time he didn't make sense and the other half he was lying and feeding me "druggie stories." I finally told him he had two choices: go to rehab, or stay out of my life. We must have had ten major fights about rehab and how he wasn't interested and he had a right to live his life however he wanted and I had no right to try to control him, I was supposed to love him unconditionally, blah, blah.

After our last fight, when he punched a hole in my wall before he ran out the door, I saw clearly that I was getting nowhere and that he was going to die unless someone, or Someone, got through to him.

I called at 3:30 A.M. and left his name on your Prayer Chain hotline. I knew I didn't have to say what the problem was, but I did. I guess I wanted to warn you all that this one wasn't going to be easy.

Sylvia, a miracle happened. He wasn't magically cured, but less than 24 hours later he showed up on my doorstep and asked if I would help him get into rehab, that night if possible, because he didn't want to live like that anymore and he didn't want to die. Thanks to the support group, I knew what to do, and he was checked into in-patient rehab by the next afternoon.

That was almost four months ago. He's still there, and he's doing GREAT! Oh, Sylvia, you and all those people who prayed for him were like a safety net who caught him just in time before he hit the ground in a free-fall. You saved a good man, too. He'll "pay it back" in a hundred ways.

Thank you, thank you, thank you.

from Sonny

My sister was near death with encephalitis on a Monday. I put in two urgent calls to your Prayer Chain hotline. The doctors and nurses who said that all we could do was wait it out saw with their own eyes that she went from total delirium on Monday to complete lucidity and a 95% overall improvement by Wednesday afternoon.

Please find my information enclosed and my request to become a part of your Prayer Chain. Now that I've received, it seems like the best way to say thank you is to give, and it would be a joy to become one more "link" in a chain of God's power in action.

from Warren

Dear Sylvia,

When you called me for my phone reading a few years ago, I was a newlywed who'd just found out I needed a heart transplant. You told me you were going to have your massive prayer chain pray for me, and it moves me to tears to this day when I think of it or tell people about the miracle you and God made happen.

I never got my heart transplant. It turned out I didn't need it. My same heart, the one I was born with, is back to 90% normal. One person in every 100,000 recovers from my situation without a transplant. And I am that "one." Lifted to that position by people so kind and loving that they'll take time out of their own busy lives to pray for a stranger. I am in their debt, and yours.

from Ariella

Dear Ms. Browne,

I run the cancer support group in my community, and I wanted to share a success story that was due to your book *The Other Side and Back.*

I'm a family physician who helps patients deal with mind/body/spirit issues. I've done a lot of work with Hospice and lecture annually at a spiritual healing conference. I've written two books on mental health, primarily dealing with individuals suffering from the borderline personality disorder (BPD). I see borderlines from 35 states and 11 countries. I treat them as human beings who matter, explain their symptoms and help them spiritually. In order to have a great life, they have to have a spiritual belief that gives them hope and a reason to let go of past behaviors.

In his book *Where God Lives,* Dr. Melvin Morse describes the right Sylvian fissure of the brain as being where God and spirit attaches to us. The BPD is a disorder where a seizure temporarily cuts them off from God and spirit.

Last fall a woman joined our cancer support group. She'd just been told of her third ovarian cancer recurrence and was getting quite depressed. I explained that depression was a physical problem, not a weakness, and showed her fascinating pictures of the brain both depressed and recovered. An anti-depressant helped her enormously to cope with her poor prognosis and to be receptive to new ideas.

Her oncologist strongly recommended chemotherapy, but she insisted on waiting so that she wouldn't be debilitated through the holidays. At a subsequent support group meeting, we talked about how the near death experience can help us find peace within ourselves and take charge of our lives. I recommended she read *The Other Side and Back.*

Her heart was moved by your book. She did the white light and green light imagery diligently. I'm writing this letter in mid-February, and at our support group meeting last week she looked absolutely radiant. It seems her latest tests showed that her cancer was completely gone—and might I add, she never had the chemotherapy.

from Dr. L. H.

You'll read more about children and their inherent psychic natures in the "Our Loved Ones on Earth" chapter. But for now, we'll focus on what often feels like the ultimate miracle—the healing of children.

Just as the Other Side is still fresh in children's memories when they arrive here—and they'll refer to it and describe parts of it if you'll listen closely—their past lives are still very accessible to their conscious minds too. We've all heard of prodigies, born to parents who can't read a note of music, who are composing complicated sonatas at the age of five, and the occasional first-grader who's working calculus problems while his classmates are just being introduced to adding and subtracting. Does it really make sense to you that those children are blank slates when they're born, and those extraordinary abilities simply happen, by some "fluke of nature" or something? (Don't you love how some "experts" would rather use the word "fluke" than insist on getting to the bottom of a phenomenon they can't scientifically explain?) Or, for more ordinary examples, I'm sure you've known children who, from the time they were born, have been breathlessly fascinated with trains, or astronomy, or horses, or the Civil War, or the *Titanic,* or airplanes, with no cues from anyone or anything around them. (More "flukes," I guess.) And then there are the fears children come in with, of anything from dark water to heights to confined spaces to lightning storms, whether or not they've ever been exposed to those things in this life-time or not. Again, what could be more logical than that those fears have simply been carried over from some past life that's as current and relevant to a child as yesterday is to us?

We discussed cell memory at length in the chapter on health, so I'll simply remind you here that it's all the accumulated knowledge our spirit minds possess, infused into and acted on by every cell of our bodies. And children, with their past lives so hard for them to separate from this new life they've just entered, are more susceptible to the neg-ative affects of cell memory than we adults are.

David was only five years old when I answered an urgent request from his parents to visit him in his hospital room. He was dying of leukemia, too weak to move or speak as he lay there attached to a web of tubes. His doctors didn't believe he'd see his sixth birthday.

Never forget that no matter how ill, weak or diminished the physi-cal body and brain might be, the spirit mind in each of us is eternally alive and well. David's body couldn't talk to me as I stood beside his bed, but his spirit came through loud and clear and gave me the key to the cell memory that was threatening to take him.

I leaned close to him and began working on that cell memory, knowing that just as the spirit of a seemingly unconscious person can speak, it can also hear.

"David, listen to me, what's happening to you now isn't meant for this lifetime. It's from another life, in another time, in another place, when you died of blood poisoning. You remember it, I know you do, and you think that because you're in a body again, your blood must still be poisoned. That's not true. It's in the past, it's over, you've already been there, done that and moved on. You've been Home since then, to be with God on the Other Side, and you've come here in a brand-new body that's clean and pure and whole, free of poison, ready to live a long, healthy lifetime. Let this blood poisoning, and anything else you've brought over from a past life that can harm you, be resolved and absorbed into the white light of the Holy Spirit so that it can never hurt you again."

I prayed, I surrounded him with God's glorious cleansing white light and the green light of healing, and most of all, I assured him over and over again that he'd already died from what was killing him and he didn't have to do it again.

He was five years old. Not expected to see six. David still stops by to say hello from time to time when he's traveling to and from college for the holidays and summer vacation. He's a healthy, happy, handsome twenty-year-old young man with a brilliant future ahead of him. I didn't heal him. His own spirit mind did, with God's help, by hearing and acting on the truth about cell memories of a past life that had no place in the life he's living now.

As all three of my children slept this afternoon I was reread-ing Sylvia's book *The Other Side and Back* and came across the discussion regarding the Prayer Chain. It reminded me to write an overdue letter of thanks.

My six-month-old daughter Isabelle was born with a duplex left kidney—two tubes run from her kidney to her bladder and the secondary tube is 70% blocked. She'll be on a daily-prescribed antibiotic until she's three years old. A tummy ache for Isabelle might mean a fatal infection, and there is no such thing for her as a "slight" fever.

Last Thanksgiving at 1:00 A.M. Isabelle developed a fever. By 4:00 A.M. it was rising at an alarming rate, and we rushed her to the hospital. They were sure she had a bladder infection, but only a catheter test would provide a sample pure enough to specify the antibiotic she needed. Her fever rose and fell and rose and fell as we rushed her downtown to the children's hospital for the catheter test, which was its own nightmare.

That night when we finally got home I rocked an exhausted Isabelle and cried and prayed my heart out to Father God, Mother God, the Archangels, the Principalities, Isabelle's Spirit Guide, my Spirit Guide—anyone and everyone I could think of. And once she was sound asleep in her crib, I went straight to the computer and put Isabelle's name on the Prayer Chain on Sylvia's website.

The next morning by 10:00 A.M. her fever was gone. It was after that that the hospital called with the test results and a prescription for an antibiotic for the rare strain of infection she'd somehow contracted. Her doctor was and is still mystified about how Isabelle went from a raging, persistent fever to no fever at all prior to receiving the medication she needed.

I know it was the Prayer Chain that saved her life. I'm certain my prayers were heard, but the Prayer Chain lent them the weight that I alone couldn't give them. I've been fastidious with both my prayers and Isabelle's antibiotics ever since, and she's never been rushed to the hospital again.

Please feel free to share this "thank you letter" with anyone who questions the validity of the Prayer Chain.

from Georgia

Dear Sylvia,

I've read many of your books, and among the many things I learned was the power of praying to Azna, the Mother God. Then I had the opportunity to find it out first hand.

My child is a gifted dancer and takes ballet classes several times a week. One morning she got out of bed complaining of pain in the back of her right ankle, and it progressed to the point where she couldn't put any weight on her right foot, or bend her ankle at all.

The doctor examined her and x-rayed her and told us she had Achilles tendonitis. He said it would take two to four weeks to heal, and in the meantime she was to eliminate all physical activity. She was heartbroken at the idea of missing her ballet classes for a day, let alone a month, and I was heartbroken for her.

As soon as we got home from the doctor I put my daughter to bed and then immediately went to my room and prayed and prayed to Azna for a healing, not really knowing what else to do.

I know how unbelievable this sounds, but I witnessed it, and I'll swear to it—an hour later my child was completely back to normal, walking fine and her pain was gone. Not only was it gone, but it never came back.

There's no question we were blessed with a miracle from Mother God, and I thank you, Sylvia, for introducing me to Her and making this miracle possible.

from Samantha

I attended a healing service of Sylvia's at a time when I was in deep despair over my 7-year-old granddaughter Laurie. The Stanford University Eye Clinic had diagnosed her with toxoplasmosis, a parasite that destroys the back of the eye. It had caused a large lesion across the pupil of her left eye, to the point where that eye had no forward vision and only slight peripheral vision, which was diminishing. Another lesion was starting in her right eye. The best her doctors were hoping for was to stop the progression of the parasite—they'd already broken the news that improvement was not something we could look forward to or hope for.

Sylvia's healing service offered prayers and comfort and an opportunity to put my granddaughter on the "healing board," where she would continue to be included in prayers from loving strangers all over the world in the weeks ahead. I can't honestly say I was confident that it would do any good after so much discouraging news from the doctors, but I can say that I believe strongly in the power of God.

At Laurie's next appointment a few weeks later, her doctors were astonished to find that the lesions were actually shrinking. The vision in her left eye had gone from a dismal 20/200 to a miraculous 20/100. They had no explanation for it. I did. It really was a miracle, God saying "yes" to all those united voices asking Him to help heal a beautiful little 7-year-old girl.

from Joyce

Dear Ms. Browne,

You may not remember my writing to you about my son Nick, but I still have to send an added note to thank you from the bottom of my heart. Nick had brain surgery just over a month ago, and he's doing better than his doctors ever imagined, to the point where they're calling him "their little miracle." I know in my heart it's because of all those wonderful, generous strangers who prayed for him. He has a long, healthy life ahead of him thanks to all of you, and mostly to God, of course, and you'll never know how much you've helped me and my family with our lives and given us hope.

from Johnnie

My dearest Sylvia,

I just wanted to update you on my condition since you added my name to your Prayer Chain.

I'm Ty, diagnosed with testicular cancer. I was out of my mind with fear when I got the diagnosis, and sometime during my panic I thought to grab the phone and ask for the help of your Prayer Chain. That was last Monday.

Yesterday, a week and a day later, my doctor did further blood tests, and every one of them came back showing no cancer markers anywhere in my system!

Just to make sure, my radiologist is going to do a CAT scan, but it really looks like God heard your amazing group loud and clear. I'll let you know, you can be sure of that!

from Ty

To appreciate this next story, you need to be introduced to Raheim. Raheim is a powerful, highly advanced spirit, my Spirit Guide Francine's good friend on the Other Side. He was a great teacher and a Sikh in his last incarnation, and he occasionally channels through me for special trance sessions, lectures and services at my church, Novus Spiritus. Raheim is not a second Spirit Guide of mine, or the constant companion and adviser Francine is. He simply visits from time to time, while I step aside as I do when I channel Francine, to share his wisdom and other profound, extraordinary gifts from Home.

And so one night Raheim was the "guest lecturer" at my church, which obviously means I was "absent." Fortunately, a woman named Regine was there, and her letter tells the story:

I brought my five-year-old daughter Maggie to a trance session with Raheim in the hope of a miracle after Maggie was diagnosed with cancer. Raheim focused exclusively on Maggie for several minutes, holding her and praying. And we got our miracle—at Maggie's next doctor's appointment after that evening with Raheim, her doctors could find no signs of cancer in her at all.

What was almost as awesome to me as that true miracle was the fact that Maggie told me and her doctors that she was healed by a "man," that she absolutely saw a "man" healing her, even though of course it was Sylvia's physical body that was holding her. I've never corrected her, and I never will. She knows what she saw, and it's not the first time that her "vision" has been a lot sharper and clearer than mine.

I occasionally schedule evenings at one of my churches to trance Francine. She teaches her audiences about life on the Other Side, about spiritual and philosophical issues far deeper than I can offer, and about any subjects that might come up as the audience members ask her questions. As I've said, I have to temporarily vacate my body in order for Francine to use it to communicate easily, always with my permission, so unless I read a transcript or hear a tape of the evening afterward, I have no clue what goes on during an evening with Francine.

And so I have to rely on fifty or sixty eyewitness accounts and a few amateur audiotapes to tell this story of healing, of the divine, miraculous power of Home.

Our small church was completely filled that night. Francine was in the middle of a lecture when she noticed and focused on a woman who was seated near the front of the room, holding a very pale, heartbreakingly thin little girl who looked to be about three years old.

Francine stopped what she was saying, looked into the woman's eyes and said, "Bring her here."

The woman began to cry as she carried the fragile child to Francine. "This is my daughter Anna," she explained. "She's only three, Francine, and she's dying of bone cancer. The chemotherapy isn't helping. The doctors say she maybe has six more months. I'm begging you, if there's something you can do, please help my child."

No matter what happens to be the issue at hand, Francine's voice never changes from a slow, very deliberate, completely emotionless monotone. "Lay her across me," she said without moving from her chair. "I will let my energy pass to her."

The woman gently placed the child in Francine's lap and held her there. Francine closed her eyes, and her lips were moving, although no one but Anna could hear what she was saying. After several minutes Francine looked at the mother again and simply said, "You can take her now."

Within a week Anna started showing signs of improvement. Within a month her doctors were mystified, and in awe, when they were unable to find a trace of cancer in her body.

Anna, who was given six months to live at the age of three, is now a thriving twelve-year-old. She still sends cards and photos from time to time, to Francine in care of me.

A WORD ABOUT THE PRAYER CHAIN

As you read again and again in this chapter, there's awesome force to be found in a choir of voices asking God in unison for His compassionate healing power. If you'd like to be a part of our Prayer Chain, or need our services, you'll find all the information you need online on my websites, *www.sylvia.org* and *www.novus.org*.

Basically, the way it works is that every morning at 6:00 A.M. (Pacific time), my staff collects messages from my designated twenty-four-hour voice mail line and from my website. The messages include the names of people all around the world who need to be included in that morning's prayers. We never ask the details of anyone's specific problems, nor is it necessary to share such personal information unless you want to.

The names are immediately passed along to the ministers of my nondenominational church, Novus Spiritus. Each of my ministers passes the names to fifty members of the Prayer Chain, each of whom passes them to fifty more, and so on. At the same time, the list is being distributed through the cyberministry on my website.

And then, at the triple Trinity (the Trinity of the Father, the Son and the Holy Spirit, multiplied by three) hour, of 9:00 A.M. (Pacific time), no matter where any of us Prayer Chain members are around the world, we pray for each and every name on the list:

Dear God,
in the mind, body or soul, wherever their pain resides,
may it be released with Thy help
into the healing white light
of the Holy Spirit.
Amen.

Chapter 11

CRIMES AND MISSING PERSONS

I gave a speech one night many years ago to a gathering of homicide detectives in northern California. I'm proud to say I'd developed a reputation for being discreet, accurate and generous in donating my time to help solve crimes that were defying what we'll politely call "more conventional" investigative tools. (In other words, when all else failed in an investigation and desperation set in, the police and sheriff's departments would grit their teeth and put in a call to that weirdo psychic Sylvia Browne woman on the unlikely chance I might be helpful. And after all, I came free of charge and never embarrassed them by publicizing my involvement, so what did they have to lose?) The speech went well, my plainclothes audience was far more respectful than I'd dared to expect, and my phone was ringing off the hook when I arrived home that night.

"I really appreciated your presentation this evening," the caller said after introducing himself, "and I'm wondering if you'd be willing to help us with the Ski Mask Rapist case."

There was no way I was going to turn down that request. The Ski Mask Rapist was one of the most notorious unsolved cases in the San

Francisco area at the time. During the previous three years, he'd brutally raped at least twenty-six woman. He never left fingerprints, he used a variety of untraceable cars, and he struck everywhere from school playgrounds to office buildings to, incredibly, a church confessional. His victims ranged in age from sixteen to eighty-three, making it impossible to anticipate where and whom he might strike next. He did have several trademarks, though: he always wore a blue ski mask, his attacks always involved a gun, he always bound his victims before sexually assaulting them, and he never left without demanding money, jewelry and ATM cards. The Bay Area was understandably terrorized, and law enforcement was understandably beyond frustrated by the lack of evidence or a reliable description of the suspect. Remember, this was in the days before DNA, so the semen samples collected from the victims did nothing more than establish that a rape had taken place and the consistent blood type of the rapist to help tie the cases together. The police wanted him off the streets and in prison—or, better yet, under it—and so did I.

I told the caller, a detective with the Los Altos Police Department, to count me in, by all means, and we sat down together the next day. We were both eager to get started, and I'm not even sure we bothered to formally introduce ourselves before he asked, "What can you tell me about this guy?"

The rapist came into sharp, instant focus in my mind. "He's Caucasian, but his features have a subtle African American hint to them. He's husky, he has dark hair, and I'm not getting his full name, but his last name starts with S." Another piece of information came flooding in, and I wanted to get it said before I talked myself out of saying something so preposterous out loud. So I interrupted the description with "I know it sounds insane to use the words 'rapist' and 'gentleman' in the same sentence, but as vicious as these crimes are, he's almost polite to his victims when he's finished brutalizing and robbing them."

The detective looked up from the notes he was taking. "We've withheld that from the press, but you're right," he said. "Victim after victim has told us that he's apologetic, even when he's threatening to kill them. 'I've killed before and I can kill again, but I'm really sorry about this kind of thing.'" I definitely had his attention, and he flipped to a fresh blank page in his notepad. "Anything else?"

"He works for the city," I told him.

"How? In what capacity?"

"Something to do with streets, actually *under* the streets. And there are lines involved with it somehow. He does something for the city having to do with lines under the streets." I was stumped. So was the detective, but he wrote it down anyway.

Then something else hit me, something much more specific. "Redwood City," I said. "He's planning a rape in Redwood City. You need to focus there and double up on your resources, because that's what he's got in mind, but thank God, you'll catch him in Redwood City before he has a chance to pull it off."

Twenty-six-year-old George Anthony Sanchez was arrested a few weeks later, on November 30, 1987, while attempting to break into the Redwood City home of a single woman who lived alone. Sanchez was a sewer repairman for the city. A search of his home revealed a blue ski mask identical to the one he was wearing, hidden near a cache of possessions belonging to the twenty-six known victims of the Ski Mask Rapist. George Anthony Sanchez was formally charged with more than one hundred felonies, and he's currently serving a sentence of life without the possibility of parole.

Like every other psychic who works with law enforcement, as I have for almost forty years, I would love nothing more than to have the spirit world at my beck and call, ready to give me instant, direct solutions to every crime and detailed maps to every missing person. I've been asked a hundred times, as have my colleagues, "If you're so psychic, who killed JonBenet Ramsey? Who killed Chandra Levy? Where is Natalee Holloway?" Every one of us wishes it were that simple, just as every member of the law enforcement community wishes all they had to do was run fingerprints or DNA through their data banks, get a "hit" and poof! Case closed.

The good news and bad news is I can only work with and share the information I'm given. It's bad news in that it's not always the specific name, address or license number of the perpetrator. Sometimes it is, and that can make life so much easier for everyone involved—law enforcement can start from there and work backward building their case. Imagine the public outrage if someone could be arrested or prosecuted on nothing more than "Because Sylvia Browne says so." And I would personally join that outrage, believe me. No one should have that much power, or be saddled with that much single-handed responsibility, and if there's no evidence beyond my say-so, there is no case, nor should there be. That's why we psychics always emphasize that we might have been one of the investigative tools that helped to solve a case, but it would be an outright lie to say we solved it all by ourselves.

The good news of only being able to share the information I'm given is that I'm given any at all. Clues, images, initials, anything and everything that comes through me from the Other Side about crimes and missing persons are nothing I consider myself entitled to. They're an honor, gifts that God and the Christ Consciousness make possible and offer in Their own infinite wisdom, time and pace, far beyond anything I would ever pretend to second-guess, let alone judge.

I also have strict rules against soliciting cases, being an ambulance chaser or joining the ranks of the trauma groupies who attach themselves to whatever mystery happens to be getting media attention. There are some very notorious cases I've been heavily involved in, but if my name is ever mentioned in the publicity surrounding them, it's not because I initiated it. I don't have a publicist, and I never will. I also never intrude. If I'm working with law enforcement or a victim's family, it's because I was asked, not because I injected myself into someone else's tragedy because it's where the spotlight happened to be. When I do get a "hit" on an unsolved high-profile case, as sometimes happens, I call the appropriate authorities, and/or my friends in the FBI who can contact the right people. No one else. And most certainly not the press.

There's another aspect to my work with law enforcement—every bit of which I do on a strictly pro bono basis, by the way—that's important to mention as another part of the answer to questions like "Why haven't you solved JonBenet, or the Natalee Holloway disappearance?" In addition to not having been asked for my input by the investigators of those cases, I also have more than two hundred unsolved cases sitting on my desk right now, every one of which is as devastating and urgent to the victim's loved ones as those well-publicized cases are to their families and friends. I can't imagine anything more obscene than sorting through those two-hundred-plus files I'm currently working on and prioritizing them based on which ones I've seen on TV and which ones I haven't. I wish there weren't other murdered six-year-olds, or missing twenty-year-olds, whose loved ones are asking for my help. Obviously, that's a wish that won't come true, and there will never be any such thing as a case that comes to me that I'll consider less important than any other for any reason, let alone because of something as arbitrary as media attention. If the day comes when I think the only cases worth solving are the famous ones, that's the day I'll retire.

One of my current cases, for example, is a death you've never heard of and probably never will. A lovely twenty-eight-year-old woman was due at a restaurant early one morning to meet friends to go bicycling along the Pacific Coast Highway. She never showed up. Her car was found. Her bicycle was found. And finally her body was found, in a construction site a few miles up the coast. Her clothing had been partially removed, and it appeared she'd been raped. It's officially classified as—ready?—a hit-and-run. I've met her lovely sister, who was also her best friend, so I've personally seen the anguish this unsolved death has caused. And to make it even more cruel, the anguish has been an open wound for the sister, the family and a wide circle of friends since the murder happened, on an early morning in 1981. Could you look this sister in the eye and say, "Sorry, too long ago, and

I don't see any publicity potential in it, so good luck and good-bye"?
Neither could I. I know this young woman was murdered, I know it
was by an acquaintance, and it won't be easy (the bicycle is long gone,
and the clothing she was wearing that morning is currently being
searched for). But like every other case on my desk, there's not a
chance I'll give up on it until this family has more answers than they
have at the moment, after twenty-five years of being told, "Hit-and-
run. The end."

Of course, with this case, just as with every other case and every
other area of my work, my participation won't mean a thing until and
unless the information I pass along is validated. And sometimes the
validations are almost as dramatic as the cases themselves.

One of the most bizarre validations in my career came in the aftermath
of one of my *Montel Williams Show* appearances. Two grief-stricken
parents I'll call Bill and Elaine were seated in the audience, wanting
my help with the unsolved murder of their daughter. Montel and I have
said this a million times, both on and off the air, but it's worth repeating here: unless we indicate otherwise during the show, I'm never given
information ahead of time about that day's featured stories, and I'm
kept carefully sequestered from that day's guests. So Bill, Elaine and
their heartbreaking tragedy were as new to me as they were to the rest
of the viewers when Montel introduced us on national television.

Rather than reopen old wounds for Bill and Elaine and other innocent parties involved by going into details about the crime, I'll leave it
at the headline that their daughter "Amanda," in her late teens, had
been violently killed in her home in a small southern town. The local
police had several suspects. What they didn't have was enough conclu-
sive evidence to narrow it down to just one, let alone make an arrest,
and after more than a year the case was in danger of slipping into the
vault of "cold" files.

"Can you tell us anything that might help steer police in the right
direction?" Bill asked me.

"Do you know who did this? Can you give us a name?" Elaine added.

I know you've been in situations in which you've been struggling to recall a name that's familiar to you, that you know is floating around somewhere in your memory bank if you can just bring it into focus, and suddenly it comes to you, clear as a bell. You can't quite describe the form in which the name comes, whether you heard it, or visualized it, you're just aware that one moment you were a blank and the next moment you knew it with absolute certainty.

That's the best description I can offer for that moment when Elaine asked, "Can you give us a name?" It came to me. I knew it with absolute certainty, even though I had no idea who the suspects were, or any names involved at all except Bill, Elaine and Amanda.

"Richard," I said. "They should be focusing on Richard."

In the edited version of the show, the version that aired, the name "Richard" was muted so that it was never heard. But the camera was focused on me when I said it, and you didn't have to be a skilled lip-reader to figure it out. Nor did you have to be psychic to see from Bill's and Elaine's shocked reaction that "Richard" was a familiar name to them. In fact, they explained, a young man named Richard was among the friends and acquaintances of Amanda's who'd been questioned early in the investigation.

The episode aired about three weeks later. A few hours after it aired, the Richard in question committed suicide.

Further investigation by the local police confirmed that Richard was indeed Amanda's guilt-wracked killer. Murder solved, case closed, validation accomplished, bittersweet as it was.

Bill and Elaine remain in my prayers, as does Richard's family.

A heartbroken young man named Paul and his mother, Rita, were in Montel's audience after the "Richard" experience, wanting help in solving the murder of Paul's younger sister, Erin. This time not only was the audio muted but the camera stayed on Paul instead of me, and his eyes immediately widened in shocked recognition when I gave him and Rita the first name of the killer, passed along to me by Erin herself, I was sure.

This time the validation was less violent and more appropriate. Paul and Rita were invited back to Montel's audience a few weeks later. Montel showed the clip of their first appearance, without the audio muted, so that the viewers in the studio and at home could clearly hear me say that the killer's name was Alex. Paul and Rita then gratefully announced that an arrest had been made in Erin's murder. The alleged killer's name was Patrick McCarthy, but he was known on the street by his middle name—Alexi.

I'm sure I won't be compromising Mr. McCarthy's Constitutionally protected right to a presumption of innocence by predicting ahead of time, in print, that he'll be convicted of this murder if he's foolish enough to plead "not guilty" and let this case go to trial. After all, I'm just a psychic. What do I know?

On February 26, 1993, a Ryder truck rumbled into the underground parking garage of the North Tower of New York City's World Trade Center. At 12:17 P.M. the fifteen hundred pounds of explosives hidden inside the truck were detonated, killing six people, injuring more than a thousand and putting a shocking end to the American myth that terrorists only attack on foreign soil.

My friend Ted Gunderson at the FBI, with whom I'd worked on other cases, called me after three of the bombers, all Islamic terrorists, had been arrested. Ted had learned to trust me and my information over the years, and knew I would never delude myself into believing that I'm smarter than the FBI; I'm just one of many alternative investigative tools at their disposal.

Ted's FBI intelligence prevented him from being even slightly surprised when I assured him that there were five, maybe six men involved in the attack, not just the three in custody. I was formally interviewed on videotape by the FBI on March 16, 1993. Because portions of the tape have aired on national television since then, I'm free to reveal an excerpt from the transcript:

> BROWNE: One of the men you need to look for has a short build . . . wiry . . . black hair . . . black eyebrows . . . There's an m on there . . . S-a-l-z-e-m something . . . Salzemon . . . Salzemon . . . m-o-n. Okay, Salzemon.
>
> GUNDERSON/FBI: What about future bombings by this group?
>
> BROWNE: I don't know that much about it, but I'm concerned about an embassy problem, I'm concerned about a department store problem, I'm concerned about a bridge problem.

The FBI ultimately arrested a total of six Islamic terrorists for the 1993 bombing of the World Trade Center. They were convicted in 1997 and 1998 and sentenced to an average of 240 years each for their crimes. Among them was a short, wiry man with black hair and thick black eyebrows named Mohammed A. Salameh. I was off by a few letters here and there, but when Ted called to tell me about Salameh's arrest, I was so thrilled I may have shattered poor Ted's eardrum when I involuntarily shouted, "You've got him!"

One of the only times I insinuated myself into a case, and moved heaven and earth to do it, was when I was overwhelmed by a tragedy I knew was in the making and knew I had to do everything in my power to avert it.

Ronald Reagan was in the White House. Along with several American and United Nations diplomats, he was planning to attend an October 6, 1981, parade and celebration of the Camp David peace agreement between Egypt and Israel facilitated by President Reagan's predecessor, Jimmy Carter. Egypt's president Anwar Sadat, who shared the Nobel Peace Prize for that agreement, was to be a featured honoree at this extraordinary event. From the moment I read about the upcoming celebration, I was so assaulted by visions of violence and potential fatalities at that appearance, including an attack on President Reagan himself, that I managed to have a personal phone conversation with First Lady Nancy Reagan and share the information the Other Side had passed along to me.

President Reagan canceled his appearance at that event.

Tragically, President Sadat didn't. The military parade proceeded as planned, with all its dignity and precision. Sadat was in the reviewing stands, saluting the passing troops, when a small group of them burst from one of the parade vehicles and opened fire into the stands with a horrifying barrage of machine gun blasts and hand grenades.

Anwar Sadat was killed instantly. Twenty others were seriously injured, including four of the American diplomats with whom President Reagan would have been seated.

I'm enormously proud of my work with the FBI and other law enforcement agencies on crimes throughout the world, including the famous and infamous ones. But I'm every bit as proud of my help with those unsolved crimes you don't hear about on the news or read about in the papers, the ones that are brought to my attention in the privacy of my office by those who are suffering from the aftermath and looking for answers. As I said earlier in this chapter, there is no such thing as an "unimportant" victim, and the grief of these victims' loved ones is every bit as deep as any you'll see in the glare of media spotlights.

Dear Sylvia,

I had a telephone reading with you concerning my son who disappeared two years ago. You told me that he was schizophrenic, not bipolar; that he was alive, not dead; that I would see him within a year; and that he was in Tennessee.

I admit I was pretty skeptical, especially after hearing the part about Tennessee. Two years ago when he "vanished," he was in Las Vegas. I wouldn't go so far as to say I disbelieved you, but I didn't have a lot of renewed hope, either.

That is, until yesterday, when I received a letter addressed to my son. It was a letter from a car insurance company to each of their customers, and it was postmarked from Nashville, Tennessee! It gave no indication about his current residence, but it absolutely validated that, just as you promised, he is alive, and he was or is in Tennessee! And since this is the first time he's used my address since he's been gone, I'm now full of renewed hope that yes, maybe I will see him within a year.

God bless you for your gift and the good you use it for, and thank you again.

from Ethel

I went to Sylvia in the hope of finding and reuniting with a man who was the great love of my life. I've missed him every day of the almost thirty years we've been apart, and probably unfairly compared both my ex-husbands to him and decided they didn't come close to measuring up. My first question to Sylvia about him was whether or not he's still alive. She said, "No, dear, he's not."

I didn't believe her for one minute. I was sure the problem was that I had only given her his first name, so she couldn't possibly know what she was talking about.

To prove her wrong, I finally thought of starting a search on the Internet. Within a day I found his name on the Social Security website, where he was listed as having died in 1989.

I was devastated. And I still can't find any information on where he died, or what the circumstances were. I'm mad at myself for being so stubborn about this with Sylvia. I've believed in her for all these years, enough so that she's the one I turned to for help with something that was important to me, and the minute she said something I didn't want to hear I "shut down."

If I'd accepted the probability that she was right about his being dead, I could have asked her all these unanswered questions, and I'm sure she would have been right about those too.

from Arlene

I received a call from my father-in-law today, who saw Sylvia on *The Montel Williams Show*. An audience member asked Sylvia if the twin boys she gave up for adoption were alive and well. They were born in 1980 in a small town called Lima, Ohio.

Sylvia told the woman that the twins were fine and successful and living in Florida. She said one of the boys was in construction, and the other boy was in engineering.

My wife and I are the adoptive parents of those twin boys, born February 1, 1980, in Lima, Ohio. We moved to Florida in 1984. The boys are indeed fine. One is in construction as a home builder, and the other does AutoCAD engineering. They both live in Jacksonville, Florida.

I'm sure Sylvia doesn't read her e-mails, but you may want to pass this one on to her.

from Tom

Back in the early 1980s I contacted Sylvia for help in finding a missing friend. His name was Mel. He had left on Mother's Day on a trip to Mt. Diablo and was scheduled to return on Father's Day. When he didn't come back I contacted the sheriff's department and the state park service, and his daughter filed a missing persons report with the police department.

Sylvia said Mel was still on the mountain, that if you looked at Mt. Diablo from the San Francisco Bay, he was on the left side. He was near where there had been a "campground" that was used for picnicking, camping, etc. She said there had been "cabins" and a "general store," as well as a stream or creek.

Helicopter searches had found nothing. I went to the Marsh Creek Fire Department, where my father had once been a fireman, and shared Sylvia's information, knowing they had a horseback search team. But it couldn't be dispatched without an order from the sheriff's department, which the sheriff's department refused to give. Based on maps, though, they thought they knew the area Sylvia was referring to, and they put me in touch with a family who lived on the mountain and was very involved with the Trail Ride Association.

That family and some volunteers from the Trail Ride Association organized their own search, following Sylvia's description and their knowledge of the mountain. Within a few hours they found Mel's body, in a creek near the site of an abandoned campground.

That's Part I of Sylvia's importance in my life. Part II was much harder to take.

It was the morning of the Trail Ride Association search. My 12-year-old daughter and I were on our way to the site where the riders were going to meet when she quietly and matter-of-factly confessed that the possibility of Mel being dead wasn't making her unhappy because he'd been molesting her for years. Needless to say, I was horrified. When his body was found, I can't begin to describe my feelings—my stupidity for genuinely thinking this man was my trusted friend, my guilt for bringing someone into my home who would even dream of hurting my daughter, my apparent blindness toward my own daughter, who'd kept quiet about it because she didn't want to hurt me.

I struggled with this for twenty years, hating a dead man and feeling that he'd died without being punished for what he'd done.

Then I read one of Sylvia's books, in which she says unequivocally that anyone who hurts children or animals will get their own special "reward" from God. I know that's true, and I take comfort in it.

Thank you, Sylvia, for making more differences in my life than I have words to express.

from Tina

I was watching you on television when a gentleman in the audience who was a Loomis Armored Car guard in Seattle asked if the gunman who killed his partner would ever be caught. I paid close attention to that story because I remembered both the guard and his partner from my years in the Seattle area banking industry.

You assured the guard that yes, the gunman would be apprehended, in another part of the country, on an unrelated crime, and then connected to this murder.

I happened to pick up the *Seattle Times* on 11/16, not long after your television appearance, and came across an article I knew you'd be interested in. (I've enclosed the first part of it.) As you'll see, it says that a Michigan man, after being arrested on an unrelated case, has been charged with conspiracy to commit first-degree robbery during which a Loomis guard was killed in a suburb of Seattle.

from Juditha

Hi, Sylvia.

Enclosed please find an article that will interest you. A relative of one of these missing men was in the Montel Williams audience recently and asked if they could be found, and if so, where. You said they would definitely be found, and it would be in water.

The first paragraph reads "A truck belonging to three men from Massachusetts who vanished in 1998 while on vacation was found in a retention pond Monday night, police said. There were occupants inside the truck, although police could not confirm how many."

from Ronnie

I had a private reading with Sylvia to ask about my father, who had disappeared six years before the reading, despite exhaustive searches by family, friends, law enforcement authorities and private investigators. Sylvia told me we would find him within two years, in a wooded area, near water. A year and a half after my reading we finally found his remains, in thick underbrush among a grove of pine trees beside the river that runs through our town. Please thank Sylvia on behalf of everyone who loved my dad. We've now been able to say a long overdue farewell. Hard as it is, it's blessed peace compared to the hell of not knowing.

from Shirley

IN CLOSING

I don't need to tell you that it's been fifty or so years of great highs and lows and I sometimes wondered if I'd find my way through. But it's God, the Christ Consciousness and all of you who have kept me going and will keep me going until my last breath in this body.

There's a private collection of letters I keep for those moments when, like everyone else, I doubt myself, and wish I'd done more, or done it better, or known sooner than I did, or, or, or—all those questions we humans ask ourselves when we're feeling far from Home. All I have to do is read one of the letters in this private collection and I'm reminded that there is a world full of genuinely wonderful people out there I've had the honor to somehow touch, and in return they've touched me and made my spirit fuller and richer than I ever dreamed it could be when I was that odd, frightened, confused little girl in Missouri.

That's what we do, we brothers and sisters, children of God that we are. We touch each other and magnify each other's light, joining ours with the glorious white light of the Holy Spirit and dispelling the darkness together.

I share this letter from my private collection with my love and gratitude to every one of you who, because you brought me your light, made mine so much brighter.

Dear Sylvia,

Hello, how is life treating you these days, my friend? To introduce myself, I'm a legally blind poetic writer. I thoroughly enjoy reading your books, which captivate my attention like a porch light to a moth. I love your approach to spiritualism and try not to miss your appearances on the Montel Show.

There were times in the past, before reading some of your books, I would ask God, "Why did I have to be born with my eye condition and become visually impaired?" Well, after reading through some of your literary works I understand the "blueprint" (chart) in which you say we all construct and map out another life here on earth before we leave Home! Understanding this concept and knowing the fact that while in my spiritual body on the Other Side I chose to be born with an eye condition makes me feel better about myself as a person because I know I did it to test my physical life. Also, knowing this has made me pull back the "metaphoric finger" toward our Father above, because He gives us options and choices of what we want to work on before we leave our spiritual Home to return to the physical side again.

You know, Sylvia, I get tickled sometimes when I listen to your books on audiotape because the reader does such a good job of projecting your emotions from letters on a page to an ear-catching treat. What gets me tickled mostly is when you get frustrated with your Spirit Guide, Francine. For example, in your book *The Other Side and Back,* when you found out that the Other Side was just superimposed over our world on earth and got upset with Francine for not telling you sooner, she said, "You never asked." HA! OH, MY GOSH, that was just the pick-me-up laugh I needed for that particular day.

I love to laugh and feel inspired, so Ms. Thing—hope you don't mind me calling you that, Sylvia—but you have such a special way of inspiring all those you come in contact with, directly or indirectly.

THANK YOU! for filling me with hope and spiritual assurance. Being assured of a reunion with loved ones and going Home to be with God fills me with joy.

God bless you, Sylvia, and continue inspiring and helping guide us along in our journey. I love you, and if I never get to meet you in person to give you a big hug in this life, I hope I get to do so back Home on the Other Side.

P.S. Tell Francine I said hello and to keep you straight and on the right track, okay? (smile)

ABOUT THE AUTHOR

A professional psychic for nearly fifty years, Sylvia Browne has written many tremendously successful books, including *The Other Side and Back* and most recently *Phenomenon*. She appears regularly on *The Montel Williams Show*, and her frequent lectures attract thousands of attendees. She lives in California.